Delusional Democracy

**Fixing the Republic Without
Overthrowing the Government**

Joel S. Hirschhorn

Common Courage Press

Monroe, Maine

Library of Congress Cataloging-in-Publication Data is available from
publisher on request.
ISBN 1-56751-380-8 paper
ISBN 1-56751-381-6 hardcover

ISBN 13 9781567513806 paper
ISBN 13 9781567513813 hardcover

Lyrics from "Everybody Knows" and "Democracy"
by Leonard Cohen used with permission.

Common Courage Press
121 Red Barn Road
Monroe, ME 04951

207-525-0900
fax: 207-525-3068

www.commoncouragepress.com
info@commoncouragepress.com

First printing
Printed in Canada

Contents

Preface

Waking Up and Shaking Up the Status Quo

CNN's *Lou Dobbs Tonight* did a poll in November 2005 and found that 89 percent of people would welcome joining a viable third party. The following day MSNBC found that 71 percent felt it was time for a major third party. This was good news because like so many other Americans I have concluded that the two-party duopoly is hopelessly dysfunctional and counterproductive to the kind of democracy we deserve. The two-party status quo must be crushed. One condition should help. The pillars of American democracy are cracking.

If you pay attention to language you will notice that "status quo" is one of the most commonly used phrases in all spheres and modes of communication. It is used in statements about changing or preserving current conditions. This book is about changing what is bad, about fighting status quos that do more harm than good because they undercut American democracy. It presents a dissenting view about the United States. Namely that American democracy no longer works for the good of its citizens. It no longer is the best in the world, or the envy of citizens of other democracies. American democracy is dying right before Americans' distracted and delusional eyes. And it has been dying for decades through the acts of Democrats and Republicans.

This is the question that Americans should ask themselves: How can I turn my discontent into a force for good to rescue and revitalize my democracy?

Many Americans are frustrated because their desire to give meaning to their lives by "making a difference" has been thwarted. So much talk about change is tossed around, but stubborn opposition to significant change flourishes. My own career journey embodies these hopes and frustrations. When I joined the Congressional Office of Technology Assessment in 1978 a top boss told me that I could choose a job that gave me money, power, or influence, but this job only offered a shot at influence. At the time I applied for the job, I had the security of being a tenured professor at the University of Wisconsin, Madison, where I had described my successful career as "publishing *and* perishing." I embraced the opportunity to improve my country and traded security for challenge.

I chose this path because the 1960s had had a profound influence on me, though I was older than my revolutionary-minded college students. Counter-culture books and thinking filled me with a desire to change the status quo values of American society. By the late 1970s I concluded that the counter culture revolution had failed; there was no fundamental or systemic change in society. Revolutionary changes in politics, government, public policies and the consumer culture were still needed. Rampant consumerism had only gotten worse. Corrupt elected officials had become the norm, not the exception.

For some years my work for Congress was satisfying. Then it became clear that impartial government analysts offering sound information, ideas and public policy options could not compete with well-funded "special interests" for access to members of Congress, their staffs, and the news media. Even when good ideas surfaced, received public attention and were incorporated in laws, federal agencies undermined them. Bureaucrats were corrupt or incompetent, or both. I helped get a federal pollution prevention law passed, but the U.S. Environmental Protection Agency never earnestly implemented it. The public obtained few positive changes and benefits. Fraud, waste and abuse were far worse than the public realized. Changing the status quo was a lot harder than I had ever anticipated.

The U.S. offers incredible personal freedoms, yet has become resistant to true societal improvement. How can this be? My answer is a society obsessively focused on materialistic consumption, driven in large measure by incessant mass marketing and advertising, technological change, and corporate power. By intention, citizens are kept distracted and largely disengaged from their government, and too busy to be agents of change or to support them. The public has become numbed by a political-corporate system that uses Americans as worker bees and consumers, and that serves special interests rather than public interests. American society needs change—not tweaking, but genuine change. Money protects the two-party status quo.

When baby boomers and older Americans reflect on how greatly the world has changed in their lifetimes, it is easy to miss the point that most of the change is related to consumption, not improving quality of life and achieving a more civil and honorable society. There is far more pseudo-change for consumers than meaningful change for citizens. As explained in my previous book *Sprawl Kills—How Blandburbs Steal Your Time, Health and Money*, America's progress has taken us backward by trading quality of life for materialistic consumption. Worse yet, few people challenge this.

Yes, many people in other nations either want to live in the United States or copy our lifestyle. But are immigrants mostly seeking voracious consumption? Perhaps, in time, they will learn that compulsive consumption gets in the way of political freedom.

I take the status quo busting theme to its ultimate application by presenting the case for millions of Americans joining together, particularly disgusted and angry left-wing progressives and right-wing conservatives, non-voters, and lesser-evil voters. United Americans can bust the two-party duopoly with a new third-party that rises above social issues, and finds common ground on principles—principles to guide the rebuilding of our representative democracy and wiping out the corporate corruption and abuse of government, the workplace, and the marketplace. Rather than wait for a politician to be a "uniter," Americans must unite themselves.

Many excellent previous books have discussed ugly truths about failing American democracy with the intent of motivating fixes in it. They have failed. William Greider's *Who Will Tell the People—The Betrayal of American Democracy*, first published in 1992 stands out as an excellent example of the case for change. Yet this and others have not awakened large numbers of Americans. Things have only gotten worse, despite endless government and corporate scandals. Americans seem to expect less and less from their government and even less from corporate America, and they get it. Americans have not yet taken back their government. As a big fan of Jon Stewart's *The Daily Show* and *America (The Book)*, as well as Bill Maher's shows, like so many others, I have found solace in cynical comedic revelations about the faults of our government and society. Like fiddling while Rome burns, many Americans are laughing all the way to a fake democracy. This comic relief is like self-medication. But the good news is that the popularity of such shows, and witty books by people like Al Franken, reveal a deep dissatisfaction with the status quo. Many people want a better political system. Their dissatisfaction can be seized on to invigorate American democracy.

A note about style: I provide many quotations from a truly diverse set of past and present people to show the breadth and depth of accurate views of American society's vulnerabilities and decline. We dissenters have lots of company. My contribution is in pulling many facts and ideas together, and weaving them into fresh themes that support a compelling call for change through a politically smart strategy. Unlike other books, American democracy is examined from political, legal, psychological, economic, historic, and cultural perspectives.

There are two parts to this volume. First, is the case for change, then what needs to be done to fix our republic. Chapter 1 probes the meaning of democracy and outlines our democracy deficit. Democracy decline is the theme of Chapter 2 along with discussions of our current shortcomings in all three branches of government. Chapter 3 offers a unique psychological analysis of why people have difficulty facing the truth about American democracy and how lies are crafted to deceive people. The enormous problem for democracy of a culture of lying is the theme of Chapter 4. Democracy cannot be examined without attention to the failure of America's mainstream media to protect it, the subject of Chapter 5. Ending Part 1 is an account in Chapter 6 of the bizarre story of an undisputed bulge on President Bush's back seen in several 2004 televised debates that the mainstream media refused to cover seriously. Part 2 begins with a detailed presentation in Chapter 7 of eight election reforms, the nitty-gritty of strengthening American democracy. Next, Chapter 8 pays special attention to the current options for direct democracy—ballot measures and constitutional conventions. Following, in Chapter 9, is a broad view of today's problems, challenges, and solutions from the historical perspective of American democracy's roots. The final chapter presents details on how a national movement to fix our democracy can take form through actions centered on revitalizing our democracy, promoting citizen participation, and stopping corporate aristocracy and corruption, and through a new third party.

Can this book succeed where others have failed? That depends on you. Americans must vent their private discontent through public outrage. Relax your defenses. Open your mind. Feel the pain. Help make a revolution.

Part 1—Fueling the Fire of Discontent

You may be angry and even despondent about our nation's current state, especially its political system. No matter how well informed you are now, this section is likely to enrage you more. That's the goal—to raise your blood pressure, make you mad, and get you in a frame of mind to see the need, even moral and civic responsibility, for becoming an activist dissenter.

Chapter 1

Facing Our Democracy Deficit:
From Anger to Action

There is a serious "democracy deficit" in the United States at every
level—local, state and national.

—The Center for Voting and Democracy

W hat we face today should frighten Americans. To paraphrase
Abraham Lincoln: A government NOT of the people, NOT
by the people, and NOT for the people shall perish from the earth.

Thomas Jefferson was right. He saw the need for Americans to
be truly engaged with their republic. He believed that "making every
citizen an acting member of the government, and in the offices nearest
and most interesting to him, will attach him by his strongest feelings to
the independence of his country, and its republican constitution." Today,
who has time to be an "acting member of the government"? Do you think
that's what politicians really want?

Our political system is exactly opposite to what Jefferson believed
necessary. Americans are too busy working hard to maintain a decent
standard of living, spending endless hours in traffic congestion, fighting
stress about financial and health care uncertainties, and being compulsive
credit-card-consumers to also be acting members of the government.
Politics and politicians have turned them off.

Yet democracy remains a core American value even though
Americans are not getting what they need from their government. And
because the democracy has not received what it needs from its citizens,
we have a disgraceful democracy deficit—unrecognized and untaken
repairs. Think in terms of two kinds of people.

Countless Americans know the system stinks and that corporate
interests have replaced citizens as acting members of the government.
They see severe problems in government and terrible elected officials.
They see America's failing democracy. But they have not stepped up as
Jefferson believed necessary and accepted their personal responsibility to
fix the republic they see in disrepair. They are not yet political activists.
Venting, ranting and blogging on the Internet don't count as system-

changing activism though they help keep many people sane and ready for revolution. Most have lost hope in changing the system through the current system; they await its collapse. They are defeatists. They are passive dissenters.

Other Americans do not see American democracy's serious decline. They hide behind a bright but false patriotism. They do not think outside the ballot box. Voting for the right people is their priority. They are more sanguine about America's economic opportunities. Despite abundant evidence, as in the first stage of grief, they are in denial about our democracy deficit and political plutocracy. Their hope rests on putting "their" true believers in office. They are likely to believe God is on their side. They are false or delusional patriots

Here are some comparisons:

Passive dissenters' delusion is that nothing can save the system from itself—they do not extrapolate many historic and positive American upheavals to our future. False patriots' delusion is that nothing is fundamentally deficient in American democracy and that we are headed in the right direction.

Passive dissenters are likely to be quixotic but alienated independents, distracted non-voters, frustrated third-party supporters, and lesser-evil voters for Democrats and Republicans. Delusional patriots are likely to be loyal Democrats and Republicans.

Passive dissenters suffer with their discontent; they could use a dose of political adrenaline. Delusional patriots embrace their anger; they could use a shot of political methadone. Both have bipolar tendencies in response to the ebb and flow of political events.

With their passionate enthusiasm, nationalism, and right-wrong-clarity, delusional patriots tend to be louder and more entertaining than pensive passive patriots, giving the deceptive impression that they have the winning hand—think right-wing talk radio and cable Fox News.

Practically speaking, the majority of Americans are neither loyal Democrats nor Republicans but conscientious objectors—bystanders to the political decay of their democracy, unwilling or unmotivated to fight to save it. Though several hundred thousand Americans may be passionately engaged on various issues related to protecting and fixing our republic, their political dissent is fragmented and marginalized, like disconnected and sometimes competing dissent-cells. Most political dissent is personal and silent. The political status quo is far too strong to be overcome by disjointed and passive dissent. Nothing short of a well-organized legion of outrage-driven Americans will fix our republic and beat the prevailing two-party duopoly.

Nowadays, when the government or politicians take an action that actually serves the public interest, it is the exception to the rule—the rule of corruption that serves corporate and other special interests. To understand current events in the political system, see them as distractions to keep public scrutiny away from what really is going on. Beyond entertainment and consumer spending, an important function of popular culture is to distract Americans from horrific political realities, not just abstract ones, but ones that directly impact the lives of most people. People may hear about the escalating national debt, but few grasp the negative impact on their own economic security, for example.

Can our extremely materialistic and superficial society be a real democracy? Change merely to promote more consumerism and corporate wealth has inexorably weakened American democracy. People use too much time and energy being good consumers to also be engaged citizens. America needs some important changes, not just obtained *through* the current system, but from some revolutionary changes *in* the system.

Here are simple criteria to evaluate America's representative democracy:

Are elected government officials in executive and legislative bodies honestly representing and protecting public interests?

Is the judiciary acting in an independent, non-partisan, and fair way to interpret state and federal constitutions and laws, and not legislating from the bench in a biased manner?

Is the constitutionally protected free and independent press truly safeguarding citizens from government excesses, failures, propaganda, lies, and corruption?

In the following pages, through ample data and information, the answers to these questions are a clear "No!" American democracy gets failing grades because citizens have no basis for trusting these institutions that are the pillars of our democracy. Think of this failure as if we were a large family living together for a long time in an old house. We have ignored many maintenance and repair needs or given up on successfully addressing them. Then, one early morning someone bangs on our door screaming for us to wake up. Our house is actually falling down, as if some storm surge or tornado had knocked it off its foundation. Such is my deMOCKracy message. As soon as possible, many more Americans must wake up and reclaim their sovereign power and fix their republic. Fast action is imperative. It is up to the citizenry.

In 2004 Peter Hart asked cable TV viewers if they agreed with this: "People like me do not have any say about what the government does." The results showed Americans' discontent when 46 percent agreed. Also, 65 percent wanted increased access to ballot initiatives and referenda to represent themselves when necessary. Paul Jacob commented: "People know how to solve this 'democracy deficit.' …The voters want to be represented and they are smart enough to know that they aren't being represented today." Survey and poll results are one thing, but they do not measure the depth and passion of views nor the propensity for taking action because of those views. Stimulating broad citizen action is a difficult challenge. It helps to have specific changes that citizens can understand and actively support; these are detailed in later chapters.

Welcome to Political Porn 101

You expect the President of the United States to understand exactly what kind of government he's in charge of, especially when he is selling democracy to other nations. In his February 2005 trip to Europe, President George W. Bush bragged with Texas bravado:

> We believe that the voice of the people ought to be determining policy, because we believe in democracy.

What hogwash. In democracy-marketing such false claims are common. Maybe it comes down to what people Bush was thinking of. Even conservative columnist Patrick J. Buchanan reacted incredulously: "But does Bush really believe this? …Would Bush himself let a poll of Americans decide how long we keep troops in Iraq? Would he submit his immigration policy to popular vote?"

For born-again Bush, the voice he hears is more likely from his God, financial backers, and sycophants, not the voice of we the people. For Bush, democracy means whatever he wants it to mean. How could the United States president get it so wrong? He was selling democracy by hypocrisy, telling a global audience what he thought they should hear and might buy. When the president of the United States publicly tells the world such stupid stuff about American democracy, it reveals just how empty and corrupted the word democracy has become.

When an important word loses its meaning from overuse and intentional misuse, what it refers to is in jeopardy. Democracy is a soft and fuzzy word, abused and misunderstood, meaning different things to different people. Several dictatorial communist regimes have used the word in their names to give them an aura of respectability. Trivializing "democracy" for marketing purposes is common. NBC Nightly News broadcast its 2004 presidential election coverage from "Democracy Plaza." Right wing demagogue Rush Limbaugh calls himself the "Doctor of Democracy"—which means what? Nothing, it's just a way to paint himself a patriot. Better to think of Limbaugh as the "Doctor of Deception."

Republican congressman Ron Paul has said; "We must reassert that America is a republic, not a democracy." Such people are playing a semantic game. Why? Because the dictionary definition of republic describes what common sense tells you is a form of democracy: "a government in which supreme power resides in a body of citizens entitled to vote and is exercised by elected officers and representatives responsible to them and governing according to law." You may have heard the "we-are-just-a-republic" semantic ploy to excuse the failings of American democracy. As columnist William Penn Fallin asked: "Why the GOP fixation on assuring us we "ain't" no Democracy we're a Republic! ...why is there such a need to blather on and on and on about being a Republic inferring we Democratic People are too stupid to be charged with caring for 'The Republic'!" What we must stay focused on is the quality of American democracy.

Forget semantics. We are both a republic and a democracy. The real question is: What is the quality of our democracy? Particularly, what's wrong with our representative government? Voters do not choose public policies but policymakers. For our democracy to work, our policymakers must be trusted to serve the public interest and tell their constituents the truth. Participation in a democracy through representation is like sexual experience through pornography. American citizens are more spectators than players in the political pornography our elected representatives star in—our illusory political system.

An unfunny thing happened on the way to America's future: Over decades of both Democratic and Republican reigns, elected representatives we Americans entrusted with our democracy sold us out—not just figuratively, but literally sold us out. Nevertheless, politicians love to talk democracy. This has only made the term more vague and its use more farcical, as in Bush's statement given above. Empty democracy talk is worse than useless. It is harmful. American democracy is not just in trouble semantically, it is in serious trouble as a political system.

While democracy is drummed into our heads to the point where the mere suggestion that we do not live in a great democracy elicits defensive rejection, the question remains: just how great is it? Trust in American democracy is physiologically embedded in people's brains, actual neural networks. Let's be clear at the outset. Contrary to popular belief and considerable democracy-worshipping, the United States is not a great democracy in theory or practice. Our Founding Fathers hedged their bet on democracy by limiting the power of "we the people." They chose a representative republic over a direct democracy, because they feared the will of the majority. It pays to remember that the word democracy does not appear in our Declaration of Independence, Constitution, national anthem, or pledge of allegiance.

Delusional American patriots incessantly talk feel-good "democracy" to keep people *thinking* they live in a great democracy. Just like Fox News endlessly describes itself as "fair and balanced" to keep viewers *thinking* they are getting truthful, unbiased news. Just like Bill O'Reilly says he is a "no-spin zone" to keep his viewers *thinking* they are getting the truth. But what people think is true does not make it true, especially in our sound-bite culture.

As a thought experiment, examine how you fit into the passive dissident-delusional patriot formulation presented earlier. Consider the following beliefs, be truthful and give yourself a score from 0 to 10, with 0 being total disagreement and 10 full agreement:

- Not only is the U.S. the world's only superpower, its democracy is the best *and* the envy of the world. Score_____

- Despite too many inefficient, ineffective, and unnecessary government programs, our representative democracy still works in the public interest. Score_____

- In our capitalist system economic inequality provides the incentive to work hard and be successful, *and* is a vital part of America's democracy. Score_____

- Private money in American politics allows the truth to be heard, reflects our constitutionally protected freedom of speech, is good for democracy, *and* must continue. Score_____

- To serve the public interest our elected representatives can be trusted to listen to the voice of the people as expressed through public opinion polls and surveys. Score_____

- The Democratic-Republican two-party duopoly provides valuable political stability that sustains our democracy. Score_____

- There are ample opportunities for third-party candidates to build public support for their political ideas and win elections if people really supported them. Score_____

- The most wealthy and influential Americans with the most to lose will never let American democracy be defeated by foreign or domestic enemies. Score_____

- Americans are living up to Thomas Jefferson's ideal of an engaged, sovereign citizenry that through their individual and organized actions protect the republic's democracy. Score_____

- Our In-God-We-Trust-democracy depends on patriotic Bible-obedient Americans to defend it against satanic and snooty anti-life, anti-religion, and anti-family intellectuals. Score_____

First, add up your total to see whether you are a low-scorer (less than 40) or high-scorer (greater than 60).[1] Second, reflect on whether being classed as a passive dissenter or delusional patriot is mostly correct—but be open to the remainder of this volume that will probe these two orientations. Third, set aside your score, and imagine millions of Americans who agree wholeheartedly with most of these statements— the high-scorers, the delusional patriots. Though they are less likely to

---

[1] In developing this admittedly simple instrument and having a politically diverse set of participants it was found that respondents fell into these two groups that correlated with their political outlook.

read this book they should be understood by those with low scores, the passive dissenters, and vice-versa. Think of two Americas and a culture war between these two political outlooks rather than between liberals and conservatives, Democrats and Republicans, blue and red state Americans, rich and poor.

Pretty clearly, this book's point of view is that the above beliefs are false and harmful myths—personal delusions reinforced by right wing propaganda bursting out of talk-radio and cable TV hosts and evangelical screamers, their mouths acting like injection needles shooting doses of deception into peoples' brains. These iconic beliefs are the building blocks of our delusional democracy. The more that people cling to them, the more they keep out painful realities. It is an addiction. Deluded Americans feel compelled to believe that America's current democracy is great and worth selling to the rest of the world; all they need is more control of it. They get their next "fix" by turning on the radio or TV to get another shot of deception aimed relentlessly at removing the toxic influence on our society of wrong-headed Americans (including abortion-friendly Liberals, marriage-minded homosexuals, United Nations-loving disloyalists, and anti-Christian smut peddlers). Their battle goes well as long as they stay alert to the threat by faithfully listening to the likes of Sean Hannity, Rush Limbaugh, and perhaps a favorite evangelical preacher. To let in information about American democracy's decline would produce painful withdrawal from false patriotism.

Millions of delusional patriots explain how a 1996 survey found that 80 percent of Americans were either very or fairly satisfied with the way American democracy works. On the other side of reality, however, are many bleaker realities that will be highlighted in the remainder of this volume, including low voter turnouts, that comport with other information, such as the survey taken before the 2000 election that found only 27 percent believed that Americans possess a spirit of "citizenship and participation," versus 62 percent that saw Americans as cynical and apathetic. Indeed, there are many millions of Americans whose survival doses come not from talk radio but from prescription drugs and compulsive consumerism.

Now consider the many low-scoring passive dissidents. Many have sunk into their own self-delusion: Though they believe that nearly everything vital to American democracy is in terrible shape, they also have convinced themselves that nothing effective can be done short-term to fix the system. They wait for the system's eventual and inevitable collapse. Many fit into the "progressive" class and vote for Democrats as lesser-evil candidates. With an as-Rome-burns capitulation they laugh at Jon Stewart's and Bill Maher's jokes, take heart that Michael Moore shows the truth, savor the writings of progressive sages like Noam Chomsky and Michael Parenti, listen to dissenters like Amy Goodman and Al Franken, and click on Commondreams.org, Counterpunch.org, and scores of other progressive Internet sites.

However, other passive dissidents are on the far right, are old-fashioned fiscal, small-government, and balanced budget conservatives and libertarians who may vote for Republicans, more as lesser-evils than as true-believers. Many were attracted to Ross Perot. They do not necessarily fit in with the right-wing social conservatives, notably fundamentalist evangelicals. There are many groups (the Cato Institute) with Internet sites for these people who like more independent or maverick pundits and politicians on the right, including Pat Buchanan, John McCain, Joe Scarborough, George F. Will, and perhaps Newt Gingrich who once declared "I am a genuine revolutionary."

For all passive dissidents, daily does of truth keep gloom and doom despair alive. Most discontented, blogging and passive dissenters are not yet ready to become activist New American Revolutionaries committed to fixing the republic without overthrowing the government. To be fair, first-it-must-fail, pick-up-the-pieces discontents lack what is argued for later in this volume, a viable new political party focused on restoring American democracy in the immediate future by waging war against the two-party duopoly, corruption, dishonesty, distractive consumerism, and corporate welfare. Few people have seen the opportunity of joining passive dissenters from the political left and right as well as independents, which will be examined later in this volume. What we must contemplate and aim for is making passive dissidents aspiring revolutionaries.

With democracy in mind, here is a non-partisan way to see the United States. It is a complex mix of a greedy oligarchy—government by relatively few people; a self-interested plutocracy—government by the powerful and wealthy; a commanding corporatist state—government under the control of business interests; and a gestating theocracy—government increasingly under the dominance of those believing they are divinely guided. All these are at odds with true democracy and Americans' traditional notion of democracy. In reality, a privileged class has usurped the power of citizens and made a mockery of voting, giving us our deMOCKracy, a delusional democracy where voting is placebo patriotism. The elitist privileged class should not be seen as Republican or Democratic, or conservative or liberal, because they can be either. They should be seen as the rich and powerful. So don't expect President Bush or other politicians to proclaim: "We believe that the voice of the relatively few, God-fearing rich and powerful ought to determine policy, because we believe in plutocracy." Elites protect American plutocracy from American democracy. For elites, the priority of U.S. foreign policy is protecting the profits of America's oligarchy, not the safety of America's democracy.

In our electoral or representative democracy we have the trappings of idealistic democracy more than the right stuff preached to us in our classrooms and touted to the rest of the world. Voting is necessary but clearly not sufficient for democracy. In a culture where making and spending money are paramount, there is no economic return for individual participation in democracy through voting like there is for business interests acting not through voting, but through lobbying and campaign financing. To the contrary, citizens voting against their own economic interests, because they focus on social issues, values, and religious mandates, receive a negative return on their democracy investment. They put the elites in power and suffer the consequences, pointing their anger in the wrong direction, mostly at cultural culprits rather than at moneyed interests.

Time to face the truth: We have a pseudo-democracy headed towards a fake democracy under the influence of delusion-pushing fake patriots who explicitly or unintentionally serve the interests of power elites. Accepting this truth is like taking a dose of intellectual penicillin to fight America's infectious propaganda; it is better than placebo voting for corrupt, dishonest, and lesser-evil politicians, but more painful than tolerating or supporting the status quo. The revolution we need must not be dreamed of or waited for, *it must be started.*

Give Me Stuff, Lots of Stuff

You might not guess it from the current state of American society, but people are probably genetically wired to shake up the status quo. Of course, change can take individuals and society backward, not forward. Seeking change for personal or community benefits or idealistic reasons may uniquely define humans. Think about it. What other animals seek change in the world around them because they consciously want to improve their condition? Without change, life is less satisfying. Change is the product of intellect and conscience. It reflects awareness that a status quo—the past—can hold us back when the future should pull us forward. Status quo loyalty can make us time-blind, causing us to suffer avoidable future grief.

As to democracy, the importance of change was summed up by Lewis H. Lapham:

> Democracy allies itself with change and proceeds from the assumption that nobody knows enough, that nothing is final, that the old order (whether of men or institutions) will be dragged offstage when its prescriptions no longer fit the facts.

Just as important at the personal level is balancing the innate desire for change with the human desire for stability, to conform, to fit in, to be accepted by others. Conformity accommodates trivial changes, when more profound ones are needed. Conformity creates common beliefs, political correctness, and herd behavior that support negative status quo conditions. *Conformists share the status quo.* They share the consequences. Conformity is the path of least resistance. Our society rewards conformity and presents status quo values as if they are natural and automatically good. "Good Americans" accept the cultural emphasis on compulsive consumerism, self-absorption, and competitive trendiness. Cynical conventional wisdom is: Why bother, you really can't change the political system. Don't make waves. You can't fight big money government.

Conformity comes easy especially when the desire for change can be channeled into consuming different things. Most Americans are seduced and sedated by consumerism. Ingeniously, the American consumer economy makes trivial changes in consumption of goods and services the easiest way to satisfy the instinctual craving for change. Forget need.

Consumption is used to fight boredom and mental stress. Consumerism does more. It pacifies and numbs the population; it distracts people from civic engagement. How long will Americans remain malleable members of the consumer economy? Until they understand the price they are paying for this distraction.

Status quo conformists serve the political-corporate system, whether or not they know it and admit it. Staying neutral, being an observer, and playing it safe support the status quo. This is so much different than knowing the difference between right and wrong, between status quo acceptance and making things better, and reaching inside oneself for moral conviction to take action. Agents of change are willing or compelled to be non-conformists and suffer the consequences. In this book, status quo busters work for change in society—because they see the political-economic system as not delivering its promises fairly across the population. They not only perceive democracy's erosion and government's failings, they fight for specific reforms. I call these people 21st century New American Revolutionaries.

Our materialistic consumerism status quo is strongly promoted, despite the endemic problems of massive consumer debt, national debt, trade deficits, and jobs export. It serves the corporatist state. Less consumption would allow people to work less, save money, have more time with friends and family, be engaged politically, and think more about the future. Extreme consumerism harms American democracy, so it is time to forsake the consumerism, not abandon the democracy. Short-sightedness is part of the consumerism status quo. Being time-blind to future consequences from current actions goes hand-in-hand with being a compulsive, conforming consumer. *Paradoxically, status quo conditions maintain short-term economic stability even as they push America towards large-scale economic instability.* Unsustainable status quo conditions produce surprises, whereas thoughtful, deliberate change prevents sudden catastrophe or crisis. A status quo that serves the present but does not protect the future is very dangerous; it is time-blind.

In *Luxury Fever*, Robert H. Frank made this important observation about compulsive consumption:

> If the defenders of the status quo are correct, we should expect to find at least some indications that further accumulation of material goods continue to provide significant increments in satisfaction, even after

countries achieve levels of affluence like those currently enjoyed in the United States. But...the scientific literature provides no support at all for this position.

In other words, it makes little sense to keep working, sacrificing and trading-off on the assumption that more consumption offers corresponding rewards. Beyond some level, rising consumption does not produce rising happiness. Worse yet, it keeps attention away from oncoming problems for democracy, government and culture. Conforming consumerism trumps civic engagement. Exactly what our oligarchy, plutocracy, corporatist state, and theocracy welcomes—but it does not support genuine democracy with collective decision-making about collective action for the common good. Personal freedom exists within our pseudo-democracy. Perversely, we pay for our consumer freedom with our sovereignty—our SELF-government. Perhaps this explains why so many Americans cling to the belief in American democracy's greatness. Freedom feeds SELF-delusion about American democracy. False patriots, such as Sean Hannity and Rush Limbaugh, falsely conflate freedom with democracy. They fuel knee-jerk citizen anger but not introspection and enlightenment.

Heroes Wanted

America's political system is stuck on corruption; the economic system is stuck on compulsive consumerism; the culture is stuck on dishonesty. To get unstuck we need more citizen revulsion that triggers political revolt.

Besides an amazing marketplace offering unparalleled opportunities to consume, we have more freedom to be angry and cynical than to bring about change. Freedom to consume is not the same as freedom to choose uniquely qualified candidates and freedom to actively participate in a democratic government. American culture teaches us to channel anger and disillusionment into consumption: from food for pleasure, to pharmaceuticals for stress relief, to cosmetic surgery, frequent new clothes and new vehicles for ego boosting. Wars against poverty, drugs, racism and now terrorism decorate the status quo with the illusion of looming change for the better. Maintaining that illusion, more than making change satisfies politicians. "The more things change the more they stay the same" rings true because there is little true, systemic change. The Model T Ford car got better mileage than the average Ford vehicle today. Most trips by jet airplane take as long today, from door to door, as they did decades ago in slow propeller planes. Change-inducing technological innovations are worshipped because they make money, unlike societal changes that improve quality of life.

The American way of thinking is not to let the good be the enemy of the better. We are trained not to be content with what is adequate or sufficient. Improvement has become buying what marketers tell us we should have. *In more we trust.* Make more money to consume more, to replace, to modernize, to update. If contentment with the good was more highly prized, there would be a lot more Amish in America. The Amish protect their status quo through isolation rather than consumption. Imagine an American economy based on Amish patterns of consumption. It does not compute. Our culture promotes consumption, more compulsive than conspicuous. Our economy depends on it. Striving for contentment and happiness without consumption is odd at best and subversive at worst. It is non-conforming behavior that inherently challenges the distractive consumerism and political status quo.

Mainstream public and private institutions automatically protect the "business as usual" status quo, unless money can be made from change. Corporate capitalism pushes consumption, and politicians protect business to maintain political stability—theirs. Progress is now not so much about changing economic or social status. It is about wanting more stuff. Call it sustained disappointment, a craving that never gets satiated. There is always something newer, better or bigger. The poor have fewer opportunities to change their status compared to what the affluent have to protect theirs. The American working class remains impotent against the powerful and privileged. Wal-Mart does not help lift its workers and customers up the ladder of success. It keeps them in an unsatisfied consumption-craving status quo. They are not working to afford more consumption, they are struggling just to survive and maintain a meager standard of living. Americans whose lives center on working doggedly to survive or afford more consumption are unlikely to become involved citizens or angry agents of change.

Busting negative status quos means battling institutions, organizations, and the people who surrender their individuality and independence to serve them. These groups resist change to maintain their success. And the more successful they are, the more they resist change through lobbying and campaign contributions. They build rules and legal structures to block change. Government's main function becomes preserving the status quo. Those content with the status quo identify, penalize and oust mavericks, troublemakers, insubordinates, dissenters, free-thinkers, extremists, rebels, whistle-blowers, spoilsports, nonconformists, misfits, subversives, radicals, provocateurs, and agitators.

Some Americans see status quo busters positively. Popular author of *Sin City* Frank Miller said: "My heroes tend to be loners against the status quo. And in 'Sin City,' I set up about the ugliest status quo that I could." A youthful view came from Loyola University student Ryan Lee: "No great leaps forward have ever been made by maintaining the status quo. Our forefathers broke the status quo when they declared our independence from Great Britain. The right of women and African Americans to vote and desegregation are more examples of breaking the status quo." More people need to reconnect with America's status quo busting heritage.

Time changes truth. As Ralph Nader observed in 2000:

> Change invariably begins with people whom the defenders of the status quo denounce as agitators, communists, hippies, weirdoes. And then, 10 or 20 years later, after the changes have taken place, the Chamber of Commerce discovers that everybody's profits have improved.

Political correctness means staying within acceptable boundaries that protect the status quo. Original-thinking innovators do not fit into most organizations; they make conventional thinkers and conformists uncomfortable. So they become entrepreneurs, outcasts, dropouts, bloggers, or status quo busters. Agents for larger scale, societal change are sometimes called social innovators or social entrepreneurs.

What irony. Our Founders were misfits, revolutionaries, and status quo busters. They conquered nature and the British to build a new nation where personal freedoms are constitutionally protected. Samuel Adams was right when he said "it does not require a majority to prevail, but rather an irate, tireless minority to set brush fires in people's minds." Adams had defined status quo busters. Consider what Mark Green said more recently:

From Walt Whitman's description of America as 'always becoming' to the GE slogan that 'progress is our most important product,' America is based on the notion of challenging the status quo in order to progressively do better.

Authentic political leaders would be challengers to the status quo. Instead, politicians have become opponents to political dissent and protectors of the status quo, totally contrary to our political roots. Worse, they challenge the patriotism of dissenters, conflating dissent with disloyalty. What American politicians don't want American democracy needs: deafening dissent.

Our Constitution purposefully made change in and by government difficult, giving us a politically stable society -- except for that nasty Civil War. Disinterest in voting and public service has risen as more Americans see too little chance of positive societal change through governmental action. Making money has become far more appealing than making a difference. Consumption has conquered idealism and promoted citizen apathy. Role models for young people are pop culture and sports stars with their own barrage of marketing messages. As *Vanity Fair* editor Leslie Bennetts observed: "Today's musical superstars seem more interested in hawking their clothing lines and name-brand perfumes than in any meaningful form of political action. Far from protesting the status quo, they're the foremost exemplars of how to exploit it to the max." Even though many young people are highly critical of our government, too few want to emulate successful agents of change. A lot more teenagers want to be Britney Spears or Brad Pitt, not Ralph Nader, Bono or Nelson Mandela, and more college students want to be Donald Trump or Martha Stewart, not Robert F. Kennedy, Jr.

Democracy of the Damned

In post-truth America used cars are sold as pre-owned, crime suspects are called persons of interest, prostitutes are called sex workers, illegal immigrants are called undocumented workers, and the president says we have a direct democracy. From the lowest to the highest, it seems that everyone is playing word games.

Innocent inaccurate statements are far and few between. Lying has become the currency of the realm. CNN reported that the average American lies once a day. Imagine how many times a day lobbyists, politicians and PR people lie. When everyone lies, of the many ways to think about American culture, the most disturbing way is to see it as a "culture of lying." We must question whether a culture of lying is consistent with a genuine democracy.

The dictionary says a lie is making an untrue statement with *intent* to deceive. Are people unsure about the *untruth* or the *intent* to deceive when they use every euphemism imaginable to avoid calling an untruth a lie and its presenter a liar? Yet, when politicians and their minions use untruths, it is reasonable to presume that they did so intentionally—it is *winning by deception*. Facile "I misspoke" excuses are usually just more lies. Appearing on Al Franken's radio show in May 2004, FOX News contributor Linda Chavez admitted that she "misspoke" when she denied having called Senator John Kerry a "communist apologist." Chavez denied having called Kerry a "communist apologist" during an interview on *FOX & Friends*, just four days after her nationally syndicated column calling Senator John Kerry a "communist apologist" appeared in newspapers and on The Heritage Foundation's website Townhall.com.

Today, it is perfectly valid to presume intent to deceive for public statements by radio and television commentators, as well as political and business leaders. Now, the ends justify the lies. Americans should presume intent, and when they observe untrue statements an L-word should spring forth. Presumption of innocence is proper in criminal proceedings. But with so many untrue statements being tossed around, sensible Americans should presume intent to trick, misinform, and mislead, once statements are shown to be incorrect. Sad to say, but in our culture of lying, accidental or innocent untrue statements are rare.

Most troubling, there is little moral indignation and outrage about dishonesty outside of family. American society has institutionalized dishonesty and corruption, despite so much religiosity among Americans. No longer is "honesty the best policy." Noted researcher on lying and honesty Bella DePaulo concluded: "Lying is a routine event. It has become part of the fabric of our lives, almost a necessity of our social and professional life." Today, keeping up with the competition supports keeping up with lies. The truth no longer sets you free; it puts you at a disadvantage. And the more time-poor you are, the easier it is to lie and believe lies. Speaking and finding truth takes time—democracy requires time. As Gar Alperovitz said: "democracy becomes meaningless if people do not have time to participate." In America's workaholic-fast-food-speed-dial-mouse-click-away culture lying is a seductive expedient and democracy is its victim.

In 1960, 58 percent of Americans believed that "most people can be trusted." Not all that impressive. It has gotten much worse; it dropped to 40 percent in 1998, and is probably a smaller *minority* now. As to public perception of large corporations, a 2004 Harris poll found 75 percent of Americans believed they were either "not good" or "terrible." This was consistent with a 2000 *Business Week* poll that found 82 percent agreed with the view that "Business has gained too much power over too many aspects of American life." Considering the powerful influence of business on government, the lack of trust in business is relevant. Why? Because democracy requires trust and honesty. Commonplace, congenital lying—a cultural status quo—must not be condoned. It must be fought. The fight for honesty is crucial to restoring American democracy.

Rampant lying undercuts laws, rules, accountability, and civic obligations. It fosters time-blindness, the inability to see future consequences of current acts. People lie to themselves about the future. When you can't trust your fellow citizens and elected officials, who are left to protect fragile democracy? Can you trust the news? Can you trust the courts? Can you trust social security to be there when you need it? Can you trust products to work and prescription drugs to be safe? Can you trust banks and the stock market? Can you trust the government to come to your aid after a natural disaster? Can you trust vaccine availability? A free society with too much freedom to lie is democracy damned.

Americans have every right to be cynical, which my dictionary illustrates by referring to people "who say that democracy cannot be honest and efficient." Politicians and business leaders have become "sinical," which I propose means not caring about the public's disgust with dishonesty and corruption. *Sinics are sinfully contemptuous of Americans, seeing them as helpless, uninterested, or gullible.* In 2005, several senior aides to Kentucky's governor were charged with hiring people on the basis of politics rather than merit, but even before they could be brought to trial the governor pardoned all of them. The governor was a sinic. Sinics send these messages: Trust us, not your lying eyes. Leave the nation to us. Vote for the choices we give you. Keep spending. Take another prescription drug to feel better. Believe that things are getting better. Trust laws and courts. Believe that the economy will benefit you. Ignore so much personal and national debt. Entrust your democracy to us, not yourself.

Do As We Didn't

The bad news is that in the 2004 election young people age 18 to 24 had the lowest voter turnout at 47 percent. Fortunately, many young Americans see the contradictions and injustices in our deMOCKracy. Listen to the wisdom of Jonathan Pattishall, a 15-year old high school freshman in Durham, North Carolina, as he saw the world in 2004, as published in *The Independent*:

> I am terrified of inheriting an undemocratic system of government. I am petrified by the thought of having no real choice or say in what happens in our supposedly 'democratic' country. ...I noticed that, according to the [dictionary] definition of a free republic, it is necessary for a government to be truly representative of the citizens of the country. So what happens if the two main political parties in a two-party system don't represent the people of a country anymore? You need to have choice—serious, honest choice. ...the only parties that get attention are the Democratic and Republican parties. No third parties or independent candidates get any meaningful attention. ...They don't get recognition in the media because corporate interests do not back them. They are trying to invigorate the armchair activist to get out and not only vote, but possibly become involved in local politics. They are asking Americans to reclaim their heritage of democracy, because democracy requires the serious participation of the people.

Here is how college student Tony Torres saw the world, from an article in Virginia Tech's *Collegiate Times*:

> The American people do not benefit from a two-man race or our two-party system. The American people deserve real choice. ...For the past 60 years, both the Republican and Democratic parties have largely pushed the same policies, run on the same platforms and supported nearly identical foreign policies. While it's true there have occasionally been slight differences on tax policy, the environment or labor laws, the reality is the differences are far less relevant than the similarities. ...Enough is enough. Let's take back our country from a two-party system that, in many ways, far more resembles a single party dominating our lives and our government.

Temple University student Nadeem Muaddi also wrote in the *Temple News* about political reality:

> The last time I checked the U.S. government was created 'by the

people, for the people.' Doesn't that mean that the President owes his allegiance to the general public? ...If we swallow our pride and vote for the less un-ideal candidate, then we're basically being forced to vote for someone that we wouldn't want as our president under any other normal circumstances. ...Let's set the bar for what a president should be."

Will young people with this kind of insight hold on to their integrity and become status quo busters? Will they revitalize our democracy? Or will our democracy continue to slide downhill and our nation's democracy deficit, like our trade and budget deficits—keep rising?

Democracy is hard, even when it's easy. Actually when it just seems easy and is taken for granted or merely griped about. Let's hope that America's youth can do what their parents did not—restore American democracy to its promise.

Chapter 2

Democracy's Arrow: From Personal Seething to Restoring Democracy

America will never be destroyed from the outside. If we falter, and lose our freedoms, it will be because we destroyed ourselves.

—Abraham Lincoln

The Greeks said that the peak is the moment of descent. Making progress means the arrow of change points up. If things go wrong, at a critical time the arrow turns and points down. How soon can you know through experience that the peak has been reached? It requires awareness of decline. One must resist smiley-face optimism, believing that our nation is still improving. It comes to this: Can Americans face facts about our democracy's deficit and decline and become energized to turn democracy's arrow up again? Yes, but it will take compelling information that moves people beyond sentiments revealed in surveys and opinion polls to a much deeper and stronger commitment to personally assist changing many negative status quo conditions. The case for change follows.

Rulers Have Their Own Rules

No democracy is perfect. At any time every democracy is getting better or getting worse, because democracy is not a state, but an intention and process. Democracy must be personal. Democracy must be who we are and what we do. For each of us, democracy is our responsibility. You can hate politics and politicians, but democracy always comes back to each of us. We the people must create the opportunity to regain control over our destiny by taking away the control now held by the power elites. Active political dissent must create political destiny. "Dissent is what rescues democracy from a quiet death behind closed doors," said Lewis H. Lapham. Dissent is the *duty* of citizens of a democracy.

For a long time, American democracy was getting better, striving for perfection. There were effective self-correcting mechanisms to maintain the effort to fulfill a proud American vision of democracy. Progress was comfort enough for accepting a less-than-perfect democracy. We once could be proud of being on the path toward making our noble constitutional vision a reality, especially when social progress was being made. Now, the self-correcting mechanisms hidden beneath the visible, self-congratulatory trappings of our electoral democracy are thoroughly corroded. We have beaten our foreign enemies but not the evil, greedy, and corrupt among us.

Historians will eventually debate exactly when the deflection point occurred, when American democracy peaked and then started to decline. But it clearly had happened late in the 20th century. From the 1950s through 1964, surveys found an impressive 75 percent of Americans trusted the federal government to do what was right nearly always or most of the time. You would expect this in a great democracy. With Watergate and the Vietnam War mess this level of faith in government dropped and stayed around 22 to 33 percent through 1994. The problem was that more Americans felt that politicians were dishonest, were only out for themselves, said one thing and did another, and didn't represent the people. In 1995 it was just 15 percent. In the late 1990s it started to rise, was 38 percent in 1997 and reached 44 percent in 2000. Also in 2000 a poll found cynicism running high with 49 percent believing that "quite a few" of those running government were "a little crooked." After the September 11, 2001 catastrophe the public's faith in government surged for awhile, reaching 75 percent in early 2002. But it dropped back down to 29 percent in 2005. A survey by *The Economist* in 2005 found only 17 percent of U.S. voters believed that their elected officials represented their priorities.

The good news about democracy's decline is that many Americans feel it viscerally. Loss of trust in government sets the stage for doing something about it. If only academics, policy experts, and activist dissenters were conscious of the decline but not the broad public there would be little hope for repairing American democracy. The challenge is to convert widely held cynicism, skepticism and alienation into citizen engagement for change. Hope rescues cynicism. If Americans have been duped, it is that the solution to what they perceive wrong is electing better people from the two-party duopoly, or that somehow economic benefits offset a lower quality democracy, or that threats like terrorism justify chipping away at democratic processes and protections.

Everyone should be shaken by what the 2005 survey by the Program on International Policy Attitudes found on Americans' views about U.S. democracy. As to how much influence the views of the majority of Americans *should have* on the decisions of elected federal officials, on a scale of 0 to 10 (0 meaning not at all influential and 10 meaning extremely influential) the mean response was 8.0. In contrast, when asked how much influence the majority of Americans *actually has*, the response was only 4.5. Sounds like a democracy gap. When asked what percentage of the time Congress makes decisions that are the same as the will of the majority of Americans, the mean answer was just 39 percent—less than chance. No wonder that the evaluation of how democratic the U.S. government is was just 6.2 out of 10 (completely democratic). The study concluded that there was "a lack of confidence that the U.S. is an ideal democracy." Not ideal is one thing. Incompletely democratic is disheartening. A continuing democracy decline is an intolerable, worse predicament. But a growing awareness that things have gone too far downhill offers hope for mobilizing demands for specific changes.

Such is the state of the union. A distrusting majority and a gap between the people and their representatives document the turning of democracy's arrow downward. How did we get here? After World War II the country needed mass consumerism, but after a few decades unbridled consumerism produced citizen distraction that allowed politicians to become increasingly dishonest and corrupted by corporate interests. Vietnam and Watergate also had a lot to do with the downturn in Americans' trust and confidence in government. Waking up to what's wrong, however, is not the same thing as determination to fix the republic.

Patriotism demands we turn the arrow of democracy from down to up. But, before that can happen, there must be broad public recognition that American democracy is much less than it could and should be—and that it is feasible to repair it. After all, you don't fix what is not broke. As Aldous Huxley said:

> The greatest triumphs of propaganda have been accomplished, not by doing something, but by refraining from doing. Great is truth, but still greater, from a practical point of view, is silence about truth.

Walking away from politics is not the answer. And personal seething but public silence about declining American democracy is ruinous.

Discontent must produce active dissent. Otherwise, we are headed inexorably toward a fake democracy. Americans must extrapolate their personal insights about what is wrong to the future. They must see active dissent as protecting their personal future, not just an altruistic effort for the good of the country. They need to buy into a long-wave theory of politics by which revolutionary change is eventually realized. They must see themselves as political descendents of the Founding Fathers.

To get into a fixing mode people must understand the multiple forces behind our democracy's decay. They range from meaningless elections resulting from corrupt redistricting, to corporate campaign financing that corrupts politicians, to false patriotism and distractive politics. Here's how each in turn have contributed to a decline with a lot of momentum.

Pushing democracy downhill was the loss of competitive races for the House of Representatives, because of hyperpartisan redistricting. In the last three elections, the incumbent reelection rate was over 98 percent. Not what our Founding Fathers envisioned. Such low turnover is not a sign of great public servants; it signals democracy dishonor. That level is what "we expect to see in countries like North Korea or China, not the United States," decried Charles Lewis of the Center for Public Integrity.

Redistricting is a serious impediment to democracy, but no discussion of our problems would be complete without understanding how campaign financing corrodes the political system. Through financial investments, corporate corruption of politicians and government has steadily shredded our democracy. Though there is a long history of corporate corruption of American government, at some point it achieved unprecedented pervasiveness and produced the deflection in democracy's arrow. Complicating perceptions is that American corruption is different than in other countries, out of sight of most people, dominated by power elites and elected officials, with little opportunity for most Americans to participate. In a nutshell, money begets corruption, corruption begets power, power begets money, which begets more corruption, which begets more power, which begets more money, and on and on. Cancerous self-replication eats away the authenticity of American democracy.

Central to this cycle are the obscene legal ways used by members of Congress to obtain funds from corporate interests, despite attempts to make the public believe that there are tough federal restrictions. Only stupid and careless lawmakers occasionally get nabbed for breaking a rule or law, like Representative Randy "Duke" Cunningham who got nabbed in 2005 for taking over $2 million in bribes from defense contractors. Getting money for travel from legitimate sources is commonplace. From 2000 to 2004, 628 lawmakers made 6,242 trips worth $18.3 million, according to the nonpartisan PoliticalMoneyLine. The split was 57 percent Democrats to 43 percent Republicans. There are all kinds of nonprofit groups and academic centers that provide freebees to members of Congress including the Congressional Economic Leadership Institute, the Congressional Sportsmen's Foundation, the Burns Telecom Center at Montana State University (named after Senator Conrad Burns), and the Trent Lott National Center for Excellence in Economic Development and Entrepreneurship at the University of Southern Mississippi.

On any typical day when Congress is in session there are 20 to 40 fundraisers, ranging from receptions with food and drink, charity tournaments, fishing and hunting events, golf outings, sports events, and boat trips. In these many ways, business groups, companies, and corporate lobbyists funnel goodies to those they want to influence, both lawmakers and their staffers. This is American style corruption—a part of the accepted status quo, the dollar-driven, cheating culture. As Bill Allison of the nonpartisan Center for Public Integrity summed up: "Some of the most outrageous things that happen in Washington are perfectly within the rules." Rules that serve the rulers.

Three of America's greatest politicians shared the same basic fear. Thomas Jefferson wrote:

> The spirit of the times may alter, will alter. Our rulers will become corrupt, our people careless.... We must crush in its birth the aristocracy of our moneyed corporations, which dare already to bid defiance to the laws of our country.

We did not listen, so our democracy has become more like a corporate theocracy and fascist feudal state in which "we the serfs" serve the corporate state as workers, consumers and docile, distracted citizens. Misrepresentative government and corporatism dispirit our times.

Ponder the following prescient statement of President Abraham Lincoln in a letter to Colonel William F. Elkins in 1864:

> I see in the near future a crisis approaching that unnerves me and causes me to tremble for the safety of my country...corporations have

been enthroned and an era of corruption in high places will follow, and the money power of the country will endeavor to prolong its reign by working upon the prejudices of the people until all wealth is aggregated in a few hands and the Republic is destroyed.

Decades later, President Franklin Delano Roosevelt echoed this fear:

The first truth is that the liberty of a democracy is not safe if the people tolerate the growth of private power to a point where it becomes stronger than their democratic state itself. That is, in essence, fascism—ownership of government by an individual, by a group, or by any other controlling power. Among us today a concentration of private power without equal in history is growing.

Here we are in a new century and corporate power is still growing. Already, power elites own a private government that controls the public government. A disappointed FDR would see today that fascism is alive and well in the USA.

Compounding the problem of democracy's decline is dishonesty and false patriotism. Today's most powerful political leaders do not talk truth, not because we have escaped the danger that Jefferson, Lincoln and Roosevelt contemplated, but because we have succumbed to it. Our elected "representatives" are silent about what is most disturbing and destructive in our society. Most hypocritical are Republicans and conservatives—especially talk show hosts—with loud reverence for our Constitution, but who do not walk the talk of democracy.

Democracy's decline has also suffered from the successful Bush and right-wing strategy of recent years: the "politics of distraction." It is the intentional political distraction of the populace. The Iraq war, social security reform, social issues like abortion and gay marriage, stem cell research, and now the doctrine of spreading democracy to the Middle East, keep attention away from the most important problem—the unraveling of our own democracy. Often, what is distractive also serves another purpose. The preemptive Iraq war served the large providers of military equipment and the petroleum industry. Social issues serve the religious right. In political physics, distraction destroys democracy. Distraction is a weapon for dismantling a democracy as surely as a military coup is. Awareness of a rotten state of the union as revealed in polls and surveys is one thing. It does equate to citizen action. One problem is that distracted citizens are largely unaware exactly how power elites surreptitiously use military power, foreign policy, and free-trade globalization to increase corporate profits that finance more corporate corruption of government. This distraction strategy has worked so well for so long that we are now an almost inconceivable distance from the democracy originally envisioned by people like Thomas Jefferson.

Strong forces propelling democracy's decline require equally strong forces to reverse it. Reversal has not happened because dissent-driven demand for change has not been loud and organized enough, or contagious. Consider the irony that consumer spending accounts for a whopping 70 percent of the national economy. Yet this market clout has not translated into collective power over the political and economic systems. Ordinary Americans should see themselves as a potentially powerful working class able to escape the bondage of the ruling class of elites. A big problem is the hectic American lifestyle that makes it hard for people to turn their energy and economic power into political dissent. William E. Hudson in *American Democracy in Peril* made an important point about the nature of democracy decline in America and why fighting it is so difficult:

> To say that American democracy is in peril, however, does not mean that it will perish tomorrow. Military coups or dictatorial takeovers are not a feature, thankfully, of our political history and tradition. An abrupt end to democratic practices is not the sort of peril we face. …the challenges American democracy faces are much more subtle than coups or takeovers by avowed authoritarians. Each challenge produces a gradual erosion of democracy that most Americans are not likely to notice. The very subtlety of the challenge constitutes its danger and justifies the need for words like *peril, alarm, challenge*, and *danger* to describe their collective effects.

The point is that negative feelings about government do not necessarily translate into sharper understanding that America's democracy decline is as dangerous as a foreign attack or invasion. We do not need a call to arms. We need a call for vigorous dissent that reaches the hearts and minds of millions of unsatisfied Americans. One thing is certain. Don't expect Democratic or Republican politicians to put the brakes on America's declining democracy. As Robert F. Kennedy, Jr. observed, "the Republicans are 95 percent corrupt and the Democrats are 75 percent corrupt." With the two-party duopoly's continuing neglect, we the people need our own insurgency for democracy, right here in the land of freedom and opportunity.

Get the Anti-Corruption Spray

Bill Moyers was right: "People with money should not be able to buy more democracy than people without money."

Corruption is the engine driving democracy's decline and Americans have become blasé about it. Reading and hearing about corruption is a distractive national pastime. Whether Americans believe that anyone can erase political corruption is dubious.

A relatively small number of people account for most corruption in the United States. These power elites consist of the corrupted—the politicians, and the corrupters—the special interests of the corporatist state. Few American government workers are corrupt. Not so in other nations, where corruption is more flagrant and government workers openly demand bribes and payments. What Robert F. Kennedy, Jr. said helps explain why the U.S. seems less corrupt than it really is. He talked about "legalized bribery," and said: "Corporations, no matter how big they are, should not be running the government. We are in a democracy, and we should be running this government."

Idaho Republican Senator William E. Borah outlined in stark terms just how corruption works in American politics:

> Money has come to be the moving power in American politics. Some years ago, politicians got into the habit of seeking contributions from men of great wealth. ...It was inevitable, if the large sums were to be given, that large sums would have to be returned in some way. Hence, money and politicians joined forces, and money has its say in shaping legislation and in administering the laws of the country. It is a fearful national evil and will in the end, if not controlled, destroy the government of the people and substitute, therefore, a government of the few—the few who have sufficient money with which to buy the government.

This sounds like it was said today. But Senator Borah was a progressive Republican and said the above in 1926! That this statement holds today, nearly 80 years later, sends a chilling message about the strength of the corruption status quo and the failure of many attempts to change it. It also reveals the horrible transformation that the party of Lincoln has undergone from sounding the clarion call against corruption to becoming its handmaiden.

The effects of widespread corruption are pervasive. Political corruption breeds citizen alienation and apathy, and when it suppresses needed change it breeds violence. Gun ownership is prized just in case the government attempts too much change. Seekers of change, who cannot find a peaceful, effective strategy, may turn to violence. America's brilliance is to keep violence by citizens away from government and economic infrastructure. Our acknowledged violent culture has two normal faces: street and personal crimes versus greed-driven white collar and corporate crimes. The Oklahoma City bombing of a government building was so shocking because it was such an aberration, a rare case of domestic *political* violence. At some fundamental level, however, so much of the violence reflects America's class struggle between the powerful and powerless.

The American myth "of unlimited opportunity" is that we have so many paths to change. But the paths are for limited personal change. Corruption blocks political change. Affluence aside, rarely do the powerless become members of the power elites, the ruling class in our capitalist caste system. European colonialism and many later dictatorships collapsed because change was suppressed, rather than embraced so that wealth could be shared. Our war on terrorism results because so many others have found the routes to peaceful change in their nations blocked by corruption supported through our foreign policy. Less obvious is how American corruption has blocked reversal of American democracy's decline by Americans. Are we to wait for some foreign democratic nation to preemptively invade the United States and restore our democracy? Is New Zealand up to the task? When democracy fails in a superpower there is no one to come to the rescue, except its citizens.

Along this line, in November 2005 E. J. Dionne Jr. wrote in the *Washington Post*: "Perhaps we should redeploy the democracy experts we have sent to the Middle East and ask them to work on our Congress." Why? Because, according to Dionne "our national government is dysfunctional." The occasion was passage in the House of a budget-cutting bill that hit social programs hard rather than rescinding tax cuts. Representative Jim Ramstad was one of the few Republican dissenters and said: "We should cut the pork, not the poor."

Upstream Corruption

Of course there has always been corruption of politicians. Corruption has worsened over time, however, both in its form and magnitude. Corruption of individuals is not the same as a corrupt *system*. We have deeply entrenched, institutionalized and legal corruption.

Americans easily see anti-democratic systems as dictatorships (Cuba), monarchies (Saudi Arabia), and autocratic, authoritarian governments (communist China). But they are not grasping (and gasping) that their own democracy has been slipping away, even though they see problems with specific government programs, the Iraq war, and the economy.

It seems hard for Americans to comprehend that legally protected freedoms alone do not make a great democracy. The world sees a "free society" with a *misrepresentative* government and extreme social and economic inequalities. University of Michigan Professor Kenneth Boulding got it right: "A world of unseen dictatorship is conceivable, still using the forms of democratic government." Unseen dictatorship has happened right before our eyes in the United States of Delusion, in our corporatist state, in our plutocracy. It is the secretive restricted political system.

In *Dirty Little Secrets—The Persistence of Corruption American Politics*, Larry J. Sabato and Glenn R. Simpson made the case for reforms, none of which included dealing with the culture of lying and the need for status quo busting by individuals outside the political system:

> We understand that as a reflection of the undeniable darker side of human nature, corruption has been, and is, a staple of every society. But the form of government chosen by a people dramatically affects the *extent* of corruption. ...even in a relatively favorable anticorruption environment such as ours, a disturbingly widespread pattern of abuses can be found... ...By the late 1990s, repeated mini-scandals about political excesses of various sorts and overweening special-interest influence on government appeared only to deepen cynicism and broaden the torpid apathy about corruption. ...*The logical response is not cynicism but eternal vigilance against misuse of power, and a vigorous, unceasing search to expose old and new forms of corruption.*

The form of government not only affects the extent of corruption, it also determines the *form* of corruption. American corruption has sustained "torpid apathy" and "cynicism." Because so much of it is bipartisan and legal, it seems unbeatable.

Historically, "downstream corruption" has been quite visible to residents in the most corrupt undemocratic societies; corruption is no secret and it is accepted as a part of the culture—people try to get a piece of the corruption-pie or use it to their advantage. In traditional corrupt societies nearly every type of government worker can find a way to take money for doing or not doing something of value, not just from businesses but also ordinary citizens. A resident bribes a police officer for a favored parking space; a business owner bribes a regulatory official to ignore illegal toxic waste dumping; a restaurant owner bribes a local government official to sanction placement of tables and chairs on the sidewalk. Corruption is just a cost of doing business and dealing with government.

In America there is "upstream corruption" that is no less effective, but far more submerged in the complexities of the apparatus of politics, government and business. We have laws that legalize campaign financing and certain kinds of "goodies" and "freebies" to appointed and elected officials. Ordinary citizens cannot get a piece of this corruption or personally take advantage of it. They are unable to become members of the power elite who receive the gigantic financial rewards of a corrupt system. Like environmental pollution, American corruption is not prevented where it is first created, but controlled at the end of the pipe when—if outrageously illegal—it *sometimes* becomes visible and scandalous. When that happens, hands get slapped, incompetent corrupters get jailed—including a number of governors and congressmen in recent years—and corruption is reconfigured and made stealthier. Corruption is the path to money and power.

In sum, downstream corruption is accepted as a culture characteristic involving a broad spectrum of people, while upstream corruption is either legal or criminal and involves political and corporate elites.

Using data from 1982 to 1997 on more than 100 nations, a most interesting research finding was that "Unlike non-democracies, whose economic performance significantly suffers from corruption, corrupt democracies apparently grow just as fast as democracies with little to no corruption," according to an article in *International Political Science Review*. Exactly the point about "upstream corruption"—elites have crafted a high-performing economic system, but mostly for those at the top of it. Corruption fuels economic inequality.

Americans are chasing money and success more than they are chasing changes in the status quo that would remove corruption. Quality of life subtly and sometimes not so subtly declines, even as our political "leaders" remind us how wonderful life is in America. Perceptions are clouded by the status quo bias belief that Americans live in the world's greatest country. Worse yet, time-poor Americans have little time to be rebels, even though being time-poor ultimately means being democracy-poor.

A Natural Democracy Disaster

Teddy Roosevelt said many incisive things, including this:

> To destroy this invisible government, to befoul the unholy alliance between corrupt business and corrupt politics is the first task of the statesmanship of the day.

Nearly a century later—o-n-e h-u-n-d-r-e-d years, this unholy alliance is alive and well, and hurricane Katrina in 2005 showed that it gets in the way of providing the most essential services that Americans have every right to expect from their government when natural forces lash out, especially when lives are at stake.

The 2005 Katrina catastrophe should go down in American history as a wakeup call about our government's deterioration. As New Orleans quickly flooded, stranded and suffering victims asked "How can this be happening in the United States?" Television audiences saw what they are accustomed to seeing in third world countries. The flooding had been repeatedly predicted and, therefore, was preventable. The framing of Katrina by the Bush administration as the nation's largest and worst natural disaster was designed to excuse government's neglect and incompetence because it wasn't a natural disaster but one of our own making. We knew we had to build the levies stronger, we knew that larger scale preparations needed to be made. Worse than not preventing the flooding was the lack of fast aid. In truth, Katrina did not destroy New Orleans as much as bad politicians, bureaucratic bungling, and as later revealed poor levee design had. Nature throws us hazards; people turn them into disasters. Unless they take the threats seriously as the

Dutch government did. It addressed the flooding hazard with costly and sophisticated technology to safeguard their below-sea-level country's citizens.

City and state failures were evident, including: No city plans to evacuate some 125,000 mostly poor and African American residents who were known to lack the ability to leave on their own, no use of available school buses for evacuation, no quick evacuation of hospitals or tourists, no plan to maintain law and order, and no pre-positioning of necessary supplies in the city's evacuation centers. The governor failed to move National Guard units into the city when it became clear a very strong hurricane would devastate the city. Federally, the Army Corps of Engineers did not even have a plan ready to implement when levees failed. There was no communications backup critical to emergency responders despite the predictable failure of land and cellular phone systems in such a situation. As the *Washington Post* editorialized: "Given the known risks, the response of government—local, state and federal— to the approaching storm was inadequate, uncoordinated and inept. ...If the response to an anticipated risk is so poor, what, then, would happen in the face of a surprise event such as a bioterrorism incident or nuclear attack?"

Mike Parker, former civilian head of the Army Corps of Engineers emphasized: "I blame a lot of our leaders over the past 40 years." With more adequate funding, he said: "Levees would have been higher, levees would have been bigger, there would have been other pumps put in." A senior Corps official admitted: "The design was not adequate to protect against a storm of this nature because we were not authorized to provide a Category Four or Five protection design." However, Katrina was only a Category Three when it hit New Orleans. Thousands of deaths and injuries, hundreds of thousands of terribly disrupted lives, and a national cost well over $200 billion could have been prevented by spending some $20 billion for both wetlands restoration south of New Orleans and beefing up the city's levee system. What fiscal insanity.

Disturbingly, in 2001 the Federal Emergency Management Agency (FEMA) had said that a hurricane striking New Orleans was one of the top three likely major disasters facing America. Also in 2001, an article in *Scientific American* was entitled "Drowning New Orleans." Among the notable things it pointed out were: "A major hurricane could swamp

New Orleans under 20 feet of water, killing thousands. ...New Orleans is a disaster waiting to happen. ...A direct hit is inevitable. ..Thus far, however, Washington has turned down appeals for substantial aid." A federal plan had been created after a 1965 flood, but the project was never funded to completion.

Nevertheless, President George W. Bush said this a few days after the calamity: "I don't think anybody anticipated the breach of the levees." Anybody? Was this a lie or was Bush's staff ignorant of what every knowledgeable person knew? Tim Russert on *Meet the Press* asked incredulously: "How could the president be so wrong, so misinformed?" Apparently, he could not bring himself to add "or lie so outrageously." The director of the National Hurricane Center said he had informed top federal officials 32 hours before landfall that Katrina's storm surge was likely to cause catastrophic flooding. Better yet, John Breaux, the former Louisiana senator and close Bush ally, said that he had spoken to Bush about the potential for failed levees the year before.

Despite all the evidence of what was inevitable and required, there was a drastic cut in funding for the New Orleans flood control system by the Bush administration because of the Iraq war funding needs, tax cuts, and corporate handouts. Funds that the Corps wanted for preventing a flood catastrophe were slashed by 44.2 percent from 2001 through 2005. In early 2005, the Bush White House opposed funding that the Louisiana congressional delegation sought for flood control. It also drastically cut funding for FEMA. Despite these facts, White House spokesperson Scott McClellan claimed that "flood control has been a priority of this administration from day one." This lie matched the Bush lie for chutzpah. After some FEMA staff whistle blowing and widespread criticism, about six weeks later the Bush White House admitted "It turned out we were all wrong."

In Katrina's aftermath corporate looting ran rampant. Billions of dollars were quickly given through no-bid contracts with waivers of liability to companies with ties to the Bush administration (including Halliburton, Fluor and Bechtel). On the one hand, great sacrifice was asked of workers—laws about wages were gutted temporarily and permission to hire illegal immigrants was granted, further depressing wages. On the other hand, large corporations from outside the region were handed profitable new business and were not asked to make any sacrifices.

A "natural" disaster quickly became a democracy disaster as then House Majority Leader Tom "The Hammer" Delay rejected federal spending cuts to offset the high costs of rebuilding New Orleans, fixing considerable Gulf coast public infrastructure, and assisting more than a million displaced Americans. Delay said, "there is no fat left to cut in the federal budget," a Katrina-size lie, considering the multi-billion dollar pork projects and corporate welfare he had recently championed in the House. When Congress did get to some budget cutting the Republicans headed straight for social programs, not corporate pork.

Who made a connection made between the Katrina disaster and its aftermath and the democracy failure? Only on Internet blogs; here are two examples:

> Democracy is a bit of a crude instrument. Public officials have strong incentives to direct funds away from dull-but-worthy endeavors and toward well-financed interest groups. …Unless voters and the press demand the heads of officials who screw up, future screw-ups are guaranteed.
>
> The destruction of New Orleans represents a confluence of many of the most pernicious trends in American politics and culture: poverty, racism, militarism, elitist greed, environmental abuse, public corruption and the decay of democracy at every level.

Katrina should become a metaphor for America's corrupt corporatist state. When the House voted for a $51.8 billion aid package the National Republican Congressional Committee quickly issued a press release attacking 65 Democrats for voting against the aid. In fact, they all voted for it, while eleven Republicans voted against it. Just political scamming as usual. Maureen Dowd rightly called our post-Katrina nation the United States of Shame for providing too little too late to devastated citizens.

Compassionate Corporate Cronyism

Corruption by corporate interests plagues Republicans and Democrats. As part of then House Speaker Newt Gingrich's Contract with America campaign, Congress passed the Private Securities Litigation Reform Act. Before this law, auditors could be held liable for all damages resulting from corporate fraud, but now it is necessary to show *intent* by auditors to defraud, which is difficult to prove. President Bill Clinton vetoed it. But unrelenting industry lobbying successfully moved

Congress to override the veto with the help of 20 Senate Democrats and 89 House Democrats.

More recently, in 2005, Congress passed bankruptcy reform sought by the credit card industry for years. Downtrodden Americans would suffer. Half of the 1.6 million personal bankruptcies in 2004 resulted from crushing medical costs. Industry profits in 2004 were $30 *billion*, much coming from various outrageous fees, not interest charges. The industry extended $3 *trillion* in credit to Americans in 2000, which surely is much higher today. Not surprising, considering that credit card companies bombarded Americans with 5 *billion* mail solicitations in 2001, and surely more today.

Like their government, Americans spend what they do not have. Average credit card debt for an American family rose 53 percent between 1989 and 2001, but rose 184 percent for very low-income families and 75 percent for middle-class families. Two Supreme Court rulings have allowed credit card companies to escape state usury laws limiting interest rates and fees. But this enormously profitable and greedy industry wanted more and got it, including the votes of 18 Senate Democrats. These weren't even needed because of the 55-Republican Senate majority, who all voted for the bankruptcy bill. Democrats also voted against amendments, including an attempt to limit interest rates to 30 percent. Keeping their campaign contributors happy revealed their moral bankruptcy. The credit card companies had spent $34 million lobbying for the law in the previous ten years and Congress gave them a high return on their investment. The *Washington Post* editorialized that "The bankruptcy bill offers a useful gauge of diminishing democracy," a rare instance of good issue framing.

Rest assured Congress takes care of business. In October 2004, in the heat of a close presidential campaign, by a vote of 280 to 141 the House passed a tax bill that provided an enormous amount of corporate handouts, subsidies and welfare—over $140 *billion*. Tax breaks went to manufacturing companies, energy producers, NASCAR track owners, mall builders, timber operations, restaurant owners, bow and arrow makers, Hollywood production companies, biodiesel producers, tobacco farmers, and others. However, on the flip side, it took away the tax deduction for the fair-value of cars donated to charities. This drove charities wild. A month before the bill passed, 259 charities asked

Congress not to do this. But charities did not get the generosity given to corporate sectors. Writing in the *Washington Post*, Steven Pearlstein summed up the event:

> This is largely a Republican bill reflecting the majority party's tax-cutting philosophy and increasingly strong corporate ties. But it says something about the moral and intellectual bankruptcy of Congressional Democrats—and their lack of political imagination—that they haven't rallied behind a Senate filibuster of this legislative abomination.

"Moral" will come up a lot in this book. Not surprisingly, the U.S. Senate passed the bill by a 69 to 17 vote, and it received President Bush's signature. Senator John McCain commented that the bill was "disgraceful" and "a classic example of the special interests prevailing over the people's interest." Senator Edward M. Kennedy said the bill "puts the interest of the big corporations above the public interests." In contrast, the majority sinical view was expressed by Senator Charles E. Grassley: "Let the record be clear, this bill is fair. This bill is balanced." First comes corruption, then the lies. The front page *Washington Post* headline was "Senate Passes Corporate Tax Bill." With journalistic integrity, that headline would have been something like "Senate Provides Corporate Handouts."

A *Post* editorial did refer to Republicans in Congress that "skew the economic playing field so as to reward their friends and fill their campaign treasuries." But the *New York Times'* front-page story did not have a quote like that of Senators McCain and Kennedy regarding the disregard of the public interest, and its editorial did not address the failed governance issue. There was no moral indignation about the loss of effective representative government or angst over the victimization of taxpayers. Declining democracy is no longer news—not because Americans don't care but because news organizations ignore it. More about the media later.

As government has shifted from serving the public interest to ignoring it, the business sector has grown increasingly obsessed with profits and to hell with their customers. Capitalism that cares little about customers would fail without government protection. Considering all the Enron, WorldCom, Tyco, Adelphia and Global Crossing corporate scandals that have devastated the lives of so many workers and investors in recent years, companies callously exporting jobs to foreign countries, companies selling unsafe products (think Vioxx), and business support for illegal immigration, no wonder Americans do not trust business. In 2002, the cost of street crime was $18 billion, compared to $250 billion from corporate crimes; there were over 16,000 homicides but over 600,000 mostly corporate related deaths of workers, tobacco users, and victims of air pollution and hospital mistakes. Arianna Huffington was right: "corporate scandal is a political scandal—corporate money corrupts politicians who by passing or neglecting to pass laws make corporate crime possible and profitable." When you think crime, think corporate supremacy.

As to the free market and capitalism, smaller and more ethical companies that are not players in the influence peddling game are at a disadvantage. Honest business people have a competitive disadvantage. They are not competing on a level "free-market" playing field. Their less ethical competitors with the help of lobbyists and campaign contributions are reaping benefits from government subsidies, tax loopholes, regulatory loopholes, and special consideration when seeking government work, like no-bid contracts. The current system has been called "crony capitalism" for good reason.

Crony capitalism makes a mockery of the free market concept. Ultimately it is consumers, entrepreneurs, and innovative start-up companies that pay for this distortion of fair competitiveness. In third world countries it is more apparent how widespread corruption means higher costs for doing business, higher prices for customers, lower pay for workers, and less health and environmental protection. In the United States, less visible and more legalized corruption is just as effective.

Money buys advantage, whether it is money to individual politicians, to the two major parties, or to other groups working on behalf of one candidate or party. Lobbyists and government relations people have only one common goal—get benefits for their business clients or employers. Just like a military arms race, special interests compete with each other on the basis of how much money they can muster. It is just a cost of doing business—a tax deduction. It is estimated that about $2 billion is spent annually on direct lobbying—personal contact with lawmakers, plus another $4 billion on indirect lobbying, such as telemarketing and issue advertising.

This is what lobbyist Robert Rozen admitted: "The general public does not even begin to understand the degree to which moneyed private interests are able to influence public policy through their campaign contributions."

There is more bad news, given not to make you depressed but to make you angry.

Another window on the state of our democracy is the health care system. Should medical care be solely a matter of personal responsibility to be paid for by those who can afford it? Or should it be seen as a survival need guaranteed to all and paid for by all through a universal health care program? The latter is used by all other industrialized, democratic nations. It says a great deal about our democracy that almost one-sixth of the population has no health insurance and that per capita medical spending is much higher than in other advanced nations. The pursuit of happiness is greatly impeded by Americans' angst over unaffordable health care.

A 2004 editorial in the *Pioneer Press* said "Money-bought influence rules health care policy," and concluded that the "status quo means 45 million Americans were without insurance this year. It means that rising insurance premiums are swamping company and family budgets. Challenge the status quo." Physician Gerry Lower attacked the influence of corporatism in the medical and health care system that "is driven, not by human rights and human needs, but by the profit motive" and that maintains "a status quo profoundly lacking in science and democracy." We need more such public connections to democracy. A vibrant democracy would have within it the mechanisms to overthrow painful social inequities. In our corrupt democracy something as profoundly critical as health care causes far too much mental stress over the threat of financial bankruptcy.

Here is a related example of using government to support corporate rather than public interests. Medicare's new prescription drug program is expected to cost taxpayers $851 billion over ten years. It was greatly shaped by lobbyists for the pharmaceutical industry, a further sign of industry power over a weakened democracy. Families USA said that the industry "succeeded in getting a bill that does virtually nothing to moderate drug costs. ...The biggest winners are the drug companies and the managed care industry." Think compassionate corporate cronyism. Besides helping their financial backers, Republicans also pushed for passage of this Medicare extension in 2003 because they thought it would increase support among older voters in 2004, which it did modestly.

Government policy on the environment also shows a weak democracy. Americans care about federal environmental policy as documented in decades of polling. They understand that clean air and water is a personal necessity. They worry about pesticides in foods as the market demand for "organic" foods amply demonstrates. They want toxic waste sites in their communities cleaned up. They take global warming seriously. They certainly do not trust corporate America on their own to protect public health and safety or the natural environment.

These realities have not deterred President George W. Bush's administration from gutting many programs to benefit industry, as documented by Robert F. Kennedy, Jr. in *Crimes Against Nature* and by many environmental groups. Areas where progress was Bushwacked include: reducing mercury pollution, reducing emissions causing global warming, controlling development on wetlands, saving old-growth trees, and protecting wilderness lands. A group of 60 leading American scientists, including 20 Nobel laureates, issued a statement in 2004 about restoring the long applied principle of honoring scientific integrity in policymaking. It said, "The administration of George W. Bush has, however, disregarded this principle."

Chair of the Senate Environment and Public Works Committee, Republican James M. Inhofe had this view of environmentalists: "They are really liberals. They're all strong pro-abortionists, they're all pro-gun control people, flying under the flag of environmentalism." Even if all environmentalists were all these things, which they are not, so what? What do hot right-wing issues have to do with the Senate's responsibility to address real environmental problems?

Greg Wetstone of the Natural Resources Defense Council saw things correctly: "What's broken is a political system that's evading science, fact and public opinion." Millions of Americans are breathing polluted air, are unable to use polluted waters, and are living near toxic waste sites still waiting for cleanup. Their government has failed them, while many industries have avoided the costs of effective regulation. Each aspect of this state of affairs runs counter to what the majority of Americans want.

Americans also endure the cost of government energy policy.

Does energy policy serve citizens or companies? That's the core issue. In editorializing about energy policy in the Bush administration, the *Washington Post* in September 2004 said that "this, as far as energy is concerned, is a status quo administration." "The priorities of the oil and gas industry always come first," said the *Post*. Nine months later, the *Post* editorialized about the "status quo" energy bill in Congress. It said that both the White House and Congress would not do what was necessary to cut dependence on foreign petroleum, because they had not "managed to overcome the pressure of the automobile, utility, oil, gas and other lobbies that spend enormous amounts of money trying to protect the status quo." Corporate supremacists ruled the day when Congress passed the 2005 energy bill. It gave $15 billion in handouts to energy companies at a time when their profits were at all time highs, again demonstrating the moral bankruptcy of America's representative democracy.

Months later, as gasoline prices started to drop from historic highs, the media finally focused on scandalous, windfall profits announced by the major oil companies. The Senate held a hearing where Republicans (who routinely received considerable funds from the industry) revealed nothing but petroleum patriotism. The heads of the five largest oil companies showed no inclination to admit taking advantage of the public. To the chagrin of the senators, they all said that the recent federal handouts would have no affect on their decisions to invest more in either oil extraction or refining.

A majority of Americans have also been shocked by their government's refusal to stop the invasion of illegal immigrants, estimated at some 3 million annually, another reason for questioning the health of American democracy. Most people have wanted something done about this massive law-breaking. These illegals place burdens on many local governments and taxpayers because of higher costs for schools and medical care.

In truth, illegal immigrants now form a "servant class" in America. A 2004 NPR/Kaiser/Kennedy School poll found that 59 percent of non-immigrant Americans say illegal immigrants have hurt the national economy, 51 percent say recent immigrants have taken jobs away from Americans who want them, 54 percent believe most recent immigrants are illegal and of these 74 percent believe that the federal government has not done enough to address the problem. If everyone is to respect the rule of law, then *illegal* immigrants must be treated as what they are: law-breakers. California State Senator Tom McClintock was right: "Illegal immigrants are in direct violation of our federal immigration laws. These laws require them to be deported, not accommodated."

Why has the federal government not taken effective action, even in the face of terrorists entering through our porous borders? There is only one answer—another form of corporate welfare. Business interests want low cost labor and their political lackeys risk national security—safety for Americans—to keep them happy. In 2004 only three companies were fined for hiring illegal immigrants. Here is what a report from investment company Bears Sterns said: "The United States is simply hooked on cheap, illegal workers. Illegal immigration has been America's way of competing with the low-wage (labor) forces of Asia and Latin America." Nice to have some truth from Wall Street. Another factor is that American companies operating in Mexico have not paid high enough wages, and globalization has resulted in manufacturing shifting from Mexico to even lower labor cost countries, especially China.

Taxation is another dimension of democracy's decline. For decades there has been talk about a radical change in the federal income tax system to eliminate gross injustices, but things have gotten worse. Citizens for Tax Justice found that for 275 of the largest U.S. companies, their effective tax rate dropped by 20 percent from 2001 to 2003 as their pretax profits jumped 26 percent; in 2003 46 companies with a combined profit of $42.6 billion not only paid no taxes, they received rebates of $5.4 billion. All this happened during a weak economy when countless Americans faced job loss and declining incomes. Republican claim that, as taxes drop, incomes rise and therefore people become both wealthier and the government gets more money from the wealth created. But the truth reveals a trend precisely in reverse. In August 2005 the official poverty rate climbed to 12.7 percent, about 40 million Americans. Republicans prefer government welfare for business and the rich rather than assistance for the poor.

Inept government does not by itself destroy democracy, but in a faltering democracy bad government flourishes. Even small status quo conditions can be deadly. Consider a freakish boat accident. A water taxi in Baltimore harbor flipped over in a 2004 storm, killing five people. Months later, the National Transportation Safety Board (NTSB) discovered that the boat had the allowable number of passengers, but nevertheless had 700 pounds of excess weight. The Coast Guard had been using an average passenger weight determined in 1960. But everybody knows that Americans have been getting fatter over recent decades. For 40 years, how could all Coast Guard officials responsible for safety not know about fatter Americans? Where was congressional oversight?

The average weight of the 25 passengers was 168.4 pounds, not the status quo 1960 average of 140 pounds. In December 2004, the Board advised the Coast Guard to "take immediate action" and use a new average of 174 pounds, which would have allowed only 20 passengers on the water taxi, which had five too many. Five died. And in October 2005 twenty people died when a sightseeing boat with close to its maximum number of passengers capsized in Lake George, New York. Soon after, it was reported that the Coast Guard had just begun rethinking its use of the 1960 weight average and that New York State used a figure of just 150 pounds. The agency had not taken "immediate action" nine months after being told to do so because "the economic impact on the industry" had to be considered. Why? Was there any uncertainty about the ludicrously inaccurate Coast Guard weight standard?

Could business interests have influenced government? By not increasing the average weight, commercial boats carried more passengers. What about packed elevators, roller coasters, balconies, bridges, and airplanes? Indeed, the NTSB had connected its recommendation to small airplane accidents resulting from excess weight.

Judging Judges Judicially

The judiciary serves as another arena for assessing institutionalized corruption and the health of American democracy.

Consider the results of an innovative study by the independent, nonpartisan Environmental Law Institute, described as "dramatic" and "troubling." In 2004, ELI reported an analysis of all 325 court cases, from January 21, 2001 to June 30, 2004, about the application of the National Environmental Policy Act (NEPA). This was a period of heightened litigation. Under this federal law the public can look at environmental impact assessments of proposed federal projects and use lawsuits if they disagree with the findings. ELI found the following:

Federal district court judges appointed by a Democratic president ruled in favor of environmental plaintiffs just under 60 percent of the time, while judges appointed by a Republican president ruled in their favor less than half as often—28 percent of the time. District judges appointed by President George W. Bush have an even less favorable attitude toward environmentalists' NEPA suits, ruling in their favor only 17 percent of the time.

When industry or pro-development interests sue under NEPA, the results are almost exactly reversed; judges appointed under a Democratic administration ruled in favor of pro-development plaintiffs 14 percent of the time, while Republican appointed judges ruled in favor of such plaintiffs almost 60 percent of the time.

[Appeals] circuit court panels with a majority of judges appointed by a Democratic president (those with two or three such judges) ruled in favor of environmental plaintiffs 58 percent of the time. In contrast, Republican-majority panels ruled in favor of environmental plaintiffs just 10 percent of the time—one one-sixth as often.

These troubling, partisan results were consistent with earlier analyses. For example, in lawsuits that attempted to hold a company's directors liable for corporate wrongdoing, from 1995 to 2002, Republican judges voted for plaintiffs 26 percent of the time, while Democrat judges did so 41 percent of the time. Between 1970 and 2002, for cases of industry challenges to environmental laws brought before the D.C. Circuit: all-Republican three-judge panels voted to accept industry challenges 73 percent of the time; for panels with two Republicans and one Democrat, challenges were accepted 50 percent of the time; and when there was only one Republican, industry challenges were accepted only 37 percent of the time. The pro-business bias of Republican judges is glaring.

So much for an independent judiciary—where trust is more critical than for the other two branches of government, because the judiciary is less accountable to the public. Of particular concerns is judicial activism whereby judges act like legislators when their task is limited to interpreting the law, not creating it. There is reason to see *partisan* justice in America, as a result of that "unholy alliance" between corrupt government and business. And more than a few Americans had this view when the U.S. Supreme Court made the decision in 2000 that resulted in George W. Bush becoming president, despite Justice Anthony Kennedy's scathing dissent pointing out that the decision by the Republican judges to anoint Bush as president would call into question the very legitimacy of the Court. Was it a political or legal decision?

Besides partisan justice, there is also the issue of outright corruption within the judicial branch of government. In December 2004, a federal judicial conduct committee changed the ethics guidelines for federal judges. Experts who follow this issue concluded that the new rules made it easier for judges, with lifetime appointments, to take more corporate-funded trips without disclosing their attendance. Douglas T. Kendall, head of Community Rights Counsel, said: "This effectively clears the path for federal judges to take lavish, corporate-funded trips." Kendall said the action "significantly weakened" the rules. New York University law professor Stephen Gillers said that the committee should have considered a clear ban on such boondoggles. And Senate Judiciary Committee member Senator Patrick J. Leahy said he would introduce legislation banning corporate-funded trips, but as a Democrat he would not likely gain enough support for passage of such legislation. Leahy made the case that there was no reason why gift disclosure rules applying to the president, cabinet officials, and members of Congress should not also apply to judges. The *Washington Post* editorialized against the new guidance under the heading "Green Light on Junkets" and concluded: "What it actually gives is permission to take trips on the dime of entities with active interests in actual cases and then hide the value of those gifts." That federal judges could take such self-serving action was yet another sign of the unraveling of democratic institutions under the corrupting rule of American corporatism.

Yet another problem is conflicts of interest for judges. A prime example was the selection of Chief Justice John Roberts in 2005 despite his decision to rule on an appeals court case [*Hamdam v. Rumsfeld*] even though he was already discussing his possible nomination to the high court with a number of senior White House officials. He voted in favor of upholding military tribunals in Guantanamo Bay, as desired by the Bush II administration. Many legal experts said he should have recused himself.

Few Americans have become disturbed about judicial immunity, which started with Supreme Court decisions in the late 1800s. In Fall 2005 little attention was given to an effort in South Dakota to get a measure on the ballot to eliminate immunity for state judges. Gary L. Zerman noted that:

> Judges are above the law as a result of the judicially created doctrine of absolute judicial immunity. …However, [the Constitution] provides NO express basis for placing the government—here judges—over the sovereignty and rights of the people. …[Judges] grabbed absolute immunity for themselves—in violation of the Constitution. …The two other independent and co-equal branches stood by and did nothing. …Reform will not come from the government. It must come from the People.

Supporters of judicial immunity argue it is necessary to protect judges' independence and not let their decisions be affected by fear of consequences. Consider the violations cited in the proposed South Dakota ballot measure that would allow citizen suits: deliberate violations of law, fraud or conspiracy, intentional violation of due process of law, deliberate disregard of material facts, judicial acts without jurisdiction, blocking of a lawful conclusion of a case, and deliberate violations of the state or federal constitutions. Sound reasonable? It is if you believe in accountability for all judges—municipal, state and federal, that no person is above the law, and depending on appeals and self-policing by the judiciary is insufficient. Critics of judicial immunity also contend that it has resulted from judicial legislation.

Yet another issue worthy of serious public attention is the loss of independence of local and state judges who are elected with the help of special interest money. The group Justice at Stake Campaign was formed because: "Special interests are spending millions to influence decisions and elect judges to serve their narrow interests." A 2001 national survey found that only 25 percent of people had a great deal of trust and confidence in their state courts and judges (26 percent for courts and judges in the U.S.), and 36 percent believed that campaign contributions had a great deal of influence and 40 percent some influence on judges' decisions. On the bright side, 57 percent strongly supported using only public funds for campaigning, an option considered in a later chapter. A 2004 survey found that nearly 71 percent of Americans believed that campaign contributions from interest groups have at least some influence on judges' decisions. Conclusion: When judges are appointed you should worry about a partisan (philosophical) bias and when they are elected worry about their special interest bias.

A new development is judges that refuse to hear cases because of their moral conflict. For example, being against abortion and not taking cases that allow minors to seek court approval for an abortion. Judges have an obligation to implement laws, not undermine them regardless of their personal beliefs about the law or religious convictions. Imagine judges that are against the death penalty recusing themselves from taking murder cases where the death penalty could be imposed. This behavior is akin to jury nullification that is abhorred by the judiciary. In both cases the law is not respected because people put themselves above the law.

The rise of the corporatist state requires judges that are pro-business in order to safeguard its interests. About selecting new Supreme Court justices, the *Washington Post* in 2005 said there was a "sea change in the way corporate America approaches judicial appointments. Ever cautious companies have traditionally left the divisive high-pressure politicking to outspoken social conservatives." No more. Business recognizes that many Supreme Court decisions affect their interests, as examples given later demonstrate. The U.S. Chamber of Commerce, the nation's largest business association, became a major player in the battle over Supreme Court justice nominations. It quickly supported the nomination of John Roberts for Chief Justice. Unlike previous candidates, he had ample experience with business clients, including Toyota, Fox Broadcasting and the U.S. Chamber of Commerce. Similarly, Bush's failed nomination of Harriet Miers should have been seen as a pro-business choice but not a religious-right ally. Keep in mind the wisdom of conservative Judge Robert Bork, the Supreme Court is now a "political institution, not a legal institution."

Switching to the executive branch of enforcing the laws, we see corruption similar to that in the judiciary. The U.S. Department of Justice is often in court representing the interests of the public. Maybe. Consider that in June 2005 headlines were made when the Justice Department suddenly decided to drastically cut the amount of money it sought in a huge case against the tobacco industry, from $130 billion for smoking cessation programs to just $10 billion. The lead government attorney had summed up the trial by saying that the government had proven "a decades-long pattern of...misrepresentations, half-truths, deceptions and lies that continue to this day." It was reported that orders for the cut came from top Justice Department officials, political appointees, some with ties to the tobacco industry. Is this what you expect from the government of a great democracy, where 400,000 residents die each year because of smoking? In November 2005 the lead career attorney, Sharon

Y. Eubanks, ended her 22-year career because of the lack of support for the case from her politically appointed bosses. They declined to give her a performance appraisal, blocking her receiving a bonus. So much for justice in the Justice Department.

When you can't trust the judiciary, you can't trust the executive and legislative branches of government and vice-versa. For example, from 1967 to 1990, Congress overturned 124 Supreme Court and 220 lower court decisions interpreting federal laws. On the other hand, in a sense, every time the Supreme Court changes its mind on an issue it is like an unofficial amendment to the Constitution. And most presidents have used their veto to curb congressional action. But when one party dominates all three branches of the federal government, constitutional checks and balances tend to fail, as during the Bush II era. For his first term, George W. Bush was the first president in 176 years to not veto anything in a full term. Some people worry about the separation of powers. More should worry about the collusion of powers.

And, following the wisdom of Howard Zinn, discontented Americans must not place undue importance on the Supreme Court as the final protector of American democracy or on the judicial system in general. As Zinn wrote in November 2005's *Progressive* magazine:

> Still, knowing the nature of the political and judicial system of this country, its inherent bias against the poor, against people of color, against dissidents, we cannot become dependent on the courts, or on our political leadership. Our culture—the media, the educational system...deflect us from the most important job citizens have, which is to bring democracy alive by organizing, protesting, engaging in acts of civil disobedience that shake up the system. ...Let us not be disconsolate over the increasing control of the court system by the right wing. The courts have never been on the side of justice, only moving a few degrees one way or the other, unless pushed by the people. ...fundamental change will depend, the experience of the past suggests, on the actions of an aroused citizenry, demanding that the promise of the Declaration of Independence—an equal right to life, liberty, and the pursuit of happiness—be fulfilled.

Will enough citizens actively shake up the status quo system?

Behind Door Number Two is the Real Government

When it comes to our government, the key question is: Just who is running the show? It's hard to decide who to blame more, corrupt politicians or those who buy them. So much goes on that we will never know. It helps to look at American reality with the aid of Michael Parenti's dual political system model.

There is the official, formal and *symbolic* political system, visible to Americans, and what they have learned about in school. It is where the political process parades. Lying politicians pretend being responsive to public interests and concerns, phony campaign debates entertain, elections are held that favor incumbents, false and misleading claims of progressive change are made, and crooks use the media to misinform Americans. It is where pseudo-democracy is played out, as staged production, infotainment to distract us.

The unofficial, informal and *substantive* political system is where hidden decisions and corruption serve the power elites. It is the pus-bloated underbelly of American democracy, waiting to be pierced by status quo busters. It is where power is exercised in private conversations, meetings behind closed doors, backroom deals, and secretive bureaucratic activities. It is where politicians schmooze with the power brokers, check-writers, and lobbyists. It is where propaganda is turned into news, political contributions earn returns on investments, and collusive special interests split the spoils and fight common enemies (like efforts to spend government money on individuals rather than corporate interests). Agreement on starting wars and pursuing international trade pacts is reached among the like-minded. It is the "dirty little secret" America, where our oligarchy, plutocracy, and corporatist state operate clandestinely. For power elites, terrorism is good, war is useful, crime is valuable, divisive social issues are handy, economic uncertainty is fine. Anything that keeps Americans fearful and distracted is good. It makes it easier to retain power, control the populace and fill corporate coffers.

For the rest of this book I will use more evocative names for Parenti's symbolic and substantive tracks of the American political system: the public *illusory* political system and the private *restricted* political system. The "voice of the people" President Bush spoke of must refer to the privileged people of the restricted political system. Power elites in the restricted system pull the strings of the political puppets in the illusory system where political theater plays out. Elites concentrate on big-picture strategy and policy, not the details of governance. They care about who is president of the United States, key cabinet officers, opportunities for privatizing government programs, promoting globalization, minimizing corporate taxes, limiting civil suits against companies, and keeping labor costs low, for example.

Besides corporate leaders, attorneys, lobbyists, and think tank policy experts, is The Carlyle Group, a prime example of a business active in the restricted political system. It is a secretive private bank and investment company; both Bush I and Bush II once served on its board of directors. Some 400 partners worldwide include many former senior government officials and military officers from the U.S. and other countries. Then there is the non-profit Council for National Policy. It is the right-wing mafia of the U.S. The secretive group has some 600 members, including top Republicans and conservatives, as well as heads of Christian right groups, including Jerry Falwell and Pat Robertson. The group's official position is that "The media should not know when or where we meet or who takes part in our programs, before or after a meeting." But it is known that George W. Bush spoke to the group in 1999, Senate Majority Leader Bill Frist received an award from it, and Supreme Court Justice Clarence Thomas was a keynote speaker in 2002. CNP's elite Gold Circle Club met May 3, 2001 at the White House with chief strategist Karl Rove and President Bush. Before the invasion of Iraq, at a May 2002 meeting the group agreed that the U.S. should topple Iraq's Saddam regime and ruled out military action against the other members of the axis of evil, Iran and North Korea. Shortly after Bush invaded Iraq, Vice President Dick Cheney and Defense Secretary Donald Rumsfeld spoke to the group.

When you watch films with convincing different worlds, such as the *Matrix,* and *Alien* movies, you know that creative people used technology and money to artfully deceive and entertain you. You paid for the deception. Now think of the power elites and their private government. Behind the scenes they guide the illusory public government. Americans are unaware of exactly how elites pull the strings, even when it means war, corporate handouts, and export of jobs. Don't think formal conspiracy. Think networked collaboration among aligned economic, social and political interests. They need not control everything, just the right things at the right times. What matters is strategic control, carefully and secretly used to avoid sparking public revolt and political instability.

As in a parallel universe, the movers, shakers, and big wheels share thinking in high-brow business groups (such as the Business Roundtable and Council on Foreign Relations), special presidential inaugural events, closed elite-fests (like Renaissance Weekend, the Bohemian Club's summer encampment, the Forstmann Little Aspen Weekend, and the Alfalfa Dinner), yacht trips, golf clubs, corporate sports stadium boxes, groups for the goliaths of globalization (like The World Economic Forum in Davos, Switzerland, The Trilateral Commission, and The Group of Thirty), and The Federalist Society for conservative attorneys. Behind closed doors corporate interests mingle with political puppets and journalist lackeys to do what voters cannot do, maneuver the system.

Our dual system is schizophrenic democracy. Just as a tiny percent of Americans have most of the nation's wealth, so too is power concentrated. Today's corporate media exploit the illusory system and market its political theatrics, while largely ignoring the restricted system. Frequent revelations of inept and corrupt government actions in the illusory system matter less than the plotting in the restricted system. Public scandals keep coming, yet the restricted system gathers more power and wealth for its members. In the end, political scandals divert public attention away from the restricted system and shock less than they entertain and distract.

In a better democracy, still with a capitalistic economy, wealth would inevitably remain unequally distributed, but political power would not mirror skewed economic power. The goal of the Second American Revolution is to rid ourselves of the *bipartisan* dual system that supports corruption of democracy through the restricted political system. Changes through voting in the illusory political system do not loosen the grip of corporate corruption on government. We must have one truthful and transparent political system serving the public interest, where money does not control politics.

Up, Up and Away: America's Rocketing Inequality

Aristotle observed that when you have great economic inequality the wealthy seek and obtain a share of power matching their wealth and thus subvert democratic government.

One of the toughest questions about the economy is how economic growth can be so good but so many Americans feel so negative about economic conditions. For example, a late 2005 Gallup poll found that 63 percent of people rated the economy as only fair or poor, and 58 percent felt the economy was getting worse. But in 2004 the economy grew by 4.2 percent and was also doing well in terms of Gross Domestic Product growth in 2005. What's happening is that real household income and wages for most workers have not kept pace with economic growth. Economic recovery began in 2001 and corporate profits jumped more than 50 percent by 2005. As columnist Paul Krugman said, "Americans don't feel good about the economy because it hasn't been good for them. Never mind the GDP numbers: Most people are falling behind." Of course some people are doing better than ever.

No respectable democracy would have the top 1 percent of its citizens receiving as much income as the over 100 million lowest income people, or tolerate many top corporate executives receiving 1,000 times what their workers receive. Over time things have gotten worse. In 1965 the CEOs of the Fortune 500 companies on average made 41 times more than the average worker. This rose to a ratio of 419 to one in 2003.

Political science researcher Frederick Solt studied the impact of economic inequality in democracies on citizens' political engagement. The results can make you sick, if you keep in mind that the U.S. has the greatest economic inequality among the world's democracies. Here are his conclusions:

> In contexts of higher inequality, people are less likely to feel that their government is responsive, to express interest in politics, or to vote. …Greater economic inequality stacks the deck of democracy in favor of the richest citizens, and as a result, everyone else is more likely to conclude that politics is simply not a game worth playing

Joseph C. Hough, president of the Union Theological Seminary, sees economic inequality from a religious perspective: "It is not at all in the spirit of American democracy to generate inequality, and to contradict equal opportunity in our society. Those are not the norms we've lived by. …It is the obscene degree to which economic inequality has taken hold in America that I think is highly questionable. …If Tom DeLay is acting out of his Born Again Christian convictions in pushing legislation that disadvantages the poor every time he opens his mouth, I'm not saying he's not a Born Again Christian, but as the Lord's humble fruit inspector, it sure looks suspicious to me. …We could ask ourselves 'What changes in the direction of this country are necessary if it really is gonna make a claim to be a democracy?' We're not asking it to be a theocracy. A democracy. That's what it's about. Politically, that's what it's about." Amen.

American society is built on the promise of equal opportunity but not equal outcomes. Distressingly, among all industrialized, first-world nations, the U.S. has the widest economic inequality in both wages and assets. As the wealthy have become richer, lower and middle income Americans have become poorer in recent years. This was not always the case, but it has corresponded to democracy's decline, deepened political corruption, and the rise of the Christian right. The power elites would have us believe that things are getting better and better, while for so many of us our own experiences and perceptions tell us things are getting worse and worse.

Newsweek columnist Robert J. Samuelson made the important point in 2005 that democracy "cushions capitalism's injustices and, thereby, anchors public support. ...A successful democracy gives people a chance to protect their interests and lifestyles." He also noted that "capitalism thrives on change," but that "Democracy resists change—it creates powerful constituencies with a stake in the status quo." He was concerned about democracy hindering capitalism when he should have decried capitalism corrupting democracy. Without effective government oversight capitalism has run amok, trampling Americans' welfare.

Capitalism has an inherent inequality, from the poorest to the richest people. "Work hard, work your way up the ladder of economic success," people are told. Wealth is around the corner. For the ladder to work fairly, however, economic inequality must not create political inequality. Otherwise, the political system (representing public interests) cannot effectively oversee the economic system (serving corporate interests) to ensure real upward mobility. Over time economic inequality has increasingly corrupted the American political system, creating political inequality (voters versus power elites). And the instrument for cloning inequality from the economic system to the political system is money— money that corrupts the political system. Heed the wisdom of Justice Louis Brandeis:

> We can have a democratic society or we can have great concentrated wealth in the hands of a few. We cannot have both.

Consider that socialist and communist states failed largely because political inequality (power) corrupted the economic system; the discontented, poor working class sought political power to get a better economy and freedom. In contrast, the U.S. system created an affluent middle class, but kept it politically distracted and docile through consumerism. However, with the rise of the American corporatist state, upward economic mobility has become illusory because the working class—both low and middle-income groups—has lost protection from the political system. The more the working class spends on products and services through choking credit, the more they unwittingly reinforce both political and economic inequality. They spend their way into economic slavery.

Do not doubt that upward economic mobility has suffered along with democracy's decline. Consider these facts. In 1980 the top fifth of families earned 7.7 times as much as the bottom fifth. By 2001 that inequality ratio jumped to 11.4. If wealth rather than earnings are used, the inequality ratio increase is far worse. Here is another window on inequality. Among children born between 1942 and 1972 fully 42 percent born into the poorest quintile never escaped that lowest rung on the ladder. In the 1970s, 36 percent of families stayed in the same income bracket throughout the decade. In the rather booming 1990s, 40 percent were stagnant, so this figure is likely rising in the new century. Lesson: the fabled rags-to-riches American dream is more like betting on a long-shot, not the favorite in the economics race.

The system is dynamic. Power elites keep expanding economic inequality (through tax cuts for the rich, corporate welfare, and actions to keep wages low) which in turn funds more political corruption that reduces oversight of the economic system by the political system—and on and on. The clever system maintains the inequality status quo, despite corporate slip-ups like Enron that create the illusion of system repair.

The most politically powerful have merged with the most economically powerful to become power elites, a true ruling class. *Their* economic system is selling out the American middle class. Wealth is increasingly transferred to the rich, power elites in the U.S. and other nations through globalization. The inevitable end point of the inequality spiral is a fake democracy with sham political parties, worthless voting, and a Wal-Martized economy for poor Americans. Citizens vote, elites control. This sounds a lot like the old communist states.

Under corporate influence our public government is selling some storybook fiction of American democracy to squeeze more wealth out of the global economy for the power elites and their multinational companies, like Halliburton and Bechtel. Intertwined economic and political inequality is being globalized, with the same game that worked here. Pseudo-democracy is on the march.

Why don't more Americans paying the price for inequality rise up in rage about worsening inequality? Other than being expectant capitalists, here's what Edward S. Herman and Noam Chomsky said in *Manufacturing Consent*:

> In a system of high and growing inequality, entertainment is the contemporary equivalent of the Roman "games of the circus" that diverts the public from politics and generates a political apathy that is helpful to preservation of the status quo.

The concept of entertainment should be broadly interpreted to include gambling, Internet surfing, and media infotainment. Distraction works for the people on top.

Gotcha Globalization

Just as most Americans cannot recall seeing a rotary phone, neither have they seen in recent memory the once proud "Made In The U.S.A." label and imprint on products. Progress? What say you?

When you think of globalization picture strong trade currents swirling around the globe filled with large-jawed shark-capitalists darting here and there to find the cheapest minerals, crops, petroleum, manufactured consumer goods, processed food, computers, airplanes, weapons, cement, wood, and cheap labor. Double-click to get educated peoples' cheap brainpower from third-world countries. Things and thinking cascade in, our dollars gush out like water from an open fire hydrant, leaving Americans thirsting for good-paying jobs, our children with mind-numbing debt to payoff. Progress?

No greater absurdity of this global trade tsunami can be imagined than the coming federal bailout of domestic automobile makers. General Motors and Ford want to offset low sales with corporate welfare. As they have closed manufacturing facilities and tossed tens of thousands of highly paid workers into our cruel economy their lobbyists have been sweet-talking members of Congress, Democrats and Republicans whom they have been giving money to for years, to save their corporate asses. They blame Japan and ignore reality, such as Toyota having trouble building U.S. facilities fast enough to satisfy demand. Here's truth: Total employment in the U.S. motor vehicle industry has remained stable over the past decade as foreign automakers expanded here, paying wages and benefits comparable to homegrown companies. So taxpayers who have chosen "foreign" cars (often made here) in our fabled "free market," even paying higher prices for them because they are deemed worth the premium, are expected to involuntarily pay billions of dollars to bail out GM and Ford. These firms made both the deals with unions they now regret, especially pension and health care benefits for retirees—and the cars spurned by so many Americans. Now they expect taxpayers to pay for their management failures. Gotcha.

If you think that globalization has been devised primarily to benefit the working class in the U.S. or anywhere else think again. Most troubling from the rising global corporatist state is an even greater shift of power to corporate interests (if that is imaginable), and even less power and money trickling down to workers.

William Finnegan wrote courageously about globalization's many dimensions in *Harper's Magazine* in 2003. Here are some of his insights:

> The idea that open markets and increased trade lead invariably to economic growth may be sound in theory, but it has repeatedly failed the reality test. ...Testifying before Congress in 1995, Lawrence Summers, then of the Treasury Department...disclosed that American corporations received $1.35 in procurement contracts for each dollar the American government contributed to the World Bank and other multilateral development banks. This was an unusually candid admission by a leading Bank supporter that one its main activities is, in fact, corporate welfare. ...the total assets of the 100 largest multinational corporations increased between 1980 and 1995 by 697 percent.... In Latin America, during the 1960s and 1970s—the decades preceding the great trade boom of globalization—per capita income rose 73 percent. During the last two decades, with trade expanding rapidly under neoliberalism, per capita income rose less than 6 percent. ...Another core belief, that lower taxes promote economic growth by encouraging people to work harder and invest more, is equally unfounded in reality. ...Even in the U.S., the foremost proponent of free trade and presumably its great

beneficiary, there are those millions of good jobs that disappeared with globalization, leaving their former holders working non-union at Wal-Mart. There is a good argument that the U.S. may be trading itself into oblivion...

The latest rise of corporate power has resulted from international trade agreements in the name of globalization, including the North American Free Trade Agreement (NAFTA), the Central American Free Trade Agreement (CAFTA), and the World Trade Organization General Agreement on Trade and Tariffs (GATT). There is no linkage between what is good for multinational corporations and what is good for working class Americans. Globalization reduces American jobs and wages. Multinational companies show no loyalty to the United States, even when they originated and are headquartered here. Wal-Mart has made communist China rich with U.S. dollars that it uses to buy our technologies and companies and to loan our government money. As Wal-Mart maximizes its profits it grows China's middle class, while American's shrinking middle class become more desperate for Wal-Mart's low prices. American money flows in a vicious cycle of economic self-destruction.

To the surprise of many, in October 2005 Wal-Mart publicly advocated an increase in the minimum wage. Why? It was feeling the impact on sales of worsening economic conditions for lower income Americans, its primary customer base.

Furthermore, these trade agreements make it difficult for American government agencies to control corporate behavior and protect citizens. American politicians have surrendered our national sovereignty. Listen to maverick Republican Congressman Ron Paul:

> The World Trade Organization, which the United States joined in 1994, has been disastrous for American sovereignty. ...Our membership in the WTO is unconstitutional, which is to say illegal. The constitution grants Congress, and Congress alone, the authority to regulate trade. Congress cannot cede that authority to the WTO or any other international body, nor can the President legally sign any treaty that purports to do so.

A National League of Cities resolution declared that such trade agreements could "undermine the scope of local governmental authority under the Constitution." The Conference of Chief Justices [the top state judges] wrote a letter to the U.S. Senate stating that the proposed Free

Trade Area of the Americas (FTAA) "does not protect adequately the traditional values of constitutional federalism [that] threatens the integrity of the courts of this country." Similarly, state legislatures in California, Minnesota, Oregon, Washington, Massachusetts, and New Hampshire, and the National Council of State Legislators, have also expressed concern over the impact of trade agreements on domestic sovereignty.

In *Who Will Tell the People,* William Greider explained how free trade globalization can erode our democracy:

> If democracy is to retain any meaning, Americans will need to draw a hard line in defense of their own national sovereignty. This is not just about protecting American jobs, but also about protecting the very core of self-government—laws that are fashioned in open debate by representatives who are directly accountable to the people. ...The gross injustices of global commerce are concealed behind the high-minded platitudes about free trade. ...laws and regulations that go beyond the status-quo consensus of the global economy are depicted as obstacles to prosperity. ...What [ordinary citizens] have seen of the global economy in the last two decades tells them to be wary and even hostile. In a functioning democracy, these popular insights...would be respected as the baseline for political debate and decision-making.

Greider wrote these sentiments more than a decade ago, and since then things have only gotten worse. More jobs are being exported, not just manufacturing and call center jobs, but higher salaried professional ones in engineering, information technology, and medical services. More recently, Michael Parenti, in *Superpatriotism,* noted:

> The plutocrats have been subverting what is left of our democratic sovereignty in a series of "free trade" agreements with other capitalist nations. ...In effect, the international moneyed interests assume a veto power over most public policy and democratic legislation.

Once you understand this, the save-our-democracy analysis is simple: The status quo globalization, free trade paradigm is a hoax perpetrated on Americans. It serves the plutocracy and corporatist state. In the long run, our children and grandchildren will pay for our Wal-Mart bargains, as we finance China's rise to superpower status. Some economists predict that by 2040 China will become the largest global economy and its military buildup is stunning. If American democracy stays weakened, China poses a major threat. History tells us that superpowers come and go.

Congress handed communist China its strength. When granting

China "permanent normal trade relations" came up in 2000, a Harris poll found that 79 percent of Americans agreed that such status should be withheld until China met human rights and labor rights standards. But in May 2000 Congress granted that status and opened the floodgates for Chinese imports. Guess what? The 200 members of the Business Roundtable had given federal politicians and their political parties $58 million in just the first five months of 2000. That money helped buy favored nation status for China, despite its human rights failures.

With more at stake, the impact of international trade on corruption became an issue. Heightened anti-corruption efforts in advanced and developing countries over the past decade have failed, despite programs by the World Bank, Transparency International and others, as well as a number of political regime changes. Corruption is buried deep within the culture and institutions of nations and now with globalization is more profitable and resilient than ever. The World Bank estimates that $1 *trillion* is spent globally on illegal bribes alone. Yet, in the U.S. nearly all "bribes" from business to politicians are legal.

Another aspect of globalization is that some U.S. courts have invoked foreign laws in reaching decisions. Sounds like outsourcing of American justice and democracy. Foreign law popped up in the Supreme Court's 2003 ruling overturning a Texas anti-sodomy law and a 17-year precedent on the issue, in the Massachusetts Supreme Court's 2004 decision to legalize same sex marriage, and in the Supreme Court's 2005 decision that struck down the death penalty for 16- and 17-year olds. For critics, citing foreign laws comes down to overstepping the domain of U.S. courts, is tantamount to making law not interpreting it, and is used selectively to support personal views. Members of Congress, Attorney General Alberto Gonzales, and others have strongly objected to the use of foreign laws in our judicial system.

Hard to imagine that we once had an economy that could stand on its own, not absurdly dependent on and vulnerable to foreign workers, power elites, and governments. Gotcha globalization puts America's genitals in foreign hands. Does anyone think that our economy will not be squeezed by intentional greed?

Keep Looking for the Exit

In light of so many years of Republican dominance, it is important to set the record straight about the true nature of Republican (versus genuine fiscal conservative) politics. Republican Representative Mike Pence observed that some Republicans think "big government is good government if it's our government." Republicans have discovered that big government works very well to shovel money to their backers. Rather than trying to fix and shrink inefficient, ineffective and unnecessary government, Republicans' anger morphed into a more self-serving strategy of perverting government to serve business and rich Americans, whose appreciation would finance their incumbency. Part of the Republican big government story is the doubling of registered lobbyists in Washington, D.C. from an amazing 16,342 in 2000 to an obscene 34,785 in 2005. Forget fiscal conservatism. Welcome the thirst for power.

People want better government. The issue is not big versus small government. Government is not a necessary evil; it can and must be a necessary good, especially for preventing harm and then helping individuals and communities when things go bad. Franklin Delano Roosevelt had this moral view of government:

> Better the occasional faults of a Government that lives in a spirit of charity than the constant omissions of a Government frozen in the ice of its own indifference.

When Americans love their country but hate their government we have a problem. People hate their government because of what the government has done or not done; its actions have been done in the name of its citizens on the presumption that it honestly represents its citizens. If it does not honestly represent its citizens (because it serves corporate interests) then its citizens have every right to be incensed. There is much more to a country than its government, and when government is far less than it should be, then the country is less than it can be. As Edward Abbey said: "A patriot must always be ready to defend his country against his government." This is how Americans must think. False patriots conflate country and government and quickly condemn dissenters, as if criticizing government and elected officials is unpatriotic. Conservative talk show hosts are especially two-faced when they condemn dissent about the Iraq war but have no qualms about criticizing social programs.

The route to better government and democracy requires redirecting our nation's enormous tax revenues to serve public rather than corporate interests and to seriously attack all the fraud, waste and abuse that have plagued government programs under both Democratic and Republican administrations. Rational Americans should be rebelling against a government that disregards their basic health, safety, economic, and security needs while serving the interests of the wealthy and power elites. Rebellion requires motivation, leadership and a plan. Right now there is motivation because most Americans know that change is needed. In later chapters the elements of are plan are presented. As to leadership, a new third-party is needed, as explained in the final chapter.

This much must be said now: The way out of our democracy decline requires breaking the corrupting influence of money on the political system and it's mangling of the economic system. *The Second American Revolution must restore American democracy with honest political and public oversight of the economic system.* We can retain our constitution and capitalism, but with fair, merit-based economic inequality, a stronger middle class, and better safeguards for workers and consumers. We must erase the restricted political system, with its private government. To shift power to the public government, NO corporate and special interest money should flow into it—absolutely nothing. More about this later.

Poetic Patriotism

Artists see our world through a different lens. They speak obliquely about our corrupt, status quo society, seeing absurdity where others see normalcy. They pierce psychological defenses and tell our hearts what our minds block out. Poet and songwriter Leonard Cohen knows that:

> Everybody knows that the dice are loaded
> Everybody rolls with their fingers crossed
> Everybody knows that the war is over
> Everybody knows the good guys lost
> Everybody knows the fight was fixed
> The poor stay poor, the rich get rich
> That's how it goes
> Everybody knows

Everybody knows that the boat is leaking
Everybody knows that the captain lied
Everybody got this broken feeling
Like their father or their dog just died
Everybody talking to their pockets
Everybody wants a box of chocolates
And a long stem rose
Everybody knows.
["Everybody Knows" in the album *I'm Your Man*.]

Almost everybody knows that the U.S. is not as good as it should be. *Almost* everybody knows that American democracy has been warped by money and corruption. *Almost* everybody knows that almost everybody knows there's too much lying going on. *Almost* everybody knows that major change is needed. But few are energized to take action. Millions of discontented Americans need more motivation and a plan.

When will American democracy's arrow turn up? When politicians get from honesty what they now get from lying: success. And citizens get what they long for: representatives and government they can trust.

And if not? What happens? Gradually and then suddenly everyone sees the elephant in the room, much more than inefficient and ineffective government—they realize that their democracy has become truly fake. And neither New Zealand nor any other real democracy will declare preemptive war and come to our rescue.

Chapter 3

Dissonance Feeds Lies: From Mental Blocks to Political Dissent

The majority of people believe in incredible things which are absolutely false. The majority of people daily act in a manner prejudicial to their general well being.

—Ashley Montague

Restoring American democracy is difficult and complicated, but, if history is any indication, definitely possible. It helps to examine several psychological concepts: cognitive dissonance, status quo bias, self-denial, and self-deception. There are psychological reasons why people discontent with America's government (passive dissidents) do not turn their cerebral and emotional dissent into action, and why others (delusional patriots) worship the forces that are ruining the nation and them economically. By understanding the psychological roots of America's delusional democracy, it becomes clear that false patriotism and extreme partisan loyalty is a protective measure to minimize personal pain.

Self-Prescribed Pain Relief

The old maxim that "the truth hurts" needs modification. Actually, some truths hurt, especially those that disturb our equilibrium and threaten our ego and self-esteem because they contradict strongly held core beliefs.

Psychologists talk about the pain and avoidance of cognitive dissonance. Think of it as a clash of conflicting and seemingly irreconcilable thoughts and information. When it occurs, it threatens mental peace and equilibrium. Objectively, information causing a conflict may be true or false. In the political world it is likely to be a lie packaged as the truth. The real issue is not the truth or falsity of the information, but how a person reacts to it. Either way, as a mental anesthetic the brain actually filters out or distorts information that causes dissonance. This is hard to fight.

Each of us has mental core beliefs and models of reality—sometimes called "frames"—that we are reluctant to abandon. People avoid information that causes dissonance by selecting information sources and conversations to participate in that are consistent with their existing beliefs. When the door cracks open and you perceive information incompatible with your beliefs, the natural tendency is to shut the door quickly—switch the channel, go to another Internet site, change the topic of a conversation, avoid the person, or turn to another newspaper article. Think self-censorship. If you rely on the mainstream media or some favorite information source, some information that might challenge your frames and overcome cognitive dissonance may not be available.

Tuning out and filtering create a false consciousness. Blocking information that clashes with status quo beliefs is a self-preservation mechanism, a form of self-medication. Valuing of the truth is defeated by the status quo. It is more than deliberately ignoring what is happening around you within earshot or in your viewscape. It is about automatic unconscious behaviors that keep disturbing information away by avoiding people, movies, reading materials, music, Internet sites, radio and television stations—anything antagonistic to status quo beliefs and emotions. It is behavioral filtering and segregation that takes people deeper into the safety of their personal status quo. It leads to intellectual isolation and affiliations that over time promote extremist beliefs. Balance, shades of grey, moderation, caveats and uncertainties give way to ideological certitude.

Most of us can think of acquaintances or friends who are absolutely and permanently "liberal" or "conservative" or "born again" or "into fitness" or "vegetarian" or whatever. You know they are not reachable with facts that contradict or threaten their core beliefs. You may think you have some incontrovertible truth that contradicts their belief, but it will not break through their defenses. Ditto for you, from someone else's perspective.

We select and maintain relationships and information sources that define our status quo support network. "Sticking with our own kind" maintains larger, collective status quos. Preaching to the choir is so prevalent because audiences self-select themselves to listen to those they already agree with, and so do speakers. Just as cognitive dissonance causes stress and pain, belief-confirming messages reduce stress and increase pleasure through the brain's release of endorphins. To disturb a person's equilibrium enough to overcome status quo bias, but not enough to cause pain that blocks new information, challenges status quo busters. Only by facing that challenge can an agent of change move beyond preaching to the choir to produce converts.

Like-minded thinking, language and people protect us from ideas and information that cause mental stress. Yet Americans have the world's highest level of mental disorders—over one-quarter of adults. Less controllable is the outside world: the stress of job insecurity, costly health care and insurance, high costs for automobile use, traffic congestion, excessive personal debt, and fear of terrorism—all things affected by the political system. Whether your core belief system supports or rejects the political system you are vulnerable. If you are being harmed by the system that you believe in, then your stress level will be low despite being harmed by it, and you will not oppose it, because doing so would cause cognitive dissonance. This explains delusional patriots. Just the opposite happens when people connect negative circumstances to a political system that is contrary to their core beliefs. They are dissenters, but not necessarily activist ones.

Dissonance Quashes Dissent

Here is a reality check. In his seminal 1971 book *Polyarchy* Robert Dahl theorized that the frustration and resentment of poorer, politically disengaged citizens "may not stimulate demands for greater equality but instead may turn into resignation, apathy, despair [and] hopelessness." As America's economic system has punished more of its citizens, neither voting nor more aggressive political action has changed the system. In 2003, Colgate University Professor Jay Mandle concluded:

> The experience to date in this country is that a "good governance" movement is too small to offset the power of wealth and correct these dismal outcomes. Appeals to fairness and democracy, disconnected from other concerns, have not proved to be sufficiently energizing to spur widespread grassroots activism. ...A powerful movement to democratize the political system will be born only when large numbers of people believe that their own interests are advanced by a political system of greater equality.

Yet many people vote against their own interests. They believe in something bigger—certain social issues and values. They willingly let others govern. Self-government has gone out of style according to Lewis H. Lapham in *Gag Rule*:

> The Bush administration owes its existence to our apathy and sloth. The successful operation of a democracy relies on acts of self-government by no means easy to perform, and for the last twenty years we have been unwilling to do the work.

The question is: What will help people let in the kind of information that will make them optimistic enough to expend the time and energy to change the political system and take acts of self-government? The right information, which is out there, must overcome defenses and get into peoples' minds. Democracy's enemy is not just the twisting and politicization of information by others, it is also the psychological mechanisms that cause vital information to be blocked or ignored by ourselves.

Inescapably, personal dissonance blocks *active* political dissidence. Delusional patriots cling to faith in American democracy's greatness; their minds block information about its failings. These include fiscal and social conservatives, fundamentalist evangelicals, and a host of anti-government, gun-loving people. They are totally committed, convinced and some would say brainwashed. They are utterly resistant to seeing America's democracy decline. Overcoming their cognitive dissonance with truth about democracy's decline is terribly difficult.

Passive dissidents see democracy's decline but are burdened with despair and hopelessness. Information and pleadings about the feasibility of successful action to improve democracy and fix government must overcome their pessimism. They are a large pool of true patriots ready for revolution.

Some in the dissent community believe that energy should be devoted not to creating change agents but rather to strengthening the belief system already held by those seeing American democracy's failings and decline. Preaching to the choir is seen as a necessary effort, as if these people will lose their convictions. However, once a belief system is in place it does not easily fade away, and repeating the same basic messages provides comfort but does not necessarily produce active dissent. This volume aims to transform a strengthened core democracy-decline belief into political action.

The predicate of this book is based on this logic. Yes, as shown previously, considerable poll and survey data document widely held negative views about our government and democracy. Moreover, a steady stream of great books has made the case for specific structural changes. Nonetheless, for decades there has been no determined collective action to fix our republic, just highly marginalized and disjointed efforts. It's not that we have had a failed revolution—a serious one has not yet been attempted! Over time the status quo dual political system and two-party duopoly have reigned supreme. Though other factors can be asserted, an overlooked one is potent mental blocking about possible successful change *among discontented Americans*. My thesis is that the strategic priority is to overcome mental blocking and energize passive dissenters to become risk-taking activist dissenters. Consider that the far right social conservatives were activist enough to take over the Republican Party, but that authentic populist progressives on the left never took control of the Democratic Party. It took quite a few years, but the conservative revolution did succeed. What the Republicans have achieved to the detriment of American democracy provides even more motivation for fixing the republic.

Yes, mainstream media have contributed to the problem, as a later chapter discusses, but there certainly has been sufficient information on our government's failings and on necessary political change during recent decades to feed a revolution. Yet an enormous number of Americans seeing the need for change have not become agents of change, nor supported quite visible ones, including Ralph Nader, John Anderson, and other third-party candidates [nor even maverick politicians like Howard Dean or John McCain]. Just as anger turned inward causes depression, so does silent dissent. Silent dissent far exceeds active dissent. Relatively few dissent-minded Americans are activists in third-parties and reform groups or are griping on Internet sites or writing books like this one. No information or vision has conquered the pessimistic mindset about actually changing America for the better. Not only do so many believe that real political change is impossible, they do not take the easiest of all actions—voting—because even that action seems useless to change the system. In 1992, Ross Perot received 19 percent of the vote for president—nearly 20 million votes, a historic third-party high, yet exit polls found that 36 percent would have voted for him if they thought he could win. And certainly Ralph Nader had many votes that never left peoples' minds.

It is too easy and facile merely to see cynical, alienated, disillusioned, and distracted citizens and pissed off lesser-evil voters and bitching non-voters. These are better viewed as symptoms of the root problem: *Psychological inertia among millions of strongly discontented Americans is rooted in a mindset that cannot foresee a successful Second American Revolution.* Yes, organizing, planning and visionary leadership are necessary, but they must all overcome entrenched pessimism that becomes a self-fulfilling prophesy. Worse than a "silent majority" is a majority of self-paralyzed and unconnected discontents who must (and can) overcome their nihilistic sense of inevitable system failure. As Hopi elders said: "We are the ones we've been waiting for." The isolated many must become the many mobilized. As Jeff Gates said in *Democracy at Risk*, we must "convert today's cynics into engaged citizens and our alienated pessimists into political optimists."

Waking up people to the truth is not the real challenge—the truth is here. It is kicking passive dissenters out of their slumbering acquiescence to a corrupt government, declining democracy, and cruel economy. Passive dissent resembles passive aggressive behavior. Archibald MacLeish said: "The dissenter is every human being at those moments in his life when he resigns momentarily from the herd and thinks for himself." Quiet, brooding dissenters, however, do not fix things. The only way to fix our atrophied democracy is to get active and exercise our freedom, as Ted Halstead in *The Real State of the Union* said:

> Like an unused muscle, collective power need only be exercised to regain its inherent strength. ...Cynics will be quick to downplay the prospects of large-scale reform, so accustomed are we to incrementalism and tinkering. ...All the requisite ingredients for change are now coming together again, at the onset of the post-industrial age. If patterns hold, our nation's next major reinvention cannot be far away.

Collective power requires united individual power. To see the next New American Revolutionary look in the mirror.

Believing Yourself into Disbelief

When we protect our cherished models of reality we open the door for manipulation by politicians, leading even intelligent Americans to vote against their self-interests. These people appear deranged and are what Thomas Frank describes as "backlash conservatives" in *What's the Matter With Kansas?* If we hear a lie that is consistent with our status quo beliefs, we are likely to accept it. Example: many people bought the lie that Saddam Hussein and al Qeada were working together, and many still believe that. Because it is easy to retreat from uncomfortable thoughts and information, psychologically protective cognitive dissonance fortifies the deMOCKracy status quo. The ugly truth is that our brains are wired for serving and protecting our status quo core beliefs. An established mindset or worldview has a *biological* basis, because beliefs and ideas are tied to long term memories.

University of Michigan researcher Arthur Lupia has studied the problem of improving civic competence, especially the difficulty of altering a person's belief system. He has emphasized that merely presenting information to people is not likely to produce change. "It is not true that 'If you build it, they will come' nor is it true that if they come, the effect will be as advocates anticipate," he said. The problem is that "Ideas are stored as activation potentials in neural networks. They represent associations between a person's body and their environment," he said. So, getting someone to change beliefs is *biologically* difficult. "The persistence of status quo biases in decision-making is but one force that renders this battle [of choice] more difficult to win than is commonly appreciated," according to Lupia. To break a status quo bias belief requires compelling, superior information that convinces someone that a new belief will deliver superior personal results or that it fits reality much better, not just that the information is better in some theoretical or ideological way. In the end, no matter what the effort, the odds are people will stay with their original tried and true belief.

New American Revolutionaries must first overcome their own psychological biases (especially pessimism about large-scale change) and than those of others. Consider these events:

> An elementary school teacher is astounded to read that his fellow teacher and friend has been arrested for being a long-time pedophile that has molested students.
>
> Parents are shocked to see television pictures clearly revealing that their son has been killed by police after he shot over a dozen fellow high school students and several teachers.
>
> A senior congressman and military hero confesses to taking millions of dollars in gifts and bribes from government contractors he has helped,

but colleagues, neighbors and supporters are incredulous.

When you hear about such reactions you naturally wonder how could the people who presumably have known the "culprit" been so surprised. Worse yet, even after the evidence is certain, you see them on the evening news in total denial. They maintain that the person seemed completely "normal" and they "can't believe what has happened." A prime explanation is a strong status quo bias belief, a prejudice. They have loved, trusted, and respected the person providing the surprise and seen them as a normal, good person. It is naïve to believe that the culprits can totally hide behind a mask of normalcy. Inevitably there are signs of bad behavior. But positive perceptions of the people block those signs and cause lies to be believed.

Here is another example of mental blocking with mind-boggling consequences. President George W. Bush told a *Washington Times* reporter in 2004 that he refrains from watching news on TV, nor reads newspapers except to scan the front page. Bush said: "I like to have a clear outlook. It can be a frustrating experience to pay attention to somebody's false opinion or somebody's characterization, which simply isn't true." Note his presumption that information from other sources is automatically incorrect. So, he purposefully blocks information that might conflict with his presumed correct information and beliefs. *Newsweek's* article "Bush in the Bubble" noted that "he does not like dissonance." Former Treasury Secretary Paul O'Neill said Bush was "caught in an echo chamber of his own making, cut off from everyone other than a circle around him that's tiny and getting smaller and in concert on everything." Surrounding oneself with affirming "yes" men and women is part of the status quo bias belief phenomenon—intellectual cocooning. We should not be surprised that so many delusional citizens in a delusional democracy elected a delusional president.

A large number of Americans now have a status quo bias belief that politicians and corporate big shots are crooks and liars, and political parties are corrupt. These are the government-corporate-distrusting Americans. Thus, media scandals about terrible behavior, lies and corruption no longer shock these people. Rather, the scandals affirm their status quo belief. However, this belief does not necessarily negate their positive status quo belief that American democracy remains strong (albeit not perfect) and the envy of the world. The problem is that these people (delusional patriots) do not fully comprehend or accept the democracy gap—the lower quality today as compared to the past, democracy's arrow pointing down and not up. Some do not have a personal measure of the decline during their adult lives, nor are they informed by schools, the media or political leaders of the decline. Their belief system from whatever source causes them to unquestioningly accept American democracy's greatness. [I speculate that far less than one million Americans have ever read any of the dozens of books like this one on our crumbling democracy.] So, there really are Americans who are rightfully distrusting of their government yet are positive and delusional about their democracy. This seems illogical, but it is so.

Now, consider a political figure that is actually honest, incorruptible and openly talks about the decline in American democracy, someone who wants a Second American Revolution. He or she may not be believed, because who they are and what they say contradict two widely held status quo beliefs. They are disadvantaged by widely held psychological defenses, with the big exception being the large number of discontented Americans who fully grasp the democracy-decline problem. It is not enough to believe that such an honest politician would be unappreciated because of what the opposition says, such as labeling him or her as disloyal and unpatriotic. The challenge for New American Revolutionaries is to overcome the status quo belief in corrupt and dishonest politicians, which is correct, and the faith-in-American-democracy belief, which is false. How do you connect to intractable "true believers" who, like President Bush, shield themselves from dissonant information about their democracy? You must work very hard with highly focused and consistent democracy-decline, democracy-rebuilding messages—more about this later. The target audiences are all those who mistrust government, both those who grasp the democracy-decline problem and those who do not.

It takes an awful lot to overcome the status quo. It is not so much that people love what they have now. Sticking with the status quo is a defensive action against a hostile, menacing and out-of-control world that in so many unpredictable ways seems to be getting worse. What is known seems safer, even if it is negative, than the unknown. A vote for the status quo is like hitting the brakes to stop bad things from getting even worse. When what is really needed is changing direction to reach a better future. Americans must love America not as it is, but as it should and could be.

Lies Work Wonders

In *The Brothers Karamov*, Fyodor Dostoyevsky said:

> The important thing is to stop lying to yourself. A man who lies to himself, and believes his own lies, becomes unable to recognize truth, either in himself or in anyone else, and he ends up losing respect for himself as well as for others.

Even delusional beliefs are reality. As Thomas Frank showed in *What's the Matter With Kansas,* the Republicans who actually coddle the wealthy and powerful at the expense of workers and small farmers have learned to lie so successfully that the latter vote against their own economic interests. George W. Bush looked out at the attendees who paid $800 a plate at a fundraiser and said: "This is an impressive crowd—the haves and the have-mores. Some people call you elites; I call you my base." In front of carefully selected crowds of more typical Americans, Bush works up the crowd by focusing on social issues. In reviewing Frank's book, Celia Bruno observed that deluded Bush-supporters are "goaded into thinking that whether they are able to own an AK-47 is more important than whether they will be able to afford a life-saving operation for their sick child. ...It is not about big vs. small government, it is about government (of whatever size) privileging the haves at the expense of the have-nots." You could show a tape of what Bush said to the elites to loyal Republicans in Kansas who are have-nots and they would not change one iota of their commitment. Such is the power of well-framed right-wing messages drummed into the brains of people that become deeply embedded neural networks of status quo bias beliefs.

Just prior to the 2004 presidential election, the Program on International Policy Attitudes (PIPA) released some fascinating findings. So called believed "facts" were determined to be more subjective than objective. The views of supporters of President Bush and Senator Kerry were compared to the objective truth. Consider these divergent views: 75 percent of Bush supporters versus 30 percent of Kerry supporters believed that Iraq either gave al Qaeda substantial support or had direct involvement in the September 11, 2001 attacks; 31 percent of Bush supporters and 74 percent of Kerry supporters believed the majority of people in the world opposed the U.S.-led Iraq war. The objective truth, as revealed in countless news reports, was that Bush supporters were wrong in both cases, as were the majority of them who believed that most of the world favored Bush's reelection. Could psychological theory precisely predict these kinds of lopsided percentages? No, but qualitatively, the ability of status quo bias beliefs to block remarkable amounts of contradictory information has explanatory power.

Indeed, PIPA itself concluded that the data showed a "tendency of Bush supporters to ignore dissonant information." Not because they are stupid, but because people normally filter out or ignore information that contradicts their status quo beliefs. The stronger those beliefs, the more effectively are "facts" rejected. Writing about these results, *Washington Post* columnist Dana Milbank said: "This past week brought confirmation that Bush and Kerry supporters live in alternate universes," and fellow columnist Donna Britt commented "we choose what we believe. We're perfectly capable of spinning ourselves." Spinning is just another euphemism for lying.

People who are unable to believe objective truth about their preferred candidate are "politicopaths." In the above case, some would argue that the false beliefs resulted from dishonest messages from conservative media and Republican propaganda. My thesis is that it is the earlier shaped psychological predisposition (status quo bias belief) to select, listen to and believe such messages that is the root problem. Inevitably, Kerry supporters were also exposed to the same lies; they were predisposed to disbelieve the lies. People do not have *time* to do careful research or even close examination of all the available information. New beliefs must displace existing status quo bias beliefs, which is very difficult. Yes, Bush supporters can be said to have been "duped." But before being "tricked" by lies, they had already tricked themselves through self-deception and adoption of a core reality model that made them vulnerable to clever politicians.

To sum up: Cognitive dissonance produces tenacious status quo bias beliefs that block new, more truthful and valuable replacement beliefs. Contrarian information literally goes in one ear and out the other. Self-delusion is the result.

An outsider having an alternative belief sees *irrational* thinking and is frustrated because using "facts" to change the other person's belief meets a brick wall. This is human nature. Contradictory facts are blocked despite spending time and energy presenting them. On the positive side, sustained passionate debate makes one's reality model vulnerable as emotions loosen defenses. Unlike people in other democracies, most Americans would rather shop, work on the Internet, play sports, or watch TV than energetically debate politics with people having different beliefs, which you are more likely to see in cosmopolitan cities worldwide.

All this reveals how politicians (and others using marketing messages) can design lies to connect and resonate with certain beliefs held by people, despite the lies being seen as blatant lies by others not holding those targeted beliefs. So a conservative candidate who really gives a low priority to government social services for the poor and disadvantaged connects with those believing in government's responsibility to care for the downtrodden by talking "compassionate conservatism," a clever and intentionally misleading slogan. Loyal conservatives do not fear future support for social service programs, but maybe some moderates and liberals buy the lie. And a liberal candidate not really supportive of more spending on defense connects to those believing in a strong military by repeatedly emphasizing his service in the military. Loyal liberal supporters do not worry about a massive military buildup, but maybe some conservatives and independents buy the lie.

The obvious problem, of course, is that connecting with one belief means a disconnection with an opposing or very different belief. So politicians are compelled to use "mixed messages" designed to appeal to opposing status quo beliefs, or to alternate contradictory messages depending on what audience is being addressed or what voters are most courted. The better partisan liar is able to con enough members of the other party and independents through his lies while holding on to his or her base of support, whose status quo bias is consistent with the candidate's true belief system. George W. Bush's promotion of the Iraq war first on the basis of fighting terrorism and then on spreading democracy—two things that most people would favor—fits this model. Of course, some keen observers would see the politician as inconsistent, flip-flopping, and dishonest. It took two years for the public to lose their trust in Bush's case for the war.

Applying this reasoning, it becomes clear that an obstacle to major or systemic changes in government is some Americans' "nationalism"—

their proud loyalty to this "great nation." Many see only the good about America and make comparisons with nations having terrible governments or economies, or focus on past American greatness. They hold on to the American dream and the promise of upward economic mobility. It is too painful to accept negative facts about our representative government and economic inequality—not merely caused by current office holders but the political economy's core functioning. They filter out these facts, thus passively sustaining our faltering democracy.

Spinning Ourselves Silly

Voters on the losing side of elections often say that those on the winning side are stupid or ignorant (and maybe a little crazy). The deeper and more disturbing truth is that people are deceiving themselves about what is true and false. Everyone is lied to by politicians. The question is whether we accept or reject the lies, and whether we accept or reject the facts when they are presented by others.

Self-denial is self-scamming. Self-spinning is an effort to hold onto a status quo worldview. We concentrate on those aspects of life and society that make us feel better. People convince themselves that if they pay taxes, give some money to good causes, and maybe vote, then they are good Americans. Many who have benefited the least from the corrupt political system, the poor, disadvantaged, and insecure members of the middle class stay loyal to the status quo system. Never underestimate the continuing power of the classic American dream; it is the rip tide of our culture, dragging us away from reality. Rather than seeing themselves in a class struggle, so many at the bottom or the middle of the income spectrum keep fantasizing that they too have a shot at being rich and, therefore, support policies that favor the rich, as if one day they will also reach dreamland. Meanwhile, they stay unwitting victims paying for a corrupt, elitist system.

Self-denial is nourished by suppressed fear, anger, and self-doubt; it requires self-deception, accepting the lies of others and lying to ourselves. Self-denial is not perfect, however, so anxiety can result because subconsciously or semi-consciously a little truth leaks in. Scientists speak of "unstable equilibrium," a condition that is susceptible to outside forces, to change. Some convictions and faiths are shakable.

This is good news for rescuing our democracy.

What George Lakoff said about spinning is relevant:

> Spin is used when something embarrassing has happened or has been said, and it's an attempt to put an innocent frame on it—that is, to make the embarrassing occurrence sound normal or good.

When people feel pain from the swirl of conflicting information and status quo beliefs they spin themselves to make the painful—not just embarrassing—occurrence seem normal or good.

When we watch partisan and professional spinners on television, we may think, "how can they keep lying with a smiling face?" Yet the challenge is examining ourselves and asking whether we are unthinkingly spinning ourselves.

Courageous Citizenship Consciousness

In his 1759 treatise *The Theory of Moral Sentiments*, Adam Smith captured the essence of the human need to avoid the pain of conflicting information: "He is...bold who does not hesitate to pull off the veil of self-delusion which covers from his view the deformities of his own conduct."

Self-delusion as the path of least resistance and pain management has been around a long time. Self-delusion is not frivolous indulgence; it is functional self-medication. Today's most important self-delusions are that American democracy is good enough and that dramatic change and reform is infeasible. You can also think of self-delusion as "self-rationalization" for getting the most you can from your life while what you know in your heart is that the nation desperately needs your civic engagement. At best, some people are waiting at the station for the fix-the-republic train to arrive so they can walk in and comfortably join in. That's like waiting for Godot.

Self-delusion—selling ourselves a false belief—results from self-deception—a fraud or trick played by us on ourselves. It is like an arms race between our unconscious (status quo bias) and conscious (awareness of contradictory information) selves. Self-deception (the process) is how we build and maintain an illusionary world. Self-delusion (the state) leads to a largely unconscious and automatic disregard of objectively true facts that would overturn a status quo bias belief. Thus, facts about the unraveling of American democracy confront love of country and can be rejected. A shared delusional personal state becomes a collective delusion supporting a delusional democracy.

Many discontented, disadvantaged, and angry Americans stick to an elaborate web of illusion maintained by accepting the propaganda and lies from politicians and the media—on the political left or right, whichever they are psychologically predisposed to trust. They trick themselves into passively accepting or actively supporting our leaders and government, despite information that should cause them to rebel against the system. Their views are rationalized by convincing themselves they are reasonable people doing the best they can with the time they have. They see only one practical choice—supporting the lesser evil, the least lying, or the least corrupted politicians offered by the status quo system—or walking away from all of it.

True political leaders would use their stature and truthful information, not lies, to change public opinion by overcoming the wrongheaded status quo bias beliefs of many Americans. But in contemporary politics, compelling arguments yield to compelling lies. As columnist Robert J. Samuelson said about the 2004 presidential race, "the candidates had positions. But these consisted mostly of appealing platitudes that said what people wanted to hear." What people "want to hear" is what produces the least cognitive dissonance relative to their pre-existing frames.

To paraphrase George Orwell: "The two-party loyalist not only does not disapprove of atrocities committed by his own side, but he has a remarkable capacity for not even hearing about them." When a large fraction of Americans share a self-delusion, they have achieved social conformity and may be the majority. They have become accustomed to being lied to and even fortify the liars. Americans' shared, bipartisan self-deception is that lying politicians are an inevitable part of the greatest nation in the world. They may get angry when a lie is first disclosed, but in time that public anger dissipates or is directed to the next stupendous political lie.

Even when people get a glimmer of the truth about lies and liars, they may hope that they are just part of political campaigning. People often convince themselves that winning politicians will return to the truth when they govern. But that just takes people back to self-delusion, because political liars invariably are habitual liars. Thomas Jefferson saw this problem in 1785:

> He who permits himself to tell a lie once, finds it much easier to do it a second and third time, till at length it becomes habitual; he tells lies without attending to it, and truth without the world's believing him. This falsehood of the tongue leads to that of the heart, and in time depraves all its good dispositions.

In the political and civic realm there are no excusable "good" lies; they are evidence of a wider, permanent problem. It is hard to figure out what information can penetrate and overturn the status quo belief of right-wing Republicans and conservatives that Americans democracy has integrity and is still improving, when it is so filled with sustained dishonesty and corruption.

The eminent psychologist and writer Erich Fromm said this in his 1979 book *To Have or To Be?*

> Our conscious motivations, ideas, and beliefs are a blend of false information, biases, irrational passions, rationalizations, prejudices, in which morsels of truth swim around and give the reassurance albeit false, that the whole mixture is real and true. ...This level of consciousness is supposed to reflect reality; it is the map we use for organizing our life.

Has Satan Made Them Theocrats?

Theocracy champion the Reverend Rod Parsley says "Theocracy means God is in control, and you are not." Theocrats have little respect for the constitutional sovereignty of the American people and their Constitution. They put all their faith in their interpretation of the Bible.

Status quo bias beliefs and self-delusion often derive from a religious faith. Religious true believers can accept and support outrageous status quo conditions, such as obscene economic inequality. Status quo defenders can and do design lies and propaganda especially for these righteous true believers. Bill Moyers has given serious thought to this phenomenon:

> One of the biggest changes in politics in my lifetime is that the delusional is no longer marginal. It has come in from the fringe, to sit in the seat of power in the oval office and in Congress. ...Theology asserts propositions that cannot be proven true; ideologues hold stoutly to a world view despite being contradicted by what is generally accepted as reality. ...For the Bible is not just the foundational text of their faith; it has become

the foundational text for a political movement. ...the country is not yet a theocracy but the Republican Party is—and they are driving American politics, using God as a battering ram on almost every issue: crime and punishment, foreign policy, health care, taxation, energy, regulation, social services and so on. ...They use the language of faith to demonize political opponents, mislead and misinform voters, censor writers and artists, ostracize dissenters, and marginalize the poor.

Similarly, Pepe Escobar wrote the article "In God—or reality—we trust," in the *Asia Times* immediately before the 2004 presidential election. "The choice now is stark, between faith-based domination and rational leadership; between a messianic cult backed by vast corporate power and the 'reality-based community.' ...Bush's trademark hostility toward the factual world just mirrors the cognitive dissonance of the crusading God-fearing armies: no wonder the Bush administration lives in fantasyland," wrote Escobar. Also, the Bush candidacy and administration was "non-reality based," according to Escobar.

Non-radical Christians are also speaking out. Baptist minister Carlton W. Veazey said: "I think we are teetering on the brink of theocracy and the Christian Right could conceivably use the battle over the judiciary and weakening support for reproductive rights to push us over the edge." He condemned the exclusion of "all other views and versions as irreligious, immoral, or wrong."

Some people refer to "Christocrats." Chip Berlet and Margaret Quigley have another good idea: "The predominantly Christian leadership envisions a religiously-based authoritarian society; therefore we prefer to describe this movement as the 'theocratic right.'" This is important because right-wing politicians under the sway of Christocrats never publicly acknowledge the theocracy goal of their supporters.

Here are some documented George W. Bush statements: "I pray I be as good a messenger of his will as possible," "I trust God speaks through me. Without that I couldn't do my job." "God wants me to spread democracy all over the World." His father, Bush I, held this democracy-limiting view: "I don't know that Atheists should be considered as citizens, nor should they be considered patriots." As to the 2000 election, General William Boykin said Bush "was not elected by a majority of the voters—he was appointed by God." Boykin became Deputy Undersecretary of Defense for Intelligence.

Is there any doubt about the drive for a Christian theocracy? Listen to Pastor D. James Kennedy:

> Our job is to reclaim America for Christ, whatever the cost. As the vice regents of God, we are to exercise godly dominion and influence over our neighborhoods, our schools, our government, our literature and arts, our sports arenas, our entertainment media, our news media, our scientific endeavors—in short, over every aspect and institution of human society.

There you have it. Nothing left out. Dominion over everything. Worse yet, here is what the Free Congress Foundation's manifesto asserted: "We will not try to reform the existing institutions. We only intend to weaken them, and eventually destroy them." As to real politics, in 2004, 48 out of 51 Republican senators voted with the Christian Coalition 100 percent of the time as did Democrat-turncoat Zell Miller. As Bill Moyers said: "So the Grand Old Party—the GOP—has become God's Own Party, its ranks made up of God's Own People 'marching us to war.'"

Bill Moyers sees the nexus between the religious right and the Republicans: "In the pursuit of political power they cut a deal with America's richest class and their partisan allies in a law-of-the-jungle strategy to 'starve' the government of resources needed for vital social services that benefit everyone while championing more and more spending on rich corporations and larger tax cuts for the rich. ...Without [the religious right] the government would not be in the hands of people who don't believe in government. ...The corporate, political and religious right converge here, led by a president who, in his own disdain for science, reason and knowledge, is the most powerful fundamentalist in American history." Just picture in your mind a meeting of the secretive right-wing Council for National Policy, the air filled with righteous rage against the plague of liberalism, plotting, scheming, and strategizing among theocratic, political and corporate elites. As senior members of the restricted political system the leaders of the theocratic right exercise their power of voter turnout to push their crusade which, coincidentally, impales so many of their followers as economic slaves.

God did NOT write our Constitution and Bill of Rights. Dissenters did. A healthy democracy requires respect for objective reality. With divine guidance, Christocrats resist objective truth. Faith is fine, but not delusion about objective reality; it is self-deception on steroids. For too many, religion is the opiate of the deceived. Intelligent design versus evolution is not science versus science, but faith versus science, an attack on objective reality. What is disheartening about Christocrats is their preoccupation with social and cultural values but not protecting and rehabilitating our democracy. Their distaste for hyper-commercialized, crass, sex-obsessed, and vulgar American culture is understandable. However, fundamentalist Christians should use persuasion, good works, exemplary behavior and their economic power as consumers to impact American society. Advocacy as citizens is one thing, supporting candidates with their beliefs is fair, but using government to serve a specific religious system defines a theocracy. Let devout Christians do and reject what they want, but respect democracy and don't seek *government* power to force others to behave like you.

It makes no sense to think in terms of a Christian, Jewish, Muslim, or atheist democracy. There is just democracy. It either works and serves all its citizens (including atheists) or does not. Thomas Jefferson's words should be honored: "History, I believe, furnishes no example of a priest-ridden people maintaining a free civil government." Jefferson fretted over "the loathsome combination of church and state." He also said: "It does me no injury for my neighbor to say there are twenty gods, or no God. It neither picks my pocket nor breaks my leg." Actually, our Founding Fathers were mostly Deists and Unitarians along with some Christians, so claims that the U.S. is a "Christian nation" are unfounded and frightening. Nevertheless, this was pronounced: "The Republican Party of Texas affirms the United States of America is a Christian Nation."

The enormous success of the theocratic right is reason enough for democracy-loving Americans to face reality. Only the fight to save divine democracy has the focus and power to win the radical right's holy war. The millions of Americans screaming with pain over the theocratic right's success with putting George W. Bush in the White House must recognize that for democracy to survive and prosper people must do the best of things in the worst of times. Yes, the Christocrats have power. So, as Frederick Clarkson asked, "What do we do with what we have learned?" His answer is simple:

> The answer to the power of the Christian Right is electoral power of our own. No excuses. Many of us have tended to abandon this cornerstone of citizenship in favor of other things. It is time to get our priorities straight. …If we believe that democracy is a good thing, we need to learn to get

very good at it. We need to be better at it than those who would destroy it. …Voting alone is not enough. The survival of constitutional democracy depends on the active participation of the citizens. …the problem of citizen disengagement and lack of participation needs to change. It's possible; and it's necessary.

Bill O'Reilly, Sean Hannity and other theocrat talk show hosts assert that "There is an anti-Christian bias in the country." On the surface this is plain nuttiness with 85 percent of Americans saying they are Christians. Take a breath and you realize what there is (and what we need more of) is a backlash among politically conscious Americans against the radical Christocrats' political blitzkrieg. Without mental blocking, non-radical Christians and others see that the Christocrats put their extremist interpretations of the Bible above our Constitution and laws. More democracy-defenders must stay vigilant and fight the theocratic right's crusade. Forget deprogramming them, however. There is no catapult large enough to hurl information high enough to overcome the psychological defensive walls of Christocrats and other backlash conservatives shackled mentally to the lies of the Republicans. They are like a cult, swallowing toxic Kool-Aid from thousands of self-professed "patriot pastors" and false patriot media kings and politicians. For them, the chorus of un-Christian political dissent is Satan's song.

What are we to do? Simply defending the Constitution and using our electoral power are not enough. And don't count on the Supreme Court to prevent a theocracy takeover. We must demand that our elected officials and judges not be on a mission for their God, only on a mission to fairly serve public interests according to the laws of the land. Taking the offensive is necessary. Religious bullies must be opposed. Our rallying and battle cry must be framed as "DEFEND DEMOCRACY OR SUFFER THEOCRACY." The battlefields are not just in the polling places but also, in Howard Zinn's words, the public places where the world can see "the actions of an aroused citizenry."

We Know Who's Crazy in Kansas

Anyone who has read Thomas Frank's *What's the Matter With Kansas?* learned how millions of Americans became the foot soldiers of the Republican revolution—what Frank calls the Great Backlash— and with great alacrity sacrificed their own economic wellbeing for the righteous defense of certain social or cultural values. The question is: Have they intentionally and knowingly created a movement to benefit the rich and powerful elites who, in turn, have shredded American democracy so prized by them? No, exploitation seems the answer. Smart Republicans hitched their fate to the culture war combatants and adopted the mantle of "values" to get the public support (votes) they needed. Here are some of Frank's key substantive points:

> [T]he backlash mobilizes voters with explosive social issues—summoning public outrage over everything from busing to un-Christian art—which it then marries to pro-business economic policies. …All they have to show for their Republican loyalty are lower wages, more dangerous jobs, dirtier air, a new overlord class that comports itself like King Farouk—and, of course, a crap culture whose moral free fall continues without significant interference from the grand-standing Christers whom they send triumphantly back to Washington every couple of years. …[The Republicans] sing the praises of the working man's red-state virtues even while they pummel the working man's economic chances with outsourcing, new overtime rules, lousy health insurance, and coercive new management techniques. …Ignoring one's economic self-interest may seem like a suicidal move to you and me, but viewed a different way it is an act of noble self-denial; a sacrifice for a holier cause. …conservatives are always hardworking patriots who love their country and are persecuted for it.

In other words, social conservatives have not won their primary battle through Bible-cleaning American culture. Yet, despite losing economically, no reality will cause them to surrender. They revel in their victimhood and persecution; they seem to welcome being burned by the Republican economy as much as they would enjoy being burned at the stake. They are blind to the primary cause of what they see as America's cultural collapse—not satanic Liberals but good old-fashioned capitalist business interests that bankroll Republicans and reap the financial benefits of every popular (but evil) cultural trend. Social conservatives are duped by the Republican's political calculus that "culture outweighs economics as a matter of public concern," as Frank noted.

In terms of the psychological framework presented in this chapter, the social conservatives of whom the evangelical Christocrats are a key component have a core belief system that rigidly and religiously fixates on social interests, such as fighting abortion and protecting the sanctity of marriage. Their powerful status quo bias beliefs block all kinds of information that causes cognitive dissonance, such as the contradiction between being pro-life and for capital punishment and a deadly preemptive war, and supporting "compassionate" politicians who work against the vast majority of ordinary folks. From an outsider's perspective they seem crazy, economically suicidal, and stupid for fighting the wrong enemy. Their patriotism is counterproductive because they support those who corrupt representative government to maintain a twisted economy that profits from all kinds of cultural crassness. Yet their belief system is as unshakable as that of a member of cult. They are not good candidates for joining a movement to fix our democracy. They have been exploited, manipulated and abused—and stick with "a working-class movement that has done incalculable historic harm to working-class people," as Frank said.

Exactly who are Satan's little helpers? Liberals? Or Republican sinics who filch the votes of social conservatives to serve the rich and powerful elites who are wrecking America's economy, debasing its culture, and dissolving its democracy?

Chapter 4

The Politics of Lying:
From Dupes to Patriots

During times of universal deceit, telling the truth is revolutionary.

—George Orwell

Delusion feeds dishonesty. Dishonesty damages democracy. Unsurprisingly, with omnipresent delusion and dishonesty, a delusional democracy results—our present state of the union. A union cannot be held together by lies and delusions. Ultimately, America's delusional democracy will succumb to stronger nations. Is this what China with its exploding economic and military power sees?

Pitiful Politicians

Here's how Americans rate the honesty and integrity of different professions in terms of the percent giving a very high or high rating according to a 2005 Gallup poll:

Nurses	82	highest
Pharmacists	67	
Journalists	28	
Senators	16	
Business executives	16	
Congressmen	14	
Telemarketers	7	lowest

Of related interest is that Americans saw some groups having too much power and influence in Washington according to a 2005 Harris poll. For big companies 90 percent felt this way, for political action committees 85 percent, for political lobbyists 74 percent. Conversely, 78 percent believed that public opinion has too little power and influence and 53 percent felt that way for opinion polls. Taken altogether the picture is that our federal representatives are not viewed as honest, and their dishonest corporate allies are seen as way too powerful while what the public wants is largely ignored. This is a vulnerable system.

Back in 1838 James Fenimore Cooper said that the word "American" equated to telling the truth. He spoke of candor as the "conviction of the necessity of speaking, and speaking it all. ...The public has a right to be treated with candor. Without this manly and truly republican quality... the institutions are converted into a stupendous fraud."

Times have changed. For today's politicians, dishonesty has become the best policy. Does anyone really believe that you can have effective democracy in a culture of lying?

First, politicians lie to themselves about their *intentions*, and then they intentionally lie to the public about the *facts*. "People who tell themselves too many lies commit a form of suicide," said Lewis H. Lapham, but lying politicians are killing our democracy, not themselves.

It is sometimes said pejoratively that elected officials use the results of opinion polls to govern. To a far greater extent, politicians use poll results to run their *campaigns*—to decide what to lie about—and, if they win, use their obligations to special interests to govern, whatever their party. First, they lie to get votes, and then they lie to justify actions that really serve their financial supporters, not the public.

Lying has been institutionalized, normalized by public servants and inflicted on the public. America's leaders have no *moral* authority at home and internationally. Everyone lies, but nobody lies more frequently, more profoundly, and with more consequences than politicians. All candidates for president and all sitting presidents lie. The connection between honesty and morals has been severed. Politicians peddling their religiosity lie with conviction when serving their financial backers. Tom DeLay and other religious-right, anti-gambling congressmen, for example, in 2000 voted against limiting Internet gambling when a lobbyist spewed money on behalf of his client.

Thomas L. Difloure wrote eloquently in a letter to *Newsweek*:

> The hubris and hypocrisy shown by DeLay and his sycophants who claim to be Christians while proudly and publicly extorting campaign contributions in return for political favors is a growing stain on our democracy that must be rejected before democracy itself becomes a meaningless expression.

Once in office, politicians continue lying to convince people that their policies and programs are consistent with their "values" and are really working. They focus on gullible constituencies willing to vote against their self-interests. They know how to selectively use the media to reach their target audiences. This works because people choose talk shows, radio, TV and cable stations with a clear political bias or slant for *confirmation* of their existing beliefs. Choosing comforting confirmation over disturbing information is a sure sign of a disengaged populace susceptible to manipulation by dishonest politicians and obliging news media.

Consider the findings of the Pew Research Center prior to the 2004 presidential election. With the "great cable divide," 70 percent of Fox News viewers supported the re-election of President Bush, compared to 67 percent of CNN viewers behind Senator Kerry. Fox News has a well-deserved reputation as being right-leaning, while CNN is a far more balanced major cable news competitor. The split among newspaper, network news and local TV users was modest, tilting toward Kerry. But those who depended on cable TV, radio and the Internet for news tilted toward Bush.

In 2003, the Program on International Policy Attitudes found that, by a large margin, viewers of Fox News were the most misinformed about the Iraq war, as compared to those who got their news from print sources or from National Public Radio and PBS stations. A 2005 study by the Project for Excellence in Journalism examined stories on the Iraq war and the extent that anchors and journalists gave their own opinions. On Fox News, 73 percent did, compared to 29 percent on MSNBC and 2 percent on CNN. Also, 38 percent of the Fox News Iraq war stories were positive, compared with 20 percent on CNN and 16 percent on MSNBC. Fox News' incessantly repeated claim of offering "real journalism—fair and balanced" is just an endlessly repeated lie to comfort faithful, but misinformed and deluded viewers. Mostly they give biased opinion.

Liars Racing Liars

Some lies are clear cut intentional incorrect facts. Others are more subtle as, for example, when George W. Bush and his minions conflated criticism of the Iraq war with contempt for our soldiers and aiding the enemy, as if dissent is unpatriotic and lying is patriotic.

In a 2004 CNBC interview, Vice President Dick Cheney maintained that he never said that it was "pretty well confirmed" that terrorist Mohammed Atta had met with an Iraqi official in Prague, a key fact used by the Bush administration to link Saddam Hussein to al Qaeda and 9/11. But a tape of a 2001 *Meet the Press* show later aired on *The Daily Show* painfully revealed that Cheney had said exactly that. Clear-cut lies are so much easier to document.

Let the race begin. Republican candidate: "My opponent will say anything to win." Democrat candidate: "My opponent will say anything to win." They both are right. As H. L. Mencken said:

> Under democracy one party always devotes its chief energies to trying to prove that the other party is unfit to rule—and both commonly succeed, and are right.

Which liar gets your vote depends on how successfully their rhetoric has caused the least amount of cognitive dissonance. In our culture of lying, what makes a good liar makes a successful "leader." A successful politician does not hesitate to lie. "Honest politician" is an oxymoron. All lies by elected officials disrespect citizens and democracy. The smaller the lie and the less its need, the greater is the evidence of a habitual liar. Dick Cheney's lie was not small. It had a purpose: To rewrite history of how Bush lied us into war. More about this later.

That an elected official truly and sincerely believes in a lie's need, benefits and higher purpose does not make the person patriotic, just dangerous. In time the person may see the lie as truth, making him or her even more believable and dangerous to democracy.

Heed the words of Vladimir Lenin: "A lie told often enough a becomes the truth." Our politicians practice this at every opportunity. Politicians who routinely lie give the very few who don't a bad name, our nation a bad government, and we the people a bad deal. A culture is in trouble when people *expect* to be lied to and accept it as *normal* behavior. Besides politicians, Catholic priests lie about their abuse of children, telemarketers lie about products, journalists lie about the facts, government bureaucrats lie about their actions, and corporate CEOs lie about company finances. A challenge for status quo busters is to be seen as truth-tellers when so few exist.

A historic con job has been pulled off by the Republican Party. In particular, George W. Bush boasted initially that he would run the government as if it was a business. Problem was that he was a failure in the business world and his record as president, just in terms of national economics, again proved his lack of talent. As author Joel Kotkin said in 2005: "The modern Republican Party can't seem to separate parochial corporate interest from the nation's larger interests." Over decades, it successfully sold the idea that Republicans provide better economic results than Democrats, because Republicans cut taxes to provide less money for wasteful government spending, often referred to as "starving the beast." In truth, ordinary Americans have not benefited economically under Republican administrations. Official data from 1959 to 2004 show that federal deficit, national debt, real per capita income, inflation, and unemployment did worse under Republican regimes. The 2003 tax cuts produced an average savings of $100,000 for households with incomes above $1 million, compared to $217 for the average family in the middle of the income spectrum.

The question is not why Republicans created this lopsided benefit, it is: Why did so many middle and lower income Americans vote for those Republicans? What spell were these Americans victims of? Perhaps they actually believed what Bush had said repeatedly: "By far the vast majority of my tax cuts go to the bottom end of the spectrum." He lied. Voters may not be fools, but they can be fooled. A 2001 *Newsweek* poll found that only half of Americans even knew that there had been a tax cut. So, it's not just that some voters are fooled; many are too distracted to pay any attention to what their representatives are doing *to* them.

Another question to ponder is: Did the Republicans do what most Americans wanted? Absolutely not. Many surveys revealed no major public support for tax cuts tilted in favor of the rich. For example, a poll conducted between the House and Senate action on the tax cut bill found that 53 percent of people wanted tax cuts for lower income taxpayers. Other surveys found support for more spending on social programs. Yet the majority Republicans did what they wanted because it served the interests of many of their core supporters, but not the majority of middle and lower income Americans. In contemporary politics, public opinion data are not used by our representatives to meet our needs; it is information around which to design propaganda to deceive us. Tax expert Martin Sullivan wrote in 2003 that the "Treasury's Office of Tax Policy may have to change its name to the Office of Tax Propaganda."

What about the Democrats? In the final vote on the tax cuts 28 of

212 House Democrats and 11 of 50 Senate Democrats voted for it and so did moderate Republicans. Those tax cuts when coupled with unbridled spending would require unbelievable borrowing and deficits.

Conservative columnist George F. Will wrote about the "Grand Old Spenders" in November 2005. He noted "the $60 billion in corporate welfare that dwarfs the $29 billion budget of the Department of Homeland Security." Also that "Federal spending…has grown twice as fast under President Bush as under President Clinton, 65 percent of it unrelated to national security." And that "per-household federal spending [is] the highest in inflation adjusted terms since World War II." Living off of federal funding are the military contractors. As Jeffrey S. Clair said in *Grand Theft Pentagon*: "The Pentagon has become a kind of government operated casino, doling out billions in contracts to the big-time spenders in American politics: General Dynamics, Boeing, Raytheon, Bechtel, Lockheed and, of course, the bete noir of the Bush administration, Halliburton." Fiscal conservatives seemed to have lost the Republican battle to corporate cronyism.

In August, 2005, the *Washington Post* editorialized about "Big-Government Conservatives." The occasion was the passage of the huge $295 billion transportation bill by the Republican-controlled Congress and it's signing by President Bush, despite 6,371 earmarks—unnecessary "pork" projects sought by senators and representatives. They will cost taxpayers more than $24 billion. Upon signing the law, President Bush said it accomplished its "goals in a fiscally responsible way." Also, federal spending jumped during the Bush II administration. Republicans' dislike for government has been converted into talent for sucking up as much taxpayer money as possible to create wealth for the few. By any yardstick, Republicans lie better than Democrats.

But Democrats share the blame for unchecked borrowing required by massive budget deficits. As Robert J. Samuelson commented in November 2005:

> Well, on the budget, most Republicans are phonies. So are most Democrats. …Countless Democrats and Republicans routinely denounce deficits, but few will repeal [the Medicare drug benefit] program that relies on literally trillions of dollars of future borrowing. …But who cares about the truth? For most politicians, the real problem is to appear principled even whey they're not.

If no one cares about the truth, then in our culture of lying it is not surprising that openly calling someone a liar is unusual. After all, how can liars cast stones at other liars? Even in the face of the biggest, boldest, most certain lies, politicians refuse to call their opponents liars because they themselves are so vulnerable. It is a mutual protection conspiracy. This is the deal among big party politicians: I won't call you a liar if you don't call me one. Politicians win, the distracted public loses. *In the two-party lies-race, no one can stop lying and risk losing; there can be no unilateral honesty.*

As Brooks Jackson pointed out on Factcheck.org, "candidates have a legal right to lie to voters just about as much as they want. ...[Candidates] can legally lie about almost anything they want." So, really good liars, repeating bold lies at every opportunity have a distinct advantage over less able and consistent liars.

Can anyone really believe that democracy functions effectively in a culture of lying? Can you have the rule of law in a culture of lying? Lying breeds distrust, and as dishonesty and distrust have worsened, American democracy has suffered from less public confidence, scrutiny and involvement. Research has revealed the connection between mistrust in other Americans and mistrust of government. A national survey in late 1995 found that nearly two-thirds of Americans believed that most people can't be trusted, compared to a majority in 1964. As noted in Chapter 2, faith in government was very high from 1950s through 1964, and then started to decline in the early 1970s stayed at much lower levels until the post-9/11 period when it peaked for awhile, but then dropped again to low levels where it remains.

Regardless of many social problems in the 1950s and 1960s, there was a higher level of civility and social capital, less partisan polarization and extremism, and more responsible media. The art of political lying was not as sophisticated or as pervasive as today. There was definitely some social turmoil but also more hopefulness about the future. There were concrete signs that government was responsive to the will of the people. It is not nostalgia. American democracy really was in a better state in the 1950s and 1960s, as I and many others can attest to.

David Wise's 1973 *The Politics of Lying* provided a benchmark in the history of American dishonesty:

> By 1972 the politics of lying had changed the politics of America. In

place of trust, there was widespread mistrust; in place of confidence, there was disbelief and doubt in the system and its leaders. The consent of the governed is basic to American democracy. If the governed are misled, if they are not told the truth, or if through official secrecy and deception they lack information on which to base intelligent decisions, the system may go on—but not as democracy.

Exactly the point—it did go on but with more lying as a fading democracy, as a pseudo-democracy. Wise went on to conclude:

> Lying and secrecy have no place in a democracy. ...For democracy to work...the governed must know to what they are consenting. If they are misled, if the truth is concealed from them by the same government that demands their sons, their loyalty, and their treasure, then the American experiment is doomed to end in repression and failure.

These ominous words should make us all question today what kind of democracy we really have. Repression and failure are upon us. Indeed, over 30 years and several presidents later, in 2004, *All the President's Spin* presented an important perspective on how political dishonesty had evolved:

> George W. Bush has created a White House that draws on techniques pioneered by Reagan and Clinton but goes far beyond them in making unprecedented use of professionalized, strategic dishonesty to sell his proposals. ...He has developed a communications strategy of unprecedented scope and sophistication centered on tactics borrowed from the world of public relations. These include emotional language designed to provoke gut-level reaction, slanted statistics that are difficult for casual listeners to interpret, and ambiguous statements that imply what Bush does not want to state outright. ...To truly understand Bush's assault on honesty, you have to look at the implications of what he says, not just the words themselves.

In other words, the very technology of lying has become incredibly more complex, sophisticated and elusive. Why? Because so many Americans have become negative about politics and politicians and it takes trickier tactics to deceive them, to keep them as non-dissenters in a delusional state or silent, repressed dissenters. Can political lying get any worse? Just wait. If aggressive action is not taken to turn democracy's arrow up, it probably will get worse.

Consider these more recent survey results on the politics of mistrust. Two-thirds of mistrusting Americans believed that government actions usually end up hurting more people than they help, compared to 29 percent of trusting Americans. Fifty-three percent of mistrusting

Americans believed that public officials don't care "what people like me think," compared to 26 percent of trusting Americans. Forty percent of mistrusting Americans believed that "people like me" don't have any say about what the government does, compared to 16 percent of trusting Americans. Just one-third of mistrusting Americans had voted in the last presidential election, compared to 60 percent of trusting Americans. Follow these data: The people who are NOT voting are the ones more likely to be distrusting, the ones who see the ugly truth about politics, politicians and government but whose dissent is expressed by staying away from elections! This just makes it easier to maintain the corrupt status quo.

In sum, as trust in each other has declined, trust in government has also dropped, contributing to our deMOCKracy. Why? Because it pushes people away from politics, away from civic engagement, and away from optimism about changing the system. Moreover, when trust and faith in government is low it is difficult for policymakers to take bold and necessary actions in the broad and long-term public interest. And it makes it more difficult for the public to trust truth-talking New American Revolutionaries who must be trusted if they are to stand any chance of motivating people to become active dissenters.

For saving our democracy, the public should be told the truth about liars, but the major corporate media do not. Producing honesty for their audience—their customers—and for their country certainly should trump everything else, but it does not. The conspiracy of dishonesty keeps many Americans duped. To turn things around, lying politicians must be made to pay a high price for their dishonesty. Honesty must be forcefully demanded and rewarded.

Spinning Out of Democracy

Forget the presumption of honesty, now "you are lying until proven honest." Becoming accustomed to lying is like a child getting used to a school bully robbing him on a regular basis. Americans are being robbed of the truth.

Signaling the collapse of our representative system is the society's acceptance of professional spinners. Accepting the "spin" of facts gives legitimacy to an activity that should enrage everyone despite it being entertaining. That the news media regularly feature spinners—political pundits—is disgraceful. Political pundits defend the lies of one party or the other to produce fair and balanced lying that is, indeed, entertaining.

If someone in office, running for office or working for a candidate or public official spinspeaks, they should be viewed as a rapist violating our Constitution and representative government. Sold as opinion, spinspeak has become normal political behavior. A radio or television interviewer, especially on the public airways, however, upon hearing spinspeak should immediately say "sorry, you are obviously lying and this interview is over—come back when you are ready to speak the truth."

With spinspeak, the two major parties have accomplished something truly Orwellian. They make themselves look like they are offering truly substantial choices to voters. The engineered differences draw people into the "race." In reality, most Americans are voting for the "best" spinners, liars, and sinics, including corporate corrupters who look straight into the camera and say that their lobbying and massive campaign contributions "are just a way of getting information to politicians and participating in the democratic process." Sinic Elizabeth Dole, when running for the presidency, looked at voters and said, "I am not a politician." Someone like Ross Perot could do that honestly, but not someone who had worked a long time in government. Governor Howard Dean garnered so much support—especially from young people—in the 2004 presidential primaries because he seemed far less a sinic and liar than most mainstream politicians. That year the massive level of spinspeak by the two parties shoved aside media coverage of third party candidates and curtailed public access to their messages.

For the two major parties spinspeak is a tool to maintain our illusory political system where rivalry between liars is made to look like competition between different principles, ideas, and visions for our nation. It is just a lying competition between liars.

An Amber Alert for Honesty

Before the 2004 presidential election, columnist David S. Broder wrote:

> In an ideal world, a president would combine the best qualities of
> both men, giving us a chief executive with firm principles, a winning

personality, an agile mind, a mastery of policy, superior political skills, and a gift of eloquence. That candidate is not in the field this year.

Aside from ignoring third-party candidates, do you see a missing quality?

Our culture needs more *honesty*, especially among its political leaders. Apparently Broder did not see honesty in either Bush or Kerry, nor think it worth mentioning, probably because he like nearly everyone else no longer *expects* honesty in politicians. Like most media stars, Broder is more of a status quo protector than buster.

Time to end the culture of lying that supports the status quo, which is constructed on lies, sustained by lies, and economically dependent on lies. When a great democracy depends on lying for its political and social stability it is in trouble. It is a house of cards, not consciously eager for systemic change, but certainly in need of it.

Listen to what William Greider said in *Who Will Tell the People*:

> Rehabilitating democracy will require citizens to devote themselves first to challenging the status quo, disrupting the existing contours of power and opening the way for renewal. ...It originates among the ordinary people who find the will to engage themselves with their surrounding reality and to question the conflict between what they are told and what they see and experience.

Stinking lies come as naturally to politicians as farts to the rest of us. People must smell the lies and stop lying to themselves about American democracy. Truth has been concealed and cheapened. Americans must find the courage to see the abundant evidence that the guts of our political system have been chewed up by lying politicians and corporate parasites. Ideally, political leaders would see truth, talk truth, and act on truth to break through cognitive dissonance defenses. With today's politicians truth-talk is not cheap—it is obsolete.

Slick Semantic Magic

Perhaps the slickest, modern form of lying is ingenious use of phrases that falsely communicate a principled position. Take abortion. The use of "pro-life" instead of "anti-abortion" is designed to convey adherence to the life-affirming principle. But are "pro-choice" believers against life? Of course not. In this semantic game, life trumps choice. Through "framing" language, the abortion debate was transformed from different beliefs, based on different "facts," to one of different "values." Then, pro-life "values" are used to define virtuous candidates. Contradictions with the pro-life value are ignored, because they cause cognitive dissonance. These include: favoring the death penalty, fighting gun controls, sacrificing American soldiers in a preemptive war, preventing import of cheaper prescription drugs, and cutting social programs and medical research that save lives. Non-Republicans should never use the term "pro-life" to describe their opponents, but consistently use anti-abortion. And instead of using "pro-choice" it would be beneficial to use "pro-freedom."

A historic example of semantic chicanery is the "less government" position, juxtaposed to "big government." Less government is designed to translate into the "values" of less intrusion of government on peoples' lives, protection of private property and freedom, and lower taxes, all things that Americans like. This seeming principled position, however, is pure hokum. In truth, the less government "value" masks political objectives of spending government money on different programs (that favor business) and distributing the tax burden differently (to favor the rich and corporations) and borrowing more money (that penalizes future taxpayers). During the first four Bush II years federal spending jumped 33 percent, the national debt skyrocketed (with foreign financing doubling to $2 trillion), and with massive illegal immigration median household income decreased and the poverty rate increased.

Non-Republicans must reframe and replace "big government" in the minds of Americans with "fair government." Republicans replaced what they attacked as spend and tax big government of Democrats with their own *spend and borrow* big government designed for winning elections by serving campaign donors. *Newsweek* columnist Fareed Zakaria was so right in September 2005:

> Bush will go down in history as the most fiscally irresponsible chief executive in American history. ...The U.S. Congress is a national embarrassment, except that no one is embarrassed. ...Public spending is... an utterly corrupt process run by lobbyists and special interests with no concern for the national interest.

That same month, even ring-winger columnist Robert D. Novak faced facts about eleven years of Republican control of the House: "[Today's Republicans] outdo Democrats on pork and are in the same ballpark on entitlements."

Republicans have been especially adept at manipulating the tax system, as when they framed eliminating the estate tax as killing the "death tax." As David Cay Johnston said in *Perfectly Legal: The Covert Campaign to Rig Our Tax System to Benefit the Super Rich and Cheat Everybody Else*:

> Perhaps worst of all, our tax system now forces most Americans to subsidize the lifestyles of the very rich, who enjoy the benefits of our democracy without paying their fair share of its price.

It comes to this: Honesty is irrelevant—actually a handicap. Bush won in 2004 by conning millions of Americans to vote against their economic self-interests. Lies worked. Here is a dose of truth: Spend and borrow economic growth is fake prosperity when spending does not serve genuine public interests. Someone has to pay for it. Increasing government spending, cutting taxes and borrowing foreign money is profoundly unsustainable.

Republicans embrace economic growth that benefits a few through contractor spending (privatized government), tax cuts for the rich, tort reform, and corporate welfare. If taxes were raised immediately to pay for Republican rip-offs, the public would rebel. Instead, the costs are pushed forward, providing profits and global power to our banker communist China. Runaway borrowing steals from the future. When Republicans say that increased tax revenues from economic growth will pay off the debt they mean future taxes from non-benefiting citizens. Taxpayers with consumer debt also bear the burden of our national debt. *Delusional democracy with delusional prosperity is a historically unique double-whammy.*

Get the Lie Detector

Sometimes an astounding level of corruption and lying in government is revealed. Consider the following condemnation of employees in the Federal Deposit Insurance Corporation, the regulatory agency that insures deposits at banks and savings and loans:

> This is a cautionary tale where the emperor has new clothes—a bandits mask. ...the record reveals corrupt individuals within a corrupt agency with corrupt influences on it... none of the individuals was

constrained by his conscience... The solution lies in requiring its staff to be dedicated, responsible, and honest. ...These people discarded the mantle of the American Republic for the cloak of a secret society of extortionists.

Were these the words of some reform group or investigative journalist? No, they were part of a 2005 ruling by United States District Judge Lynn N. Hughes, appointed by President Ronald Reagan. Hughes agreed that the suit FDIC filed in 1995 but dropped in 2002, was based on lies; he awarded $72 million to Charles Hurwitz, a Texas businessman, and others to recover legal costs incurred over 20 years in defending the suit. Hurwitz had been blamed by the FDIC for the failure of a Texas thrift—United Savings Association of Texas—and the government wanted over one billion dollars from him. Hughes said that "Hurwitz faced a Goliath-like adversary: his government. ...The drain on his entrepreneurial energies cannot be undone. The actual costs of his defense can and must be repaid." The judge's ruling was a victory for government accountability. Lies lost.

Battered Americans must admit that we no longer have the great democracy we were taught to love. In the end, accepting the truth about American's descent into fake democracy is the only way to restore it. Democracy requires honesty, especially to fight false status quo beliefs. Americans' brains must be rewired so that they hold onto their valuing of ideal democracy, but are so outraged about our current failed democracy that they commit themselves to action. Truth matters. We need more truth about lies. In honesty we must trust. Heed the words of former Senator John Edwards: "The world desperately needs moral leadership from America, and the foundation for moral leadership is telling the truth."

Against those thoughts is the stark reality pointed out by Alexander Cockburn in the article "First the Lying, Then the Pardon" in *The Nation* in November 2005 when the indictment of Scooter Libby, Vice President Cheney's chief of staff, was still making news. Cockburn outlined a past pattern of senior White House officials caught lying and obstructing justice but depending on last-minute pardons by presidents for escaping the rule of law, and how this might play out again for the Bush II administration. "If officials violating the law and lying about it know with certainty that they are going to escape legal sanction, then we no longer have a government. We have a sequence of criminal conspiracies," said Cockburn. Presidential pardons have become nothing less than a mockery of the rule of law as Bill Clinton demonstrated with his last-minute pardons for 140 people, including the fugitive criminal Marc Rich.

In November 2005 various polls found that a majority of Americans thought that President George W. Bush had lied about the reasons for starting the Iraq war. A Harris poll found that 64 percent believed that the Bush administration "generally misleads the public on current issues." Of interest was something else that the mainstream media ignored, namely that a Zogby poll found that 53 percent of Americans felt that if Bush had lied about the Iraq war he should be impeached by Congress. Among Democrats 76 percent felt this way, among independents 50 percent, and even among Republicans 29 percent. Why was the media so silent about the lying and impeachment issue? Wasn't this as significant as all the things that got Bill Clinton impeached?

Finally, nominated for Best Supporting Political Liar in 2005, Interior Secretary Gale Norton, who told audiences about the benefits of drilling for oil in the Arctic National Wildlife Refuge: the oil would satisfy the needs of Illinois for 43 years, of Florida for 29 years, of New York for 34 years, and of New Hampshire for 315 years! Wow. She dismissed the question of how many years ANWR's oil would fuel up the *whole country*. It provided a "deceiving picture," she said, apparently because the answer is just 13 to 17 months, showing that deception is (subjectively) in the mind of the liar. For this unconservation-minded conservative, partial irrelevant facts in the service of the oil industry were intentionally patriotic. Or were they intentionally deceptive political lies to manipulate environmentally-concerned Americans paying her salary?

Chapter 5

Media Madness: From Being Democracy's Guardian to a Joke

> The American press, with a very few exceptions, is a kept press.
> Kept by the big corporations the way a whore is kept by a rich man.
>
> —Theodore Dreiser

America's press is our culture's favorite punching bag. And rightfully so. Expectations for the press have always produced disappointment. Listen to what Bill Moyers, a real journalist, said in 2003:

> If free and independent journalism committed to telling the truth without fear or favor is suffocated, the oxygen goes out of democracy.

Fake journalists Jon Stewart and his colleagues mocked our press in *America (The Book):*

> Yes, our press has never been freer, its status never quo-er. By removing the investigative aspect of investigative journalism, today's modern media finally has the time to pursue the ultimate goal the Founding Fathers envisioned for newsgathering organizations: To raise the stock price of the media empire that owns them.

Seeing Through the News Scam

The Pew Research Center found that prior to the 2004 election only 54 percent of Americans rated the news media coverage of the election good or excellent. Conservative pundit George Will said in 2004 that the major news media had become "marginalized."

The public has seen enough evidence to have little regard for journalists. As shown in Chapter 4 a 2005 Gallup survey found that the public ranked journalists very low for honesty and ethics at just 28 percent. Add this: The annual survey of the press in 194 nations by the independent Freedom House found that in 2004 although the U.S. press was "free" it ranked 24th (tied with five other countries), down from 15th in 2003. It is fair and necessary to conclude that American democracy is not being adequately protected by the news media. Everybody knows.

True, some news stories describe corruption and injustice. They often depend on whistleblowers or confidential sources who leak information to reporters. "We live in an increasingly secretive environment and it's getting harder to get information out to the people," said *New York Times* reported Judith Miller in 2004 when the special prosecutor tried to identify government sources that leaked information about a classified CIA agent. In this case, Miller went to jail for 85 days to protect a source that she ultimately revealed to be Vice President Cheney's chief of staff. Scooter Libby and Bush-brain Karl Rove used reporters to attack a critic of the Iraq war, the husband of the CIA agent. Some thought Miller went to jail to redeem her tarnished reputation. She had helped deceive the public to believe that Iraq had weapons of mass destruction, which it did not, based on her use of secret "high government officials." In *The Exception to the Rulers*, Amy Goodman summed up Miller's role in the Iraq war:

> Miller's reports played an invaluable role in the administration's propaganda war. They gave public legitimacy to outright lies, providing what appeared to be independent confirmation of wild speculation and false accusations. …Miller's false reporting was key to justifying a war.

Miller later admitted: "I got it totally wrong." She blamed her sources for providing misinformation, not her own negligence, nor that of her editors. Here's what a colleague said in 2000 about her: "I do not trust her work, her judgment, or her conduct." In 2003 the *Times* executive editor decided that Miller could no longer cover Iraq and weapons of mass destruction. For crimes against journalism and democracy Miller—the Woman of Mass Deception—deserved her jail time. In November 2005 she was forced to resign from the *Times*.

No wonder that journalists have lost their integrity and public respect. Power elites routinely misinform Americans by being anonymous sources for lazy and sometimes biased reporters and columnists (not acting as whistle blowers about government crime, fraud, waste and abuse, as in Watergate). As Alison Weir, head of If Americans Knew, said:

> It used to be that anonymous sources were rarely and very cautiously used. It is essential that we return to rigorously sourced journalism. Lives depend on it, as does our democracy.

Any American who thinks they can trust information coming from the mainstream media is in a state of self-delusion. A national survey of adults in June 2005 found that Americans had grown more skeptical about military and national security news. In 1999, 79 percent of Americans said that the media kept them well informed on military and national security issues; this dropped to 61 percent in 2005. Similarly, in 1999, 77 percent of Americans believed that the military kept them well informed; this plummeted to 54 percent in 2005. Plus, more than 75 percent believed that the military occasionally provides false or inaccurate information.

What stands between the truth and the public? Censorship, but not by some government agency as in dictatorships. Here, some is self-censorship by reporters, some is corporate censorship (media companies and advertisers), some of it is uncritically used government propaganda, some of it masquerades as patriotism, and some of is done in the name of "good taste"—political correctness. Howard Rheingold summed up America's media connection to our democracy:

> We have a vicious circle of corruption and influence that subverts the right of American citizens to be informed. The process is extremely dangerous to democracy.

The rest of the world receives different information about the U.S.—information that makes the U.S. look less democratic, fair, and peace-loving. Many Americans are amazed at the negative views of the United States by much of the world's population. Some dismiss this by saying "they just hate our government, not us." But that's the point. *Our* government is *our* problem.

An effective free press in a democracy should foster dissent and empower dissidents. It must reveal the differences between genuine patriots (trying to protect and restore American democracy) and fake patriots (trying to protect the plutocracy and corporatist state); when it reports scandals, corruption and crime it must explicitly identify the implications for American democracy. This democracy-framing is rarely done.

Free Press on a Free Ride

The Founding Fathers envisioned success with three branches of government, two with elected members and an independent judiciary, plus a free press and free speech to safeguard public interest. Practice has failed theory. At times the government system has suffered from consolidation of partisan power, most recently with Republican control of the legislative and executive branches of the federal government. And with more power concentrated in leadership than committees, Congress has largely surrendered independent oversight of federal agencies and programs. Long before the Katrina calamity and the firing of FEMA's director, Michael Brown, Congress ignored evidence of FEMA's serious deficiencies, for example. Norman J. Ornstein of the conservative American Enterprise Institute summed up the situation in October 2005:

> This Congress doesn't see itself as an independent branch that might include criticizing an incumbent administration. Meaningful oversight, because it might imply criticism, has been pushed off the table altogether.

Bush I White House counsel C. Boyden Gray concluded: "Congress, especially the House, is the most unrepresentative of the American people." Plainly the executive branch is also patently unrepresentative and the "independent" judiciary has become far too partisan.

Critical to representation is giving voters an accurate picture of the world, something the media fails at abysmally. The fabled "fourth estate" has, for some time, failed Americans. The news media does reveal important information, but the major news media support the status quo far more than they are watchdogs and explainers of events, trends, and lies that damage our representative form of government. [Coverage of the Katrina hurricane aftermath was a welcomed exception, driven by the stunning visual evidence of government ineptitude and dishonesty that could not be ignored.]

Some outspoken truth-tellers and status quo busters have achieved considerable media success and access to the public. They skewer sacred cows and deflate propaganda, wherever it comes from. Besides Jon Stewart, the more famous ones include Don Imus, Arianna Huffington, Bill Maher and Lou Dobbs. But these few are not enough to spark a revolution, as time has shown.

The news media benefit from the constitutional protection of free speech. Free speech is supposed to protect dissenters, people having beliefs and messages not shared by the majority. But free speech works best when dissenters have access to the general public. The major news media provide few opportunities to dissenters, miniscule as compared to what is given to those expressing mainstream thinking. A healthy free society must *discourage* conformity and actively promote *dissent*. Our mainstream news media are not doing that. In the 19th century, John Stewart Mill was right when he said in *On Liberty*:

> Protection, therefore, against the tyranny of the magistrate [the government] is not enough; there needs protection also against the tendency of society to impose, by means other than civil penalties, its own ideas and practices as rules of conduct on those who dissent from them.

This is a warning against status quo domination and "political correctness." More recently, Robert W. McChesney noted: "For a variety of reasons, the media have come to be expert at generating the type of fare that suits, and perpetuates, the status quo." Americans, said McChesney, "are blindfolded by a media system that suits, first and foremost, those who benefit not by reform but by the preservation of the status quo." The media focus on problems and scandals, but not solutions requiring a change in the status quo.

As James Fallows said in *Breaking the News*, journalism's "fundamental purpose [is] making democratic self-government possible. …Mainstream journalism has made the mistake of trying to compete with the pure entertainment media—music, TV celebrities, movies—on their own terms. …The institution of journalism is not doing its job well now."

By putting profits over public service, superficial coverage of politics is packaged as "infotainment," more like a sports event than a democracy-preserving activity. Mainstream media have more in common with corporate interests than public interests. They fail to help Americans reach understanding, solutions and change. Robert F. Kennedy, Jr. hit the mark when he said that the media "have devolved from a marketplace of ideas to a marketplace of commerce. Journalists are not supposed to find balance. They're supposed to find truth and explain that to the public."

Explaining has given way to more profitable and often partisan infotainment. With this emphasis the media rarely dig deep into issues, democratic institutions, and truthfulness. TV news is designed to excite, not enlighten. The media do not provoke people to rethink their current beliefs. Rather than make what's important interesting, the media make what's important titillating. The coverage of sex crimes against children should be covered as moral decay in American society. Instead, it becomes almost pornographic, for example. Journalism no longer holds up an honest mirror to society to help people see complexity, ambiguity, the context of events, and the connectedness among issues. Consumer news shaped as infotainment is like a fun-house mirror that distorts reality and makes you laugh or moan, not look at reality as you would gaze at a great painting and contemplate its meaning. Infotainment displaces introspection, which American democracy desperately needs. As Robert D. Putnam observed in *Bowling Alone*: "TV-based politics is to political action as watching *ER* is to saving someone in distress. ...Citizenship is not a spectator sport." Enjoying TV politics and rooting for your side is masturbating to political pornography—not effective citizenship.

The news business is conflicted. The major media made a lot of money when some $1 billion was spent on the 2004 presidential election. The more the media made it a tight two-horse race, the more money it made. There was no financial incentive to cover third-parties. The pay-to-play business model for the media protects the two-party duopoly, protects incumbents, and constrains challengers and third-parties. As columnist Robert J. Samuelson said: "Although America isn't polarized, our political and media elites are working hard to make it so." But most people think it is polarized, because polarization makes money for the media. Filmmaker Michael Moore asked a good question in 2000:

> Is it safe in a 'free society' to have the sources of our information and mass communications in the hands of just a few wealthy men who have a VESTED interest in keeping us as stupid as possible—or at least in keeping us thinking like them so that we vote for THEIR candidates?

Fast Pitching the Rhetoric

Hector Castillo was a candidate for New Jersey governor in 2005. He named his independent party the Education Not Corruption Party and declared that the Democratic and Republican Parties "are just empty promises and they're full of corruption." His corruption framing was crystal clear. His media coverage was minimal. Of course he lost.

The daily flow of many mainstream news stories, columns, and editorials must be reframed to explicitly connect events to the decline of American democracy. Whenever corruption and dishonesty among public servants and corporate bigwigs are revealed or commented on, the story you read or hear should include something like the following:

> American democracy has suffered another blow.
> Public trust in American democracy is tested once again.
> With this new revelation, American democracy continues to decline.
> How many dishonest and corrupt elected officials can American democracy take?
> This latest scandal disgraces American democracy.

Headlines should also prominently feature attention to democracy.

And when comedians get their laughs from revealing some absurdity about our political or corporate system they should end with something like these:

> And so American democracy pulls another Katrina.
> Thanks for sharing the pain of America's democracy-delusion.
> Why vote when you can laugh about America's democracy?
> Guess what—our Constitution never says democracy!

Imagine a few years of countless and relentless framing like these. Pretty soon the status quo bias delusion of American democracy's greatness would wither.

The bumper sticker message of this book is "Unite and fight—fix our deMOCKracy."

Doped and Duped by the Media

It is difficult for democracy-believing Americans to see themselves as victims of a vast, complex, and largely invisible system that controls what news and information reaches them and how issues are framed. Some of the nation's best minds have seen the truth. Decades ago Walter Lippman said:

> The manufacture of consent…was supposed to have died out with the appearance of democracy…but it has not died out. It has, in fact, improved enormously in technique. …Under the impact of propaganda, it is no longer plausible to believe in the original dogma of democracy.

Similar is the wisdom of David Wise in *The Politics of Lying*:

> If information is power, the ability to distort and control information will be used more often than not to preserve and perpetuate that power.

According to Edward S. Herman and Noam Chomsky in *Manufacturing Consent*:

> It is much more difficult to see a propaganda system at work where

the media are private and formal censorship is absent. This is especially true where the media actively compete, periodically attack and expose corporate and governmental malfeasance, and aggressively portray themselves as spokesmen for free speech and the general community interest. What is not evident (and remains undiscussed in the media) is the limited nature of such critiques, as well as the huge inequality in command of resources, and its effect both on access to a private media system and on its behavior and performance.

This is the core of what might be called the Chomsky thesis, the power of an elite, corporate status quo-protecting system that imposes barriers to political dissent, a wider political debate, and status quo busting. Americans' thinking is numbed, pacified, and shaped through this media system. This system works in concert with the two-party duopoly and corporatist system to keep people preoccupied with being consumers rather than engaged citizens. The goal of the current media system is to marginalize—not totally prevent—dissent and minority viewpoints and it works.

In *Rich Media, Poor Democracy*, Robert W. McChesney, consistent with Chomsky's thinking, summed up current society:

> In many respects we now live in a society that is only formally democratic, as the great mass of citizens have minimal say on the major public issues of the day, and such issues are scarcely debated at all in any meaningful sense in the electoral arena.

Formally democratic sounds like pseudo-democracy. McChesney saw American society thusly:

> [T]he illusions of consumer choice and individual freedom merely provide the ideological oxygen necessary to sustain a media system (and a broader social system) that serves the few while making itself appear accountable and democratic.

Appearances are designed to deceive. The propaganda way of thinking about the media explains how in 2002 and 2003 the media was an accomplice to the preemptive war on Iraq by President George W. Bush. The war was justified with incorrect information, intentionally used to deceive—LIES. *Democracy Now!* host Amy Goodman said: "The media was a conveyor belt for the lies of the administration." Earlier, in *Rich Media, Poor Democracy*, Robert W. McChesney wrote of the "innate right of the United States to invade another nation" and how the "media will tend to accept the elite position as revealed truth and never subject the notion to questioning." Talk about a prescient statement!

The whole anti-war perspective was effectively marginalized to such a degree that in the 2004 presidential campaign and afterwards a large fraction of Americans still believed in "facts" that had been belatedly revealed to be false. In other words, the *patriotic* belief in the validity of the Iraq war, which was falsely conflated with the war on terrorism, became a patriotic status quo bias belief. More than at any previous wartime era, for the Iraq war, patriotism was narrowly defined by the government and media so that any dissent and anti-war view was cast as "treason." The media's attempt to redeem itself failed as it tilted against the Bush candidacy; because it was too late psychologically.

The propaganda machine can achieve its objectives merely by delaying the truth and first implanting lies rather than blocking truth completely. Also, the many parts of the propaganda machine treat each other politely by not using L-words, which helps suppress the truth and make the public blasé to lies. Propaganda fed through the media in the United States is different than in a totalitarian state, as explained by Edward S. Herman and Noam Chomsky in *Manufacturing Consent*:

> [U.S. media] permit—indeed, encourage—spirited debate, criticism, and dissent, as long as these remain faithfully within the system of presupposition and principles that constitute an elite consensus, a system so powerful as to be internalized largely without awareness. …[This] makes for a propaganda system that is far more credible and effective in putting over a patriotic agenda than one with official censorship.

Too few Americans have heard of retired Air Force Colonel Sam Gardiner, a propaganda expert. He wrote a report in 2003, "Truth from These Podia: Summary of a Study of Strategic Influence, Perception Management, Strategic Information Warfare and Strategic Psychological Operations in Gulf II." It made the case that an intentional $200 million propaganda effort about the Iraq war was run by the Bush administration and the British government. Fifty specific news stories were analyzed and found to be faked by government propaganda experts in a secret operation to market the Iraq war. Despite being a military expert used frequently by many media outlets, this report was largely ignored by mainstream media. Similarly, in early 2004, the nonpartisan and respected Carnegie Endowment for International Peace released a study that concluded the Bush administration had "systematically misrepresented" the threat from

Iraq's weapons program. This too received too little media attention, as did the consensus about starting the Iraq war at the 2002 meeting of the secretive, right-wing Council for National Policy.

According to Gardiner, one propaganda objective was to sell "the big lie," namely that Iraq was tied to the 9/11 attacks. He said:

> It was an orchestrated effort. It began before the war, was a major effort during the war, and continues as post-conflict distortions. …The message is more important than the truth. …Truth became a casualty. When truth is a casualty, democracy receives collateral damage.

In other words, the Bush administration lied us into war by using "weaponized information." Gardiner was very critical of mainstream news media that eagerly took the disinformation hook, line and sinker, often through leaks and confidential sources. He asked, "Why aren't they helping us get to truth?" He also wondered, "how spin got to be more important than substance." The Bush administration cared not that by targeting the U.S. public for deception through domestic propaganda it violated the 1948 Smith-Mundt Act. They sold the war just like bad products are sold through false claims. Political corporatism triumphed.

"I pain for our democratic process when I find individuals not angered at being deceived," said Gardiner. But duped Americans are not angry. Besides buying into government lies, the mainstream media chose not to show Americans huge numbers of photographs and video images of ghastly human impacts of the Iraq war on Iraq citizens and even on our soldiers, especially from fighting insurgent forces. But the rest of the world saw those images. To paraphrase an old Chinese maxim: He who knows not, and knows not that he knows not, is a victim of propaganda.

In December 2004 President Bush awarded the Presidential Medal of Freedom, the highest civilian award to three of his Iraq war heroes: George Tenet, former CIA director, who told Bush it was a "slam-dunk" that Iraq had weapons of mass destruction; L. Paul Bremer who ran Iraq initially and mistakenly disbanded the Iraq army and later confessed "We never had a enough troops on the ground;" and retired General Tommy Franks who gave Defense Secretary Donald Rumsfeld what he wanted by never asking for enough troops to prevent the ruinous post-invasion insurgency.

Richard Cohen wrote in the *Washington Post* that the White House ceremony was "absurd," "as if facts do not matter and failure does not count." The whole affair "has the creepy feel of the old communist states, where incompetents wore medals and harsh facts were denied," said Cohen. It was indeed Orwellian. It was a masterful attempt at rewriting history by the nation's Liar-in-Chief at his very best. Lying that undercut American democracy was labeled as virtuous efforts that protected freedom. The Presidential Medal of Freedom was turned into the Presidential Medal of Deception. Orwell discussed use of the word democracy and was right when he said that such political words are "often used in a consciously dishonest way," thus defining political pornography in our culture of lying.

Appropriately, on April fool's day 2005, the presidential commission that investigated the intelligence community's pre-Iraq war efforts on weapons of mass destruction released its report. It concluded that the entire intelligence community had been "dead wrong," and it said that intelligence agencies "seem to be working harder and harder just to maintain a status quo that is increasingly irrelevant to the new challenges presented by weapons of mass destruction." Ex-CIA agent Melissa Boyle Mahle observed: "The whole structure is set up to preserve the status quo." And the *Washington Post* said that intelligence officers were "more concerned about preserving the status quo than finding better ways to safeguard the nation." A powerful and destructive status quo had hammered the United States into war. And no one asked George Tenet to give back his Presidential Medal of Freedom.

In 2005 former deputy secretary of state Richard L. Armitage confessed: "Those who argued at the time that the acceptance of democracy in Iraq would be easy...were dead wrong." Or did they lie?

No democracy starts a war is a longstanding axiom. Supposedly it supports the "Bush doctrine" of seeking democracy in other nations to achieve world peace. But the U.S. initiated the Iraq war. That makes the U.S. what? A pseudo-democracy?

Homeland Deception

Besides the Iraq war, federal propaganda on domestic policy hit the fan in January 2005 when several actions by the Bush II administration became public. One practice was the production of prepackaged video news releases that were deceptively shown as real TV news, and which were created to promote administration policies and the reelection of Bush. Several federal agencies produced such deceptive releases. The General Accountability Office twice criticized the use of paid advertisements disguised as journalism, saying they were illegal "covert propaganda." A GAO official said "the viewer has no idea their tax dollars are being used to write and produce" the fake news. It is actually against the law to use federal funds "for publicity or propaganda purposes within the United States," unless expressly approved by Congress. But in March 2005, the Bush administration disagreed and told federal agencies they could continue the practice.

Even worse was the revelation that television commentator, pundit, and columnist Armstrong Williams, who had achieved success as a right-wing African-American, had received $241,000 from the Department of Education to tout Bush education policy in his "journalistic" activities. Several Democrat Senators wrote President Bush, saying "We believe that the act of bribing journalists to bias their news in favor of government policies undermines the integrity of our democracy." Alex Jones, director of Harvard's Shorenstein media center said the action showed that "the Bush administration neither understands nor respects the idea of an independent media."

Referring to the "debacles of hired and faked journalists," conservative columnist George F. Will admitted in 2005 that "government by the consent of the governed should not mean government by consent produced by government propaganda." Much earlier, in 1971, Congressman Sam Gibbons asked: "How can you give your consent to be governed when you are misled and lied to?" Lying politicians never have the consent of the governed. And no one should think otherwise.

In 2004, the $88 million spent by the Bush administration on public relations was more than twice that spent by it in 2001, indicating how taxpayer money was used to influence the presidential election. *New York Times* columnist Frank Rich got it right:

> When the Bush Administration isn't using taxpayers' money to buy its own fake news, it does everything it can to shut out and pillory real reporters who might tell Americans what is happening in what is, at least in theory, their own government.

Deception often peaks and then falls prey to the truth, because it takes too long for the media to discover and communicate the truth.

In 2005, when over 2,000 Americans had been killed in the Iraq war and some of the deception game had finally been revealed the public wised up. A survey by the Program on International Policy Attitudes found that 74 percent of Americans believed the goal of overthrowing Iraq's authoritarian government and establishing a democracy was not sufficient reason to go to war with Iraq; this was true for 86 percent of Democrats, 60 percent of Republicans, and 73 percent of independents. Some truth came late but the whole story behind the Bush determination to invade Iraq, unrelated to the 9/11 event and even to global terrorism, remained untold.

Debate Debauchery

An illuminating example of the corrupt two-party grip on our illusory political system is the degeneration of national televised presidential debates. Live debates are excellent outlets for lies—and they give viewers the opportunity to root for their side, like a sports event. However, entertaining debates are not necessarily good for democracy. They usually create optical delusions.

For a time, the League of Women Voters ran these debates and they became open to significant third-party candidates. In 1988, in response to the George Bush and Michael Dukakis campaigns entering into a secret debate contract, the League pulled out. It spoke of a "fraud on the American voter" and "the hoodwinking of the American public." After the Republican and Democratic National Committees ratified an agreement for the "parties to take over the presidential debates" the Commission on Presidential Debates was created. The two parties negotiate the rules for each series of debates. Walter Cronkite called the commission-sponsored debates an "unconscionable fraud" designed for "sabotaging the electoral process." However, the media have embraced and supported this fraud, making them accomplices after the fact.

Imagine if all the networks joined together and said, "no way, we want the debates open to significant third party candidates or we won't televise them." But no, the news media have never stood up to the open conspiracy and manipulation by the two main parties. Neither do the big-name news anchors who act as moderators for these debates. Where is the moral indignation? Why is there no boycott of these sham debates by the news media?

Locking out third party presidential candidates from televised debates maintains the vicious cycle of keeping small parties small and largely invisible to most Americans. As Green Party presidential candidate David Cobb said in 2004: "These so-called debates are an insult to democracy and the American people." Cobb and Libertarian candidate Michael Badnarik were actually arrested when they tried to attend the St. Louis debate as audience members. Cobb said: "the real crime is the corporate hijacking of our democracy." Two-candidate debates help the media race to anoint the "winner," which in 2004 did not prove significant for Senator John Kerry and did not harm Bush, the debate "loser." There is virtually no voice for restoring the League of Women Voters as the group running presidential debates.

What needs to be emphasized is that the public has consistently said that they want third-party candidates in presidential debates. In 2000, a Zogby poll found that 60.9 percent of likely voters wanted the Green Party's Ralph Nader and 58.7 percent wanted the Reform Party's Pat Buchanan in the debates. Majorities of both Democrats and Republicans wanted them in. In 2004, another Zogby poll found that 57 percent of voters wanted Nader in the debates, and a different poll found that 59 percent of likely voters and 62 percent of undecided voters wanted Nader included and 57 percent believed the debates should not be sponsored by the Republicans and Democrats but by a nonpartisan sponsor. Neither the two-party duopoly nor the media cared about what the public wanted and what democracy deserved.

An impressive effort was the creation of the Citizens' Debate Commission in January 2004 as a replacement for the Commission on Presidential Debates. It substantially lowered the barriers to third-party candidates. In August 2004, the U.S. District Court ordered a Federal Election Commission investigation of the Commission on Presidential Debates because of its rules that block third-party candidates (unless they get 15 percent in national polls, which of course is difficult without being visible in televised debates). Soon after, eleven pro-democracy civic groups issued the report "Deterring Democracy: How the Commission on Presidential Debates Undermines Democracy." It said, "the debates have been reduced to a series of glorified bipartisan news conferences, in which the Republican and Democratic candidates merely exchange memorized sound bites." And it supported using the Citizens' Debate Commission as "a genuinely nonpartisan sponsor." This alternative commission received considerable favorable national press coverage. The *Seattle Post-Intelligencer* editorialized in 2004 that the two-party debates "are designed to limit conversation and make certain voters won't learn more" and supported the use of the Citizens' Debate Commission. But the two major candidates refused to participate in a series of debates sponsored by this group. Their refusal was mostly ignored by the media.

One irony is that both parties participate in primary debates where there are often a number of participants on stage, including third party candidates.

In 2004, Internet websites revealed the intense anger of many Americans about Nader's exclusion from the debates and many state ballots. Frank Scott summed up the undemocratic power of the two major parties: "[Nader's] pro-democracy, anti-corporate, pro-peace argument and his intellectual superiority...could have spelled disaster for the status quo."

To its credit, in September 2004, *USA Today* editorialized about the injustice for voters: "[Nader] will not be an option for many voters who chose him four years ago. And setting partisan interests aside, what is democratic about that?" It also said that voters were being forced "to make the 'real' choice between George W. Bush and John Kerry...but the effect is to disenfranchise voters who think that 'real' choice isn't much of a choice at all, and that undermines confidence in the political system." The editorial provided considerable information on how states effectively block third party candidates for any office.

The lack of depth in televised debates has caused voters to focus on the personality and superficial characteristics of candidates: their looks, how they speak and walk, their spouses, and their debate performance. Superficiality breeds emotional responses, rather than intellectual scrutiny. The news media do "fact checking" during campaigns and after debates and point out numerous wrong facts spoken in debates or used in ads. But media political correctness prevents calling politicians outright liars, when that's what they are. Columnist Robert J. Samuelson savaged President George W. Bush's presidency in October 2005 and shyly concluded that "He has not been straightforward with the public." You mean he lied!

What exactly is wrong with calling liars *liars*? Edward S. Herman and Noam Chomsky provided an explanation in *Manufacturing Consent*: "It is very difficult to call authorities on whom one depends for daily news liars, even if they tell whoppers." Liars is what ordinary Americans are thinking and screaming, especially when viewing televised debates.

Size Matters

An historic exception to the media's reticence to call out lies occurred when MSNBC (pro-Kerry) commentator Lawrence O'Donnell tore into (anti-Kerry) Swift Boats Veterans author John O'Neill. Unusual honesty about dishonesty shocked viewers of *Scarborough Country*. O'Donnell referred to O'Neill's "disgusting, lying book," and made these comments:

> That's a lie, John O'Neil. Keep lying. It's all you do. ...That's a lie. It's another lie. That's a lie. ...You lie in that book endlessly. ...You're just lying about it. ...It's a pack of lies. ...He just spews out lies. ...I just hate the lies of John O'Neil. ...He's been a liar for 35 years.

MSNBC felt compelled to issue a statement condemning O'Donnell's "disrespectful insults." MSNBC said that O'Donnell agreed. But, *that turned out to be a lie!* O'Donnell later said, "I don't apologize for a single word that I said. ...People have been coming out of the woodwork to tell me how great they thought it was. There's a big 'mad as hell and I'm not going to take it anymore' contingent out there on this subject that feels I was giving voice to their position." It is true that many Americans want lies and liars confronted openly and *honestly*. And O'Donnell, as a regular TV commentator and writer-producer for NBC's successful political drama *West Wing,* really knows something about what Americans want and like.

The real distinction between mainstream and alternative media is that the mainstream media "largely acts as a megaphone for those in power," according to Amy Goodman, host of *Democracy Now!* The alternative media are sanctuaries for dissent, both progressive and conservative.

Just weeks before the 2004 election, the *Washington Post* media expert Howard Kurtz wrote the article "'Balance in a Spinning World." The first thing to point out is that Kurtz did not write about lies, lying and liars (so called L-words). Instead, he referred to "serious distortions," "falsehoods," "fundamental misrepresentation," and "misleading" statements. This by someone who also said: "Whatever their orientation, journalists are the last line of defense against public deception. If they fail to challenge distortions by politicians, they might as well join the stenography pool." Kurtz was soft on lies and liars, and was out of touch with reality—stenography pool?

Days later, another article by Kurtz was "Ads Push The Factual Envelope." Here too, rather than talk about lies other terms were used; "misleading claims" and "exaggerations" were used even though a number of outright lies were described. Similarly, around the same time, the column by *New York Times* writer Bob Herbert entitled "Webs of Illusion" was dishonest about dishonesty:

> Hyperbole is part of every politician's portfolio. But on the most serious matters facing the country, Mr. Bush's administration has often gone beyond hyperbole to deliberate misrepresentations that undermine the very idea of an informed electorate. ...A president who spends too much time spinning webs of illusion can find himself trapped in them.

Routine "misrepresentations" by politicians misinform the electorate and sustain a misrepresentative government. Why do journalists who talk about the "the last line of defense against public deception" and "misrepresentations that undermine the very idea of an informed electorate" refuse to be honest about other people's lying? Surely such media cowardice does not help our republic function honestly or fulfill the constitutional purpose of a free press. Why doesn't the media wake up and smell reality. Stop dancing around the stark truth: POLITICIANS ARE LYING TO US! YOU KNOW IT AND MOST AMERICANS SURELY KNOW IT. Are media people concerned about pissing off their confidential sources?

On Election Day in 2004, Richard Leiby wrote in the *Washington Post* about the performance of L. Paul "Jerry" Bremer on NBC's *Today* show. Host Matt Lauer grilled Bremer about the disappearance of some 380 tons of explosives from a site in Iraq, which had become an embarrassing issue for the Bush candidacy. Lauer noted a videotape that had surfaced which showed that the explosives were present at the site on April 18, 2003, which was after the fall of Baghdad on April 9. He asked Bremer: "Does it prove, in your opinion, that these munitions disappeared after U.S. forces should have been guarding them?" Brenner said "No." He maintained that "we just don't know what the facts are." When pressed, Brenner gave a long, tortuous assertion that the U.S. troops would have seen any removal of the explosives, and he knew that because: "I actually was in Iraq at the time." As Leiby noted, "Bremer didn't arrive in Iraq until May 12, 2003." Neither Lauer nor Leiby honestly described Bremer's spinning of the truth.

Millions of concerned Americans want the press to challenge *lies* by politicians, a whole lot more than challenging their *distortions*. A liar is worse than a distorter. Something that Kurtz and nearly all of his colleagues don't seem to understand. One exception is *New York Times* liberal columnist Paul Krugman. He made an important point around the same time, namely that there are important qualitative differences among lies:

> The point is that Kerry can, at most, be accused of using loose language; the thrust of his statements is correct. Bush's statements, on the other hand, are fundamentally dishonest. He is insisting that black is white, and that failure is success. Journalists who play it safe by spending equal time exposing his lies and parsing Kerry's choice of words are betraying their readers.

The point is not that Kerry was honest—he routinely lied. Indeed, a check of Internet sites revealed that there was as much hollering about Kerry's lies as there was about Bush's lies. Kerry certainly seemed to have lied on many occasions when he claimed he had met "with the entire Security Council" and discussed the Iraq situation. Media people who sought confirmation of this discovered that four of the five ambassadors on the Council claimed that neither they or their staff had met with Kerry. Kerry also drew flack when he asserted that President Bush intended to start a military draft after the election. Best of all, Kerry told Jim Lehrer: "Well, I've never, ever used the harshest word as you just did." In other words, Kerry claimed he never accused Bush of "lying." But research showed that on a number of occasions Kerry exhibited unusual honesty by saying that Bush had lied.

On the inequality of lies in the 2004 presidential race, Kurtz said: "At issue is how far reporters should go in analyzing the candidates' attacks and ads, especially if one side is using a howitzer and the other a popgun." Commenting on the race, media expert Mandy Grunwald said: "I think the Bush folks in government and the campaign make stuff up

more than anyone I've ever seen and have largely paid no penalty for it."
But towards the end of the lies-race Senator Kerry was doing more of it
to stay competitive with Bush.

The point is that mainstream news media try to balance one
candidate's untruths with the other candidate's untruths. They do not dig
deep and reveal the qualitative differences in the scope and consequences
of lies. They are unwilling to distinguish differences in the audacity of
the untruths, their different implications for democracy, and are averse to
calling any untruth a lie and anyone a liar, as if the intent is at question.
The political arena is not like the court system. There is no basis for a
presumption of honesty or not questioning politicians' intentions.

For lies, size matters. Here is a poetic expression by Gerald Bosacker
about the inequality of lies that appeared on freepress.org in October
2005:

> Bill Clinton lied about his whore,
> which was his blasphemy and sin.
> George Bush lied on the need for war,
> defends it still with Karl Rove's spin.
> Which liar, I ask, has hurt us more,
> weighing the Iraq mess we're in?

Opinionated Journalism versus Journalistic Opinion

True journalists doing something other than direct news reporting
offer a point of view supported by facts. Bill Moyers made the point
that "the quality of journalism and the quality of democracy go hand in
hand." And *Washington Post* critic Tom Shales said this about Moyers'
stint as the host of the PBS TV show *Now*: "Moyers represented reason,
deliberation, serious questioning of the status quo and, especially,
standing as firmly as possible against government encroachment into
Americans' private lives."

It has become difficult for people to distinguish news from opinion.
True journalism respects and seeks facts and truth while recognizing
different perspectives (using different facts) on an issue. Complete
objectivity exists nowhere, not in science or journalism. No journalist
should claim to have total and certain "Truth." Still, presenting personal
opinion together with false information is unacceptable. Presenting only

one side of an issue is tolerable as long as there is no deception about being balanced.

Opinion should be seen as presenting information through the lens of a particular mindset and has no obligation to offer truth. The most successful and the most highly opinionated commentators are totally partisan, with the vast majority being Republican/conservative. Notably, 90 percent of talk radio commentators are in this camp. Their success has benefited from lies, distortions and misrepresentations. Even when their lies are revealed by others, they stick to them. Many radio stations and cable channels offer nothing but right-wing opinion that is served up to audience only wanting one-sided debate and information.

Americans devoted to right-wing commentators have the highest levels of *incorrect* information, according to every independent study. Insidiously, time-poor and stressed-out Americans don't have the time and energy to seek the truth. It is so much easier to fall victim to misinformation and be led astray by lying, shouting and arrogant commentators like Rush Limbaugh, Sean Hannity, and Bill O'Reilly. These fake patriots, bloviators and pontificators talk values as they undermine our democratic values. To critics of government, dissenters and true patriots they say, "love it or leave it." But the "it" is America as it is now, *their* America, corrupted and corroded democracy under *their* influence, not what American democracy should be.

The undercurrent of hatred, intolerance and anti-democratic sentiments in these right-wing blowhards was illustrated when Bill O'Reilly in November 2005 expressed his anger over a democratic vote by San Francisco citizens against military recruiting in schools by saying: "And if al Qaeda comes in here and blows you up, we're not going to do anything about it. We're going to say, look, every other place in America is off limits to you, except San Francisco. You want to blow up the Coit Tower? Go ahead." Bill O'Reilly also condemned opponents to the Iraq war by comparing them to people who set the stage for Adolph Hitler's Nazi Germany.

Here is ironic truth: *The downturn in our democracy has accelerated during the rise of Republican/conservative commentators.* Right-wing commentators reach untold millions of Americans daily through many media outlets. They constantly reinforce each other's lies and messages, false and biased information marketed as opinion. Compulsive and distracted consumers make perfect suckers. Once indoctrinated into pseudo-religious right-wing dogma, they block truthful information causing cognitive dissonance, including the links between their media idols and the corporatist state. As in primitive cultures, millions of Americans have fallen prey to false idols. In a theocracy faith replaces facts. In a plutocracy power replaces patriotism.

A democracy can fall from attacks by outside forces or evil forces from within. American democracy is crumbling from the weight of the powerful right-wing media-political-corporate complex. It is less a takeover than a strengthening of historic power elites. Right-wing media kingpins use salacious political pornography to keep the faithful mesmerized. Diversion and distraction work. Civic engagement is lived vicariously through the fast-talkers whose personalities and rhetoric obscure the truth. Americans focus their resentment on the *illusory* political system while ignoring the *restricted* political system that their right-wing heroes secretly support. It is an incredible con game. Right-wing idols are plutocrats enjoying the fruits of the corporatist state while protecting it. In the class struggle between the powerful and powerless, the right-wing media rulers fool the latter (the public) to serve the former (the elitists). Media plutocrats do not serve their country.

Comedy Scores a Hit for Democracy

"We're supposed to live in a 'beacon of democracy,' with a highly developed political system that makes us the envy of the world. So why is the host of a self-described 'fake news' program responsible for many of the few-and-far-between moments of honesty in this year's [2004's] endless, mind-numbing, soul-deadening election campaign?" asked Alan Haas.

In October 2004, in the heat of the presidential campaign, cut-the-crap, anti-hype, and a plague-on-both-your-houses Jon Stewart, host of *The Daily Show* on Comedy Central, was a guest on CNN's *Crossfire*, where shouting heads pander, pontificate, and bloviate to either the political left or right. Stewart knows how to spot lies and parody the news media by offering fake news built around those lies. *Crossfire* producers apparently planned to add some humor to the show. Instead, Stewart was intent on delivering a serious message about the poor performance of the major news media, including *Crossfire* which he said was "bad." Stewart begged *Crossfire* hosts Paul Begala and Tucker Carlson to stop shilling for politicians and corporations. Here are the main points made by Stewart during the heated dialogue with the two defensive and obnoxious hosts (representing both heads of the two-party duopoly):

> We need help from the media, so I'm here to confront you. The media is failing miserably. It is painful to watch. You have the opportunity to knock politicians off their mark; instead you offer knee-jerk reactionary talk. PLEASE STOP! Stop hurting America. Right now, you're helping the politicians and corporations. You're part of their strategies. You are partisan hacks. You're doing theater. What you do is partisan hackery. You have a responsibility to the public discourse and you fail miserably. This is such a great opportunity you have here to actually get politicians off their marketing and strategy.

Stewart also criticized the media for spending so much time interviewing Democrat and Republican spinners after the presidential debates in "spin alley," which he dubbed "deception lane." As on his own show, positive audience reactions showed that Stewart was speaking for many Americans fed up with the major news media. *The Daily Show* is a source of news, not just comedy. Viewers learn the truth about lies because of the parodies, in contrast to the major news media that do not reveal political lies. *The Daily Show* does what the media do not—it causes introspection—and it does that as it entertains.

The honesty and correctness of Stewart's comments about the major news media on *Crossfire* became a national story. The blunt comments by *New York Times* television critic Alessandra Stanley hit the mark and validated Stewart's remarks:

> Real anger is as rare on television as real discussion. ...The fuming partisan rants on Fox News are aimed at the converted. ...news programs, particularly on cable, have become echo chambers for political attacks, amplifying the noise instead of parsing the misinformation. ...shows like 'Crossfire' or 'Hardball' provide gladiator-style infotainment as journalists clownishly seek to amuse or rile viewers, not inform them. ...[Stewart] and his writers put a spotlight on the inanities and bland hypocrisies that go mostly unnoticed in the average news cycle.

On the other coast, Rick Kushman of the *Sacramento Bee* also vented:

> "Political analysis" on TV is supposed to help Americans decide

how to vote. Instead, what it does is cloud the genuine debate and bring out raw emotion. Stewart tried to explain, between interruptions, that by turning "Crossfire" into insult theater, they allow politicians on both sides to use the show, and shows like it, to market themselves and to push their emotionally manipulative messages.

Alan Naas said:

> With the corporate journalism organized around flattering the politicians, instead of challenging them—no matter how outrageous the lies or how bloated the rhetoric—Stewart's "fake news" ends up being more truthful about the reality of U.S. politics than all the Crossfires and Hardballs piled up in a great steaming heap.

In January 2005, CNN announced the end of the 22-year-old *Crossfire* and CNN/U.S. President Jonathan Klein said that Stewart had "made a good point about the noise level of these types of shows, which does nothing to illuminate the issues of the day." Viewers need information, but "a bunch of guys screaming at each other simply doesn't accomplish that," Klein said. Stewart had accomplished far more than he ever thought possible. The salvo he fired at *Crossfire* helped kill it.

Behind the fun is an interesting reality: surveys reveal that people learn more from these satires than they do from major news shows. The Pew Research Center found that 21 percent of people 18 to 29 years old got their regular campaign news from the comedians on *The Daily Show* and *Saturday Night Live*, compared to just 2 percent from ABC News; and half said that they regularly or sometimes learn something from late-night comedy shows. An Annenberg Center survey of more than 19,000 adults found that: "Viewers of late-night comedy programs, especially *The Daily Show* with Jon Stewart on Comedy Central, are more likely to know the issue positions and backgrounds of presidential candidates than people who do not watch late-night comedy." Their knowledge rivals newspaper readers and network news viewers.

The ultimate irony is that comedic presentation of fake news—jokes about real news—offers more truth about current events than the "news" itself from the mainstream media, and more truth about the failings of the major news media than offered anywhere else. It also pierces government propaganda transmitted by mainstream media. Ana Marie Cox, of Wonkette.com, had a good take on Stewart's popularity with younger people: "It's not that young people don't like politics. The way politics is talked about in the media is alienating. They're seeing Jon Stewart as a kind of hero who will lead us out of the darkness."

We can hope that among the many fans of *The Daily Show* laughing at our laughable government and democracy are also being empowered to become activist dissenters.

Don't Buy the Snake Oil

In a 1958 speech at a radio and television industry conference Edward R. Murrow warned that the nation better "recognize that television in the main is being used to distract, delude, amuse, and insulate us." With respect to alarming political realities, rather than being informed, Americans have indeed been distracted, deluded, amused, and insulated, made even worse today with computers and myriad electronic devices. About the 2005 Murrow biographical film *Good Night, and Good Luck* the *Seattle Times* editorialized:

> What audiences should understand while viewing this movie is that democracy is in greater peril today than it was when McCarthy was bringing people before Congress on trumped-up charges of communism. The threat now is not a fear-induced witch-hunt, but one of democracy's cornerstones: the press.

Rather than fueling citizen scrutiny and sovereignty, the major news media have become status quo shills. Their main interest is in fostering a "horse race" between the two major parties, not in being a watchdog for our democracy, nor in covering third-party candidates who have something important to say. In 2000, the *New York Times* editorialized against the candidacy of Ralph Nader by saying that "the public deserves to see the major-party candidates compete on an uncluttered playing field." When third-party candidates get some media attention it is hardly about their substantive stands on issues, it is about their impact on the two-party horse race. Worse yet, their issues are usually different than the two-party candidates' issues but ignored by mainstream media.

This is the sad truth: *Mainstream media do next to nothing to promote honesty among politicians and bring public attention to failings of our representative government.* What good is a "free" press that is mostly an outlet for dishonesty? Just as factory farms use chemicals to manufacture tasteless chickens, the media uses advertising dollars to manufacture tame news.

In 2000, John Nichols and Robert McChesney chastised the media in *It's the Media, Stupid:*

> The flow of information that is the lifeblood of democracy is being choked by a media system that every day ignores a world of injustices and inequality, and the growing resistance to it. ...[The media] fosters a climate in which the implementation of innovative democratic solutions is rendered all but impossible.

Newspapers and TV news shows, especially on cable television, think that giving people representing the two major parties, directly or indirectly, an opportunity to spin, lie and deceive is all they have to do to be "fair and balanced." Writing in the *Columbia Journalism Review*, Russ Baker commented on the 2000 presidential election: "We know that the candidates stayed to their script. But did the media do the same thing? If so, were we complicit in limiting the quadrennial national debate?" It was so then, and thereafter. In fact, the two-party-media complicity defines and maintains the status quo.

Fairness Chokes on Polluted Airwaves

From 1949 to 1987, the Federal Communications Commission had implemented the Fairness Doctrine as its policy. It required radio and television stations to address significant and controversial public issues and to air all sides of them, and to give equal time to all candidates. The doctrine empowered citizens to seek fairness of the airwaves. The term "balanced and fair" came from the doctrine. People went to stations when they wanted balanced coverage of an issue and access to the *public* airwaves. Nearly always, broadcasters worked something out with those people, and rarely did the FCC get involved and when it did, it did not impose fines or dictate a solution, but directed the station to come up with more balanced coverage.

In 1969, the U.S. Supreme Court [in *Red Lion Broadcasting Co., Inc. v. FCC*] unanimously upheld the constitutionality of the Fairness Doctrine; it did not violate the First Amendment rights of the companies that owned stations. The ruling said that it is "the right of the viewers and listeners, not the right of the broadcasters, which is paramount." Nice, the Supreme Court put the public first. Bill Moyers said this about the doctrine:

> The clear intent was to prevent a monopoly of commercial values from overwhelming democratic values—to assure that the official view of reality—corporate or government—was not the only view of reality that reached the people.

In 1982, a TV station was told by the FCC that it had to air an opposing point of view to the pro-nuclear energy ads it was running. The station appealed and, in 1986, a federal appeals court, in an opinion written by conservative judges Robert Bork and Antonin Scalia, ruled that the Fairness Doctrine was not a law and need not be enforced. The court asked the FCC to determine whether the doctrine restricted free speech, even though this issue had been settled by the Supreme Court 15 years earlier. The Reagan administration, pushing deregulation, welcomed the opportunity. Reagan's appointed head of the FCC openly avowed to kill the doctrine. But then Congress passed the doctrine as a law in 1987. It passed in the House by 3 to 1, and in the Senate by nearly 2 to 1. Even staunchly conservative Representative Newt Gingrich and Senator Jesse Helms voted for it. But it was vetoed by President Ronald Reagan. Soon after, the FCC repealed the doctrine, claiming is was unconstitutional, despite the Supreme Court's ruling.

In 1989, the doctrine bill easily passed in the House. But a threat of a veto by Bush I killed it. In 1991, the measure did not move past committee hearings, because of the continuing veto threat. The doctrine reappeared in 1993 when there was hope that President Bill Clinton would favor it, but of course the Congress had become more conservative and corrupted, so it might not have passed. That year, a national survey found 60 percent of Americans supported restoration of the doctrine. But that year Rush Limbaugh mounted his paranoid "Hush Rush" campaign to kill the doctrine, as if his show was threatened by the legislation, which it was not. The industry was concerned that the doctrine would compel *stations* to become balanced, without of course threatening *specific shows*, like Limbaugh's. Limbaugh deceived the public about the threat to his show and he won. The killing of the doctrine allowed conservative talk radio stations to flourish. Stations no longer had to be "fair and balanced." They could be pure right-wing.

With the demise of the Fairness Doctrine and the corporatization of the media, principally through the actions of two Republican judges and three Republican presidents, Americans lost balanced news coverage on the *public* airways and it made it easier for cable stations and more recently satellite radio stations to also be unbalanced. The dumbing down of the news corresponded with the shift to infotainment. Today, people routinely talk about how polarized Americans are between the conservative and liberal poles. Not widely understood is that the killing of the doctrine was instrumental in fostering polarized broadcasting which has polarized politics and the public. Worse yet, American democracy took a hit, because citizens easily fell into the trap of sticking with their status quo bias beliefs and could avoid hearing from "the other side." Unmistakably, Americans have less First Amendment access to balanced information on important issues, including ballot initiatives.

Georgetown University Professor Angela Campbell said: "Now there's no recourse against a station that wants to be completely one-sided or that refuses to air a certain point of view." Several broadcast stations refused to air anti-war commercials before the U.S. invaded Iraq.

Pennsylvania State Representative Mark B. Cohen spelled out the crucial political value of the fairness doctrine]:

> The fairness doctrine helped reinforce a politics of moderation and inclusiveness. The collapse of the fairness doctrine...helped lead to the polarizing cacophony of strident talking heads that we have today.

Consider the 2003 decision by a Florida District Court of Appeals to reverse a lower court jury verdict and side with the Fox TV network. Fox argued that it had a First Amendment right to *deliberately distort, rig and slant the news.* The FCC's 50-year-old News Distortion Rule, which prohibited the broadcast of false reports, was deemed by the court as not qualifying as a "law, rule or regulation," because it had been created over the years in FCC decisions, just like the Fairness Doctrine. Five major companies filed amicus curiae briefs in support of Fox's argument, including Post-Newsweek Stations, Gannett Co., and Cox Television. Thus, stations using the public airways are now free to lie by commission or omission in news reports, and they do it because of incompetence or the desire to please advertisers or corporate station owners.

To hell with the right of citizens to get fair, honest, and balanced news from radio and TV stations, that have received free access to the publicly owned airwaves. As FCC Commissioner Michael Copps said, "No one has a God-given right to use these airwaves for strictly commercial purposes;" government licenses should mean "using public property for primarily public purposes in behalf of the public interest." Anyone who thinks the broadcast media will put the public interest ahead of their commercial interest is deluding themselves. An informed electorate is the basis for American representative democracy, but without fairness and honesty the public has been steadily robbed of what it needs to be thoughtful and engaged citizens. Worst of all, the public rarely gets coverage of necessary news media reforms that Congress should enact. Sonoma State University Professor Peter Phillips got it right:

> Democracy in the United States is only a shadow in a corporate media cave of deceit, lies and incomplete information. We stand ignorant of what the powerful are doing in our name and how the corporate media ignores key issues affecting us all. ...Without an active independent media informing on the powerful we lack both freedom and democracy.

Together with the 1996 deregulation act, the death of the Fairness Doctrine and the kind of radio it stimulated contributed to the consolidation of the industry in recent years. Consider that just seven giant media corporations own or control virtually all of the nation's 2,000 TV stations, 11,000 radio stations, and 11,000 newspapers and magazines. This corporate power has affected news coverage, particularly in-depth analysis and criticism of the two-party duopoly and corporate power and influence. The Bush II administration's FCC made it easier for a few media corporations to gain more control.

Too Much of a Good Thing

Enthusiasm about the Internet needs to be curbed. Martin Wattenberg has examined the question of whether access to incredible amounts of information will produce a more politically engaged citizenry and concluded that "it is questionable whether many citizens will actually take advantage of this new wealth of information. With countless available information sources for a wide variety of specific interests, it will be extremely easy for those who are not much interested in party politics to avoid the subject altogether. The result could well be a growing inequality of political information, with a small group of committed partisans becoming more knowledgeable while the rest of the public slips further into apathy concerning the parties." He was referring to the two-party duopoly but his thinking also applies to other groups such as progressives.

William Greider wrote eloquently about our "mock democracy" in *Who Will Tell The People*, where he focused on information-driven politics, rational policy analysis, and democracy-for-hire. Here is some of Greider's wisdom:

> During the last generation, a "new politics" has enveloped government that guarantees the exclusion of most Americans from the debate—the expensive politics of facts and information. A major industry has grown up in Washington around what might be called "democracy for hire"— business firms and outposts of sponsored scholars devoted to concocting facts and opinions and expert analysis, then aiming them at the government. ..."Information" that leads to "rational" choices is supposed to be a virtuous commodity in the political culture. Democracy, it is presumed, can never get too much of it. ...The reality is that information-driven politics, by its nature, cannot produce a satisfying democracy because it inevitably fosters its own hierarchy of influence, based on class and money.

Greider's book was published in 1992, so there was no attention to the Internet explosion. It is clear, however, that the Internet has simultaneously provided another outlet for information-driven politics, including massive numbers of people and groups who previously had very little chance of having their views published in mainstream news media or heard by politicians. In a sense, the Internet is the cyber-battleground on which information and analysis from "outsiders" does battle with powerful special interests. Using the Internet to bust status quo conditions is a guerilla operation. What Tom Leykis said about talk radio applies equally to the Internet:

> The only thing talk radio does that is positive, is that it finds the rage bubbling underneath the surface and allows people to see that they're not the only ones who feel that way.

But like talk radio, Internet use promotes self-selection—choosing comforting web sites that cause the least amount of cognitive dissonance, ones that fit status quo bias beliefs. Information for confirming rather than challenging beliefs is sought. This is self-censorship. Formal Internet sites and more informal blog sites, as well as all sorts of lists and chat rooms, are narrow-mined, exclusionary, and closed to divergent thinking. I was thrown off of a list because I was perceived as not being a "true believer." Internet activity allows people to vent and preach to the choir, but less likelihood of reaching a wider audience. Internet anarchy promotes free speech effectively in a vertical (same site or list) sense, but not in a horizontal (different site or list) sense.

The information-Internet age within the culture of lying promotes as much confusion and paralysis as it supports positive change. The Internet provides a counterbalance to the death of the Fairness Doctrine, a way for the truth to seep out. It also makes it easy to spread lies. The time needed to ferret out the best thinking and information on the Internet works against efforts to fix the republic. Contradictory information reaches huge numbers of people with little time to figure out what and who to believe. Idea competition is intellectual clutter that stultifies as much as it enlightens. The Internet just provides a new and better venue for those with money and power to cover their corruption tracks with misinformation overload.

Despite its shortcomings, the best free and independent press is on the Internet. The success of Internet news reflects public disillusionment with the major news media, both print and television, especially among younger and politically dissatisfied people. Once, angry Americans wrote letters to the editors. But getting a letter published in a major newspaper or an emailed comment read on a cable news show is like winning the lottery. Citizen journalism flourishes on Internet magazine sites and personal blogs. Raw honesty is welcomed on the unregulated and uncensored Internet. Consider the following comments.

On Weblog.nohair.net, Gordon voiced his reaction to watching one of the 2004 presidential election:

> Watching the 'debate' just confirmed my disgust with the liars and crony capitalists in the current administration. Indeed, if there was one result, it was that I no longer think that maybe Bush is a genial boob, misled by his handlers. I think the debate showed that he is liar-in-chief. Moral and ethical corruption flows from the top.

In October 2004, Fleming Funch made this incisive observation on Ming.tv:

> Politicians have always been bullshit artists. But until sometime recently it wasn't quite possible to completely disregard the truth and to deal almost entirely in double-speak. ...And what is remarkable is that even if the facts are reported, fairly visibly, at the same time, it is entirely possible for the public figures to stand up, without flinching, and say that something entirely different happened. It is like a bad magician on TV.

Half of the audience sees really clearly that he drops the card under the table, and the card he then shows you, he took out of his sleeve. ...But the other half of the audience thinks that he does real magic and it is no trick. ...Doesn't matter if the observant part of the audience insists and explains how they saw him pull it out of his sleeve. Doesn't matter at all. I am on one hand really impressed at the mastery of deception. The facility with which half a population of apparently normally functioning human beings can be brought into such a complete trance.

The following heartfelt poem by Essie Ablavsky, was written in the summer of 2004 and appeared on a poetry website. There really are Americans who see their democracy slipping away.

Our Demockracy

Secrets kept from public ears
Perpetuating long kept fears
Ignoring all the blood and tears
This is our demockracy
Money becomes scarce for some
While for others it just comes
We're Left with the lowest sum
This is our demockracy
Manipulation of our minds
gross exploitation of all kinds
And so the long kept truth unwinds
This is our demockracy
Our demockracy
when voting just becomes a scam
when the people's voice no longer stands
when truth is covered under sand
WE HAVE NO DEMOCRACY
when media is privatized
and facts kept from public eyes
when all we hear for news is lies
WE HAVE NO DEMOCRACY
When the power reaches peak
there will be no more truth to seek
Then you'll see just how unique

AMERIKA CAN BE
JUST LIKE ALL THE TYRANNY
JUST LIKE NAZI GERMANY
THAT'S THE TRUTH THAT WE WILL SEE
TOO LATE IT WILL BE
FAR TOO LATE TO CHANGE OUR WAY
AND MAKE SURE THAT WE HAVE OUR SAY
WE NEED TO IMPEACH BUSH TODAY
TAKE OUR COUNTRY BACK

Thousands and thousands of these sentiments expressed on the Internet speak for a large part of the American population that is dissatisfied, angry and ready to support a new third party.

Chapter 6

Bush's Bulge: From Wrinkle
to Pucker to Silence

The news and truth are not the same thing.

—Walter Lippmann

Having outlined the major problems with the media in terms of democracy, we can see the fine details at work in the coverage of one particular story: Bulgegate.

Mainstream media missed a golden opportunity to demonstrate their integrity and public service. This story also illustrates our culture of lying and how scandal in the illusory political system is tolerated. Be clear, this is not an anti-Bush tirade. It is about dishonesty undermining our democracy—dishonesty and cheating at the highest level of politics—and how the mainstream media refused to cover an incredible story and enlighten the public *before* they voted for president in 2004.

It all started with the 2004 televised presidential debates, and the story kept accelerating on the Internet, because of bloggers playing detective—serving as our independent press—to reveal things ignored by the major news media. Like a skit on *Saturday Night Live*, there for millions of viewers to see was the rectangular bulge on the back of President Bush's jacket during the first televised debate. It was not a fake bulge, not some optical delusion.

Watching Bush's bulging back on replays of the debate video was like watching hard-core political pornography—embarrassing and titillating—worse even than the president appearing inarticulate and ignorant. But there it was, and no reasonable person could ignore it, because it was—beyond a reasonable doubt—something curiously peculiar. Mainstream media could and did ignore it, or at least easily dismiss it.

Let's review the many "official" self-serving but fake explanations given after the initial White House position that the photos had been doctored collapsed:

Story #1—One of the first media stories on the bulge was by Mike Allen in the *Washington Post*. "Several officials, pressed for a serious answer, flatly denied that anything was fishy about the hump. These officials said they had checked and that there was nothing under Bush's jacket—not a wire, not a transmitter, not a garage door opener. Bush was not wearing a protective vest, sources said. …'It is preposterous,' campaign spokesman Steve Schmidt said. He declined to elaborate or to suggest what could have produced the unusual photo," wrote Allen. During an on-line discussion, when asked about the bulge issue, Allen said, "White House and campaign responses have been so contradictory. …Bush aides…can't explain the bulge…they say he was not wearing a vest." In the *New York Times*, Elisabeth Bumiller also wrote about the bulge: "The bulge—the strange rectangular box visible between the president's shoulder blades in the first debate—has set off so much frenzied speculation on the Internet that is has become what literary critics call an objective correlative, or an object that evokes large emotions and ideas." The deeper question of truth about the purpose of the bulge remained.

Story #2—The president himself tossed aside the odd bulge appearance on *Good Morning America* when Charlie Gibson asked "What the hell was that on your back, in the first debate?" Bush chuckled and said, "Well, you know, Karen Hughes and Dan Bartlett have rigged up a sound system --." Gibson interrupted, "You're getting in trouble --." Bush jumped in, "I don't know what that is. I mean, it is, uh, it is, it's a --- I'm embarrassed to say it's a poorly tailored shirt." Gibson asks incredulously "It was a shirt?" "Yeah, absolutely," said Bush. Gibson pushes: "There was no sound system, there was no electrical signal? There was --." Bush tries to be funny: "How does an electrical—please explain to me how it works so maybe if I were ever to debate again I could figure it out. I guess the assumption was that if I was straying off course they would, kind of like a hunting dog, they would punch a buzzer and I would jerk back into place. I—it's just absurd." Okay, the president was not under oath. But did he lie?

Story #3—Andrew H. Card, Jr., the White House Chief of Staff dismissed the bulge as nothing more than "a poorly tailored suit." A shirt problem had turned into a jacket culprit.

Story #4—Ken Mehlman, the Bush campaign manager, was asked by Tim Russett on NBC's *Meet the Press*: "This was the first debate, George Bush at the podium, the bulge in the back of the suit. All right. Come clean. What is it?" Mehlman, trying to be funny, said: "The president, in fact, was receiving secret signals from aliens in outer space. You heard it here on Meet the Press." Russett follows with: "It was not a bulletproof vest or magnets for his back or anything?" Mehlman responds: "I'm not sure what it was, but the gentleman responsible for the tailoring of that suit is no longer working for his administration." Blame the tailor.

Story #5—Mark Kinnon, media director for the Bush campaign, when asked about the use of some sort of communication device said: "The president has never been assisted by any audio signal."

Story #6—Bush campaign staffers scoffed at the attention to the bulge and blamed a conspiracy theory instigated by bloggers, and they denied specifically that it was a type of Kevlar vest. The official line was: "Mr. Bush was wearing neither an electronic receiver nor a bulletproof vest on his back. He was merely wearing a rumpled suit jacket. Who ya gonna believe—us, or your lying eyes?" Bush spokesman Scott Stanzel said: "Some people have been spending far too much time on left-wing conspiracy web sites." Blame the Internet and the bloggers.

Story #7—During the campaign, Karl Rove said, "Nothing was under his jacket." Would Karl Rove lie?

Story #8—After the election, *The Hill* reported that Secret Service sources said the bulge was the outline of a bulletproof vest. One Internet commenter raised these questions: If Bush had a vest during the debates, wouldn't the Secret Service have had Kerry wearing one? And why would Bush be wearing a vest while driving around in a pickup truck on his extremely well guarded ranch?

Story #9—A few days later, Karl Rove appeared on several Sunday news shows and claimed the bulge was due to some problem with the president's jacket, some sort of pucker he blamed on the tailor.

Story #10—A spokesman for the Secret Service refused to comment on the bulge matter.

Add to all of this that Bush's chief debate negotiator, James A. Baker III (a key player in The Carlyle Group), prior to the debates, sought and received a stipulation that cameras must not be positioned behind the candidates, although this was not honored by the media. Why would Baker want this?

The Internet Pricks the Bulge

Many Internet sites revealed detailed information about the bulge. The consensus was that shirt and jacket stories were not consistent with the same odd protrusion existing on Bush's jacket in all three debates, when he wore different shirts and jackets, and was also inconsistent with photos of Bush in many other situations showing the same type of bulge, including the photo of Bush in a pickup truck on his ranch.

Following an initial story on Salon.com, the most detailed account of the Bush bulge was a story by Dave Lindorff on MotherJones.com. [How the story was investigated reveals a great deal about our political culture. Here was a story seen by millions on TV, yet the gumshoe work was ignored by the mainstream media and fell to a lowly reporter blogging and writing for a small periodical, *Mother Jones*.] The crux of Lindorff's story was a recounting of what a NASA photo-imaging expert had discovered. Robert M. Nelson worked for NASA's Jet Propulsion Laboratory at the California Institute of Technology for some three decades and was a senior scientist with impeccable credentials. He had analyzed digital photographs taken from video broadcasts of the three debates using standard methods that sharpen but do not distort the image. Nelson said:

> In the first debate the bulges create the impression of a letter T with a small feature which appears similar to a wire under the jacket running upward from the right. In the second and third debates the jacket has a generally padded shape across a large part of the entire back which tapers inward toward the spine in a downward direction. This is consistent with the hypothesis that a pad was inserted to conceal the T-shaped device seen in the first debate.

Bruce Hapke, professor emeritus of planetary science at the University of Pittsburg examined the images and concluded: "I would think it's very hard to avoid the conclusion that there's something underneath his jacket. It would certainly be consistent with some kind of radio receiver and a wire."

Lindorff observed: "Nelson's work makes one thing abundantly clear: the White House, the Bush campaign, and the president himself have been lying about the bulge in his suit." Lindorff and others on the Internet discovered that there are relatively common systems consisting of a back-mounted transceiver, a neck loop, and a wireless earpiece hidden in the ear canal. They have been used for some years by public speakers, politicians, actors, musicians, and TV news people.

Alex Darbut of Resistance Technology, Inc. said this of the Bush bulge: "There's no question about it. It's a pretty obvious one [receiver]—larger than most because it probably has descrambling capability." It should also be noted that some Internet detectives had blown up digital photographs of the debates to reveal a thin wire on Bush's shirt.

There are four other relevant pieces of information. First, During a D-day event in France, a CNN broadcast appeared to pick up—and broadcast to surprised viewers—the sound of another voice apparently providing Bush his lines, after which Bush repeated them. Second, Danny Schechter, who operates MediaChannel.org and who had been looking into rumors about Bush being wired, became aware of concerns that others might be picking up their radio frequencies. On the first day of the Republican convention "They had a frequency specialist stop me and ask about the frequency of my camera," Schecter said.

Third, James Atkinson, a technology expert, told of a Bush visit to Boston in March 2004 when he stayed at the Park Plaza Hotel; the system Bush was using could be heard on the right frequency 1500 feet away, "and one of his advisors could be heard doing voice checks and then feeding him data about the school he was about to visit," said Atkinson, who provided details on the specific system the White House had purchased in the past few years.

Fourth, Fred Burks, a long-time contract Indonesian language interpreter working for the State Department and the White House since 1995 told of his experience working at a meeting between President Bush and the president of Indonesia soon after September 11, 2001:

> During the 90 minutes, President Bush not only covered all the [22] points, he covered them quite well and without any notes! Not once during the entire meeting did he look at any notes or receive cues from anyone present in discussing the Indonesian political situation with depth and intelligence. I was astonished! "How could this be?" I asked myself. …I am convinced that he must have been using some sort of earpiece through which someone was telling him what to say.

There was also considerable analysis of a number of Bush's odd silences and statements during the debates that could be explained by his paying attention to what was being said to him in his ear. At one point, for example, Bush snapped, "Let me finish!" But neither Kerry nor the moderator had interrupted him. There simply was no apparent reason for Bush to say that.

Media Most Cowardly

Abraham Lincoln said:

> To sin by silence when they should protest makes cowards of men.

By not giving Americans important information, mainstream news media are silent sinners. Most of the Internet Bush bulge hullabaloos centered on the question of Bush receiving "help" during the debates, which raised a serious ethical lapse issue. In contrast, the major news media tiptoed into the bulge story, mostly focusing on the Internet coverage and finding something comical about it all. They did not pursue the cause and importance of the bulge itself. Apparently, they were afraid to confront the possibility before the election that the President of the United States was cheating during the debates. Risking his job and reputation, NASA scientist Nelson had tried for several weeks to interest the media in his enhanced photos from the first debate. Several small newspapers and then the *Los Angeles Times*, the *New York Times*, and the *Washington Post* rejected the story.

Prior to the election, former *Mother Jones* editor Jeffrey Klein said:

> Major media outlets are understandably reluctant to influence an election, but in this instance, they have a certified government expert willing to go on the record; there's absolutely no excuse for their silence. All any journalist needs to do is report this news.

Another perspective was aired by Margaret Whitman on AxisofLogic.com a week before the election, namely why the Kerry campaign also ignored the bulge story and the possibility that Bush had been coached during the debates. Why didn't Kerry call for an investigation of the bulge? Possibly, Kerry did not care because he "won" all three debates. Whitman asked: "How can [the Kerry campaign] let this go with the polls being neck and neck? ...It almost seems like John Kerry is protecting his ole fraternity brother." Or was it a desire to protect the culture of lies and "the presidency"?

A few days after the election, Fairness and Accuracy in Reporting

(FAIR) put out a press release "New York Times Killed 'Bush Bulge' Story." They reported that five days before the election the *Times* had killed a story about the mysterious object Bush wore on his back during the debates. FAIR said: "The Times' bulge story is the latest example of possible self-censorship by major news media during the election campaign."

After a few more days, the *New York Times* did a story on the bulge with a humorous slant; it was titled "Cashmere and Kevlar? Bulge Affair Has Tailor Miffed." The *Times* acknowledged the bulge in all three debates and that *The Hill* had discovered the bulletproof vest explanation but afterwards the Secret Service refused to confirm it. It largely ignored the serious reporting by two of its staff and tried to make a joke about the matter. Here humor was used to deflect and minimize serious issues facing a democracy, in contrast to Jon Stewart, who uses humor to illuminate and provoke.

The logic at the *Times* seemed to be that the proximity to Election Day somehow justified not using the work of its reporters. What backwards thinking. It was the proximity to the election that made the story all the more important—it really was news fit to print.

There are many good reasons why the Secret Service would want to have the president in constant communication during some activities. So why lie about it? Why would Bush's first reaction be to talk about a rumpled shirt? Either the device was legitimate and Bush is a habitual liar or it was not legitimate and he is an uncreative liar.

But would a communication device be necessary in highly secured debate locations with Secret Service agents standing a few feet away? And if the White House somehow convinced the press to withhold stories on the Bush bulge because of national security or presidential safety needs, then the press should have its heads slapped hard, very hard. How could any reasonable journalist ignore the possibility that Bush received some prohibited help during the debates? Why did Baker want no views of the backs of the debaters? What about the other evidence of Bush's previous use of a device to get information? What about the strange silences and statements by Bush during the debates?

With so much attention, a poll of registered voters by *The Economist* included a question about the bulge shown on the second televised debate. Thirty percent thought the bulge was caused by "a radio receiver so that his team could communicate with him during the debate." This result did not vary significantly with sex, age or intention to vote, but varied considerably with party affiliation. Of Democrats, 48 percent had this view, compared to only 11 percent of Republicans. Conversely, only 4 percent of Democrats thought that the bulge was due to a fold in Bush's jacket, compared to 17 percent of Republicans. This shows how a positive status quo belief in Bush blocked disturbing information.

Surely, if revealed *before* the election, debate cheating would have impacted some voters. The major news media had a responsibility to the public to take the bulge story a lot more seriously. Ben Bagdikan, retired dean of University of California Berkeley's journalism school agreed:

> I cannot imagine a paper I worked for turning down a story like this before an election. This was credible photographic evidence not about breaking the rules, but of a total lack of integrity on the part of the president, evidence that he'd cheated in the debate... ...Cheating on a debate should affect an election. The decision not to let people know this could affect the history of the United States.

Frustrated NASA scientist Nelson said:

> The scientific community last November produced very credible evidence suggesting the president may have been cheating in the debates. ...The founders of this nation understood the importance of an informed public, but given what has just happened, one is tempted to ask: Does the term "free press" apply only to those who can afford to own one?

The nagging question remains: Why would Bush feel the need for help during the debates? The likely answer is his distaste and discomfort with unscripted, spontaneous discussions. It's not a matter of intelligence. It is about having a command of many facts and talking points—and about being quick on your feet in a stressful situation—about not freezing and smirking. Here is the scary truth: *The emperor has little information.* After all, during his first four years in office, Bush had set a record for having the fewest press conferences. In them, he would need information to publicly confront questions from journalists. Not something an information-naked president welcomes. And there were all those events where only faithful Republicans or members of the armed forces could attend to heap praise rather than challenge Bush with tough questions. As *New York Times* columnist Maureen Dowd said in 2005, the Bush people "shy away from taking questions from the public unless they get to vet the questions and audiences in advance. ...The president loves democracy—as long as democracy means he's always right." The president of a great democracy must respect and welcome dissent and embrace opportunities to substantively defend his policies. Bush's failure to do so fits hand in glove with a democracy in decay.

Little Ado About Something

In December 2004, the *Washington Post* ran the major story "Interpreter Says No To Secrecy." It was about Fred Burks leaving his contractor job for the State Department after 18 years of providing interpretation for top government officials. He refused to sign a new contract with a secrecy pledge. It certainly seemed that this was retaliation for his reporting Bush's likely use of a hidden earpiece during the meeting with the Indonesian president. The *Post* story avoided use of the word "bulge" and made only this limited connection to the earlier bulge-debate controversy:

> White House spokesman Sean McCormack dismissed Burk's allegations of a secret presidential wireless device—similar allegations surfaced most recently during Bush's election debate with the Democratic challenger, Sen. John F. Kerry (D-Mass)—with a laugh and a one-word comment: "Nonsense."

Political truthfulness is nearly extinct in the media. Everybody knows.

Part 2: Spitting Fiery Outrage

Can we stop American democracy's decline before it hits rock bottom? Yes. History's lesson is that major political and social upheaval happens when adverse conditions set the stage for new thinking and political solutions. Adverse conditions are plentiful. Time is short. Soon, optimism must overtake resignation to the current dysfunctional system and remove a self-fulfilling prophesy of national collapse. It can be flipped inside out to become a self-determined positive future of American renewal.

Chapter 7

Making Elections Matter: From Conscience to Conviction

> The crisis of modern democracy is a profound one. Free elections, a free press and an independent judiciary mean little when the free market has reduced them to commodities available on sale to the highest bidder.
>
> —Arundhati Roy

When elections don't matter nearly as much as they are supposed to a democracy is in trouble. American elections must move beyond placebo patriotism to passionate participation by nearly all citizens, as if their lives depended on voting, because they do.

For most people elections have become a pro forma exercise, a futile formality. Dissatisfaction with the current dual political system, the major two-party duopoly, and an increasingly audacious corruption-based deMOCKracy requires improvements in our election process. The goal is not just increasing the number of voters fooled by campaign lies, but to make our representative government work in the public interest. Elections must be opened up to get more "outsiders" seeking and winning public office. Elections must also give opportunities for reducing the corruption of government by well-heeled special interests. Without disbanding the restricted political system run by power elites, however, election reforms within the illusory political system are not likely to return American democracy to the people. But it's a start.

To begin with, here are three absolute necessities for making elections matter more.

First, the one proven approach for increasing voter turnout is same day registration. It is now used in six states, Idaho, Maine, Minnesota, New Hampshire, Wisconsin, and Wyoming. [North Dakota does not require any voter registration.] For those six states voter turnout was 60.6 percent in 1996 versus 48.3 percent in states without same day registration, in 2000 it was 65.6 percent versus 50.3 percent. No other approach has produced these kinds of improvements. A 2000 survey of non-voters found that same day registration was the most popular, with two-thirds saying it would make them more likely to vote. The big caveat is that several known techniques to prevent voter fraud should be used. In 2002, a ballot measure in California to offer same day registration failed by three to two, because of opposition by Republicans and conservative groups. Ironically, that year the voter turnout was an abysmal 29 percent. Also in 2002, a similar measure failed in Colorado. University of California, Berkeley professor Raymond Wolfinger believes that same day registration helps third-party candidates. For example, Jesse Ventura's win in 1998 was credited largely to young people who registered as independents on Election Day.

Second, more attention to various kinds of election and voter fraud by individuals and groups is needed. Among the minority 38 percent of Americans who believe the two major parties care about the public a full 90 percent believe in the integrity of elections, but of the majority 62 percent with no confidence in the parties only 51 percent have such faith. Election integrity really is an issue, perhaps more so with the advent of electronic voting, with only half the states requiring a paper receipt for voters. Every proof or hint of election fraud is like another dagger into the heart of democracy, draining its vitality by sapping enthusiasm for voting.

Third, what should be a no-brainer, non-debatable change is making Election Day a national holiday. The most cited reason for not voting is the difficulty of taking time off from work or school. Placing it on the weekend has also been suggested, but using a Saturday or Sunday would undoubtedly raise objections from religious groups, and perhaps even from people who prize weekends for carrying out countless personal and family needs. A far better idea, as presented by University of California, Irvine Professor Martin P. Wattenberg is to make it a holiday and, specifically, to combine it with Veterans Day on the second Tuesday in November and rename it Veterans' Democracy Day. As Wattenberg said, "what better way could there be to honor those who fought for democratic rights than for Americans to vote" on this holiday. An increase in voter turnout and enthusiasm would surely result.

Fourth, as a matter of equity, voting rights should be restored to felons who have fulfilled all their penalties, including parole and other forms of post-incarceration monitoring. There are nearly five million such Americans, or 2.3 percent of the national electorate.

But we need much more. In this volume the focus is on more

substantial or radical election reforms which are sorely needed. Consider that in the 2000 presidential election 58 percent of non-voters said they *chose* not to vote, as compared to only 40 percent who said that some procedural barrier prevented them from voting, such as a failure to register. Also note that surveys before elections routinely show that very high fractions of eligible voters say that they certainly or probably will vote—typically over 80 percent combined. Yet clearly over one-third of them do not vote. Though all of the following changes advocated in this chapter are important, they are given in order of importance:

1. Expand the use of Clean Money, Clean Election programs.

2. Provide a None of the Above option on ballots.

3. Permit fusion candidates to promote third-party candidates.

4. Reform the Electoral College or its use by states.

5. Provide Instant Runoff Voting.

6. Pass the "Our Democracy, Our Airwaves" federal law.

7. For primary elections, support an open or crossover primary that favors third-parties.

8. Make voting compulsory after other reforms

At the outset I emphasize that each reform, when taken by itself, will not have a large enough impact and may appear unexciting. Can we really rehabilitate American democracy just by tinkering with the rules? No one change will do it. But if they were all implemented, a seemingly sleepy set of reforms pushed in back room operations of dissent would go a long way to creating fundamental systemic change. Nor should there be a competition among these reforms, especially by those who have attached themselves to single options. We surely will not get them all at once, but the ultimate prize is getting them all.

Don't Let Your Conscience Be Your Guide

Here is a paradox. Surveys have found that over 90 percent of Americans believe that voting matters. They do see it as a legitimate civic duty. But still so many of them do not vote. Understanding their behavior is far more important than blaming it. When a film or play does poorly its producers are wise to rethink what they did rather than blame the public. So too with a political system. Perhaps what is more amazing at this point is why so many Americans still bother to vote.

Voting is justifiably unpopular with millions of Americans who feel their vote will make no difference to them personally or to their community, state or nation. As Martin Wattenberg observed:

> People who have an interest in who should govern and what government should do are thus more likely to feel that there is a benefit to voting, just like people with a favorite team are more likely to attend a sporting event. …It is not hard to understand why most non-voters don't vote: they are uninterested, uninformed, and uninvolved. …The psychological approach has further identified the problem to be primarily one of a lack of motivation to vote, particularly stemming from party decline.

However, the decline in association with both the Democratic Party and the Republican Party is good news, from the perspective of seeing the opportunity for a new competitive third party. And citizens being uninterested, uninformed and uninvolved surely has a lot do with uninteresting, unimpressive, and unremarkable candidates from the two-party duopoly.

Non-voters are more welcomed than you might imagine. As Paul Allen Beck and Frank J. Sorauf said in *Party Politics in America (seventh edition)*:

> The case for democracy itself rests on the wisdom of the widest possible sharing of political power and political decision-making within society. …Widespread nonvoting also casts some doubt on the effectiveness with which the political parties—the political organizations primarily concerned with contesting elections—manage to involve the total eligible electorate. …[The parties] often appear not to relish the challenges of new voters, especially those of low status. The experience of political power has made them (especially their parties in government) sympathetic to the comfortable status quo of two-party competition. They do not welcome the uncertainties that a radical alteration in the electorate would bring.

The Sunday before the 2004 election, the *Washington Post Magazine* published "None of the Above" by writer Gene Weingarten. The article went over the usual litany of reasons why people should vote, but do not. Then it explored the behavior and thinking of one "typical" non-voter in Michigan, Ted Prus, a documented non-voter, who explained his disinterest simply: "All politicians are liars." He and his wife shared three prime characteristics: they mistrust and disbelieve politicians, they tune out the news, and they don't like the way most things in the country are going. As to the presidential choice, Weingarten summed up the attitude of Prus:

> The way he sees it, a vote for either man is a vote for a liar; a member of the privileged class who will promise whatever it takes to get your vote and then do whatever it takes to keep the country safe for the privileged class. Screw 'em all.

And screw American democracy. One question remained unanswered: Would Americans with this worldview be more inclined to vote if there was a viable, honest third-party candidate or the "None of the Above" ballot option?

In a real sense, non-voters *are* voting—voting against the entire political establishment they see as irrelevant to their lives. As Wattenberg also pointed out, non-voters have been found to be less satisfied with American democracy. Lack of trust in government is consistently found in polls and surveys. A 1999 survey found that 63 percent of Americans said public opinion should rule over conscience and individual judgment of elected officials. Why? Because 80 percent believed that government "is pretty much run by a few big interests looking out for themselves," rather than "for the benefit of all the people." A different 1999 survey found that 64 percent of Americans believed that "government is run by a few big interests looking out for themselves, not for the benefit of all," and 58 percent believed that "you can't trust politicians because most are dishonest." No surprise that a 1999 Pew Research Center poll found that nearly two-thirds of Americans believed that "large political donors" have "too much" influence on which candidates become presidential nominees and 62 percent believed that "average voters" have "too little" influence. A 2002 Gallup poll revealed that two-thirds of Americans believed that "no matter what new laws are passed, special interests will always find a way to maintain their power in Washington." But a realistic view of corrupt government is not the same as a negative view of American democracy, nor should it kill all optimism about fixing it. The worst delusion is fatalistic—that the awful system is what it is and is here to stay. If our forebears had felt that way there would be no USA.

Widespread distrust in our government and hopelessness about fixing our republic defines the public's political ennui. For *most* Americans, political alienation and despair is the end; it does not lead to civic engagement or activist dissent. People turn away and seek satisfaction elsewhere, leaving power with the crooks and liars. The corporatism that undermines democracy ends up profiting more. What a system. We can leave it but it will not leave us alone.

We cannot escape the many ways this insane system inevitably stabs us. If hardly anyone fights back hard it will just keep coming at us. So here is another example (not that you may need one) of corporate welfare punishing people. Under pressure from business groups like the American Benefits Council and the ERISA Industry Committee, Congress has created an incentive for companies to break the pension promises made to employees that will not be kept. As corporatism has sunk to new lows, company executives have stopped funding employee pension programs. Upon bankruptcy the federal Pension Benefit Guarantee Corporation (PBGC) bails them out. Recent examples: $9.8 billion United Airlines and $5.7 billion Northwest Airlines walked away from. Retirees who enter the PBGC program usually get greatly reduced pensions and face severe financial problems; 44 million workers and retirees are covered by the program. One victim called it "legalized crime." Because so many U.S. companies have discovered the benefits of not funding their pension programs, the PBGC has faced skyrocketing shortfalls, from about $50 billion in obligations in 2001 to $450 billion in 2005. So it faces insolvency despite being funded by a tax on companies with pension programs. Companies are fighting higher premiums by lobbying Congress. Ultimately, American taxpayers may get hit with bailing out the PBGC (that bails out companies), just like the Savings and Loan fiasco years earlier.

The final nuttiness is that companies can legally report false figures on their pension shortfall; they can assume that their pension fund will be fully funded, while the much larger pension termination figure is reported only to the PBGC that keeps it secret until the shortfall hits the fan. Northwest Airlines chairman Gary Wilson sold company stock and collected $19.7 million before his company went bankrupt; he knew the real pension problem and that the stock would become worthless after bankruptcy, which it did. Everyone gets screwed—except corporate executives and politicians who let them get away with monetary murder.

When trust and citizen engagement are gone and deserved mistrust in government prevails, corporate welfare is made easier. As with a person, democracy can be killed passively or actively. Sometimes, raw political, police, or military power kills democracy by halting elections and closing independent newspapers. U.S. democracy has been killed more subtly and passively by dishonesty, little political party competition and corporate corruption. As said before, having considerable personal freedom does not mean you have real democracy. Conscience won't get citizens to vote as time has shown. Neither will guilt work. We must make elections matter.

Cleaning Up Elections with Clean Money

The Supreme Court's 1976 decision [*Buckley v. Valeo*] that money equals speech made it impossible to limit campaign spending. Paul Street commented: "It ignored the fact that vast private wealth invested in the political process tends to drown out the positive free speech rights (including the right to actually be heard) of candidates and parties that do not have access to vast private fortunes."

Colgate University Professor Jay Mandle has studied the politics of democracy across a number of democratic nations. He has verified how public financing of electoral efforts goes hand in hand with increased voter turnout and greater government spending on "personal security"— namely spending on education, health and pensions. The choice is between our current "plutocratic financing" and public financing. What Americans need to appreciate more deeply within their cores is that, with very few exceptions, voters currently only get to choose among "candidates who either themselves are wealthy and finance their own campaigns, or are acceptable to private funders." Not just acceptable but indebted to their financial supporters. "Public policy is thereby biased to the interests of the wealthy. This system affects the policy agenda by reducing both the range of candidates and voter participation. ...The greater the commitment to the public financing of elective politics, the more the political process is responsive to the needs of the people," said Mandle.

Face facts. Regulating all corrupting money out of politics will not work. Blame lobbyists and lawyers working for power elites.

We have an alternative. Few Americans know about a nascent movement in the United States to return "power to the people." It is the "Clean Money/Clean Elections" (CMCE) movement. The basic concepts are:

- Candidates for public office can choose to accept public financing for primary and general election campaigning, if they forego private funds.

- However, they must qualify initially, usually by raising a significant number of small contributions, often limited to $5, and perhaps signatures from registered voters to demonstrate that they are not a fringe candidate.

- In some cases, in addition to receiving a set amount of public funding, candidates in the general election may receive supplemental public funds to match significant campaign contributions received by an opponent directly or indirectly from private sources.

This is a profoundly important and effective way to remove the corrupting influence of campaign contributions and provide opportunities for Americans to run for public office without kowtowing and pandering to special interests. It offers choice to candidates and creates more choice for voters. It makes our representative form of government more open and transparent. It expands free speech. This approach is far different and more effective than any other strategy, including the McCain-Feingold reforms (officially the Bipartisan Campaign Finance Act of 2002) which the 2004 presidential election showed were essentially useless. Nor have campaign finance laws improved trust in government, according to research at the University of Rochester that concluded "the effect of campaign finance laws is often perverse, rarely positive, and in all cases modest." It is more than a little interesting that in 2004 John Kerry received $10.7 million from Republicans that had contributed to the Bush campaign.

A national poll in 2000 revealed that by a margin of 68 percent to 19 percent, voters supported full public financing. This support cut across different groups: Democrats—77 percent for/15 percent opposed; independents—71 percent for/14 percent opposed; Republicans—59 percent for/27 percent opposed; self-identified conservative Republicans

51 percent for/32 percent opposed. As to concerns about the current system, 36 percent said buying help from politicians with campaign contributions was a central problem, and 34 percent thought a central concern was politicians becoming corrupted by campaign contributions, perks, and favors from special interests. Federally, 87 percent thought that special interest contributions affected the voting behavior of members of Congress, which dropped to only 82 percent for their own representative. Senators Paul Wellstone and John Kerry and Representative John Tierney, all Democrats, together introduced federal CMCE legislation which went nowhere.

CMCE was enacted by voters in Maine through a ballot initiative in 1996 that resulted from 1,100 volunteers collecting 65,000 signatures, by the Vermont legislature in 1997, and by ballot initiative in Massachusetts and Arizona in 1998. The greater use of ballot initiatives than action by legislatures is not surprising. Because of their alliances with special interests, those already in power usually do not want to face opposition from candidates without any such obligations, and who can run as "clean" candidates.

New Jersey, New Mexico, North Carolina also have some version of CMCE, and it is receiving support in a number of other states. There is considerable information on the effectiveness of CMCE. Overall, in Maine and Arizona, about three-quarters of all the candidates for office participated in CMCE programs in 2002. In 2002, 39 of Arizona's elected officials were "clean"—22 Republicans and 17 Democrats. An astounding nine out of eleven statewide candidates won their elections using only public funds. Democrat Janet Napolitano was one of these; she received $2.3 million in public funding, and became governor by beating Congressman Matt Salmon, for whom President George W. Bush and Vice President Dick Cheney had conducted in-state fundraising events. Significantly, 62 percent of women candidates, 57 percent of Latino candidates, and 100 percent of African American candidates ran as CMCE candidates. Voter turnout increased by 10 percent that year. All these fine results provide strong evidence that Americans can positively respond to real political choices untainted by corrupt money.

Arizona Republican Mark Spitzer summed up his experience: "Clean Elections is about the restoration of democracy." The experience of Democrat Jay Blanchard in Arizona was instructive. He won a state

Senate race against the sitting House speaker who was term-limited out of office, and who became embroiled in a serious scandal in the final weeks of the campaign. Blanchard acknowledged that without public funding he would never had run and the Republican would have won unopposed. By winning his seat, Blanchard removed the Republican Senate majority and created a two-party tie.

Of course, those who benefit from the status quo of "dirty" campaigns and elections oppose CMCE. They often use the slogan "No Taxpayer Money for Politicians." A main argument is that using taxpayer money deprives government programs that benefit the public. This is the height of hypocrisy and sinicism, especially when it comes from conservative and religious right-wingers. There have been several cases of aggressive efforts to defeat CMCE in its early years, apparently trying to head off national adoption of it.

The successful Arizona law produced through a ballot measure provoked opposition. Big money special interests and right-wingers mounted a ballot initiative for the 2004 election that would overturn the original law. A grassroots coalition was formed to prevent its placement on the ballot, including Senator John McCain and Governor Napolitano. They wrote that the opposition proposition "poses a clear choice between people's interest and the special interests." The proposition proposal went to the Arizona Supreme Court which struck it down. A lawsuit was also attempted; it wanted to bar the payment of matching funds. It was rejected by a Superior Court judge. In the end, CMCE remained.

In 2000, two citizen ballot initiatives for CMCE failed. In Missouri, the Chamber of Commerce and the Associated Industries of Missouri, including leading companies such as Anheuser-Busch and Monsanto, backed the group No Tax Dollars for Politicians which spent more than $600,000 to defeat the measure. In Oregon, the group No Taxpayer Handouts for Politicians spent about $135,000 to defeat the initiative. A conservative consortium also worked to defeat the measure. The Republican candidate for secretary of state publicly opposed the measure in her campaign materials. The opposition has made one thing extremely clear: CMCE is a threat to special interests and worth opposing with large sums of money and significant resources. While proponents of CMCE may be outraged by these efforts, they should see them as a clear signal that the clean election movement is on to something important.

This is a good way to look at the real world: Candidates who do not accept available CMCE funding should be presumed corrupt. *The ultimate goal of CMCE should be to create a system that works so well that public pressure compels ALL candidates to reject ALL money from corporate and special interests.* Senator John McCain was so correct when he described our current electoral system as "nothing less than a massive influence peddling scheme where both parties conspire to sell the country to the highest bidder."

Dirty Politics De-cleaned Massachusetts

Massachusetts offers a sad story. Over some time a coalition of many citizen groups worked hard to get the Clean Elections measure on the ballot. Mass Voters for Clean Elections, with the help of 6,000 volunteers, prevailed. The entire Massachusetts congressional delegation supported the original signature drive. The measure passed with 67 percent of voters in a 1998 ballot referendum. Soon afterwards, contrary to his public support, Governor Paul Cellucci submitted a budget without any funding to implement the new law, meaning that no funds were actually available for clean campaigns. Next, the legislature tried to give incumbents the right to raise unlimited amounts of private money and also get public funding. Then the governor said he would veto both the loophole and $10 million appropriated for the Clean Elections program. After serious protests by supporters of the new law, the governor capitulated and did not veto the funding. But in 2002, the state legislature refused to allocate funds. The state Supreme Judicial Court ordered it to provide funding; the state's Republican Party was a co-plaintiff in that lawsuit, but not the more powerful state Democratic Party. But only limited funds were made available, allowing 10 legislative candidates and one gubernatorial candidate to run as "clean" candidates.

And then the final insult hit. In 2003, the state Senate under Democratic control *repealed the Clean Elections law and Republican Governor Mitt Romney refused to veto the repeal*! The Mass Voters for Clean Elections group said: "The legislature stole our voter-mandated Clean Elections system, having never fully funded it or given it a real chance to work."

How the Senate accomplished its "coup" merits attention. It took sinicism to new heights. The Senate acted through a budget amendment rather than distinct legislation, which avoided referring a bill to a committee and thus avoided public hearings. It also used a voice vote, instead of a roll call, so that citizens could not know how senators voted. The maneuver avoided any direct vote in the state House. Incumbents and their special interest supporters were determined to keep state government as *misrepresentative* as possible. There was no second Boston tea party.

In explaining the legislature's gutting of the law's reform of campaign financing, the *Boston Globe* noted the legislators' desire to maintain the original status quo which "was an incumbent protection system for the Legislature." Indeed, in the strongly Democratic state, typically 70 percent of incumbent legislators have had no opponents. The *Boston Globe* editorialized strongly on what had happened:

> The Legislature's arrogant refusal to fund the law last year...was a dark chapter in the state's political history. Even worse was the Senate action last month, attaching repeal language to the budget without so much as a roll-call vote. ...The nut of this story is that the Legislature is trying to kill Clean Elections. It is a clear case of attempted murder, and the killers are trying to walk away free. Romney has the ability to get a set of fingerprints, and he should take it.

But Republican Romney helped kill the Clean Elections law, even though to win office he had portrayed himself as a reformer and supporter of more accountability for the legislature. Through his inaction, he put the last nail in the coffin.

Remarkably, this impudent bipartisan crushing of the peoples' will in Massachusetts never became a major national news story. Legal but shameless political behavior is too common to be news. The Massachusetts story was remarkable for its demonstration of how people in power use every trick in the book to preserve their status quo. Together with the Missouri and Oregon cases, it is all too clear that CMCE faces strong opposition from status quo defenders who should be viewed as traitors, responsible for our declining democracy.

Spending to Get the Bums Out

A federal CMCE law would be historic and probably do more to restore honest representative government than any other action. But defeats of CMCE demonstrate that framing for this reform has to focus on what it does for citizens rather than on how public financing works.

CMCE is about saving our democracy, saving taxpayers' money, and obtaining a government that genuinely serves the needs of its non-elite citizens. It is about providing a "vehicle for the majority of the population to find its political voice," according to Jay Mandle. It is about turning around the perception of government as a necessary evil to government as a necessary good. It is about many Americans discovering trust for their political system and feeling good about voting.

If money matters, then people must see that the corruption status quo wastes enormous sums of citizens' taxes. No matter how much public money is spent on financing campaigns, it is in the financial interest of citizens that CMCE be used, despite other worthy needs for taxpayers' dollars. *CMCE must be sold as stopping the massive waste of taxpayer dollars.* Spending tax dollars on CMCE will surely prevent many more tax dollars being wasted because of the corruption of politicians by high-spending special interests. Corporate fat-cats are feeding off the congressional pork paid for by we the people. Depending on how it is calculated, one year of corporate welfare and tax breaks would pay for more than ten years of CMCE for the entire nation. Congressman Tierney summed up the economic benefits to special interests: "Tens of millions in campaign contributions have bought tens of billions of dollars in wasteful subsidies, dirty air, dirty water, and the push for the privatization of Medicare." Those billions of dollars are paid by taxpayers. Consider that the top eleven largest recipients of corporate tax breaks (GE, SBC Communications, Citigroup, IBM, Microsoft, AT&T, ExxonMobil, Verizon, JPMorganChase, Pfizer, and Altria) received $51.9 billion from 2001 to 2003. They spent about $10 million a year on campaign contributions for good reason. The bottom line is that they received over $1,700 for each dollar "invested" in politicians, which is a remarkable return on investment.

Unlike the materials disseminated by public interest groups promoting CMCE, a federal bill introduced acknowledged that, with the current system, democracy is undermined by "imposing large, unwarranted costs on taxpayers through legislative and regulatory outcomes shaped by unequal access to lawmakers for campaign contributions." Note that the 2003 report "Investing In Democracy" by the Center for Government Studies presented a good detailed case for CMCE, except that it did not include the economic advantage for taxpayers.

So the CMCE message should be framed as a way to cut corruption of government. We must spend some taxpayer money to save much more of it. The opponents of CMCE knew how to attack it with slogans like No Taxpayer Money for Politicians. CMCE supporters must use messages like Honest Politicians Are Worth the Cost, Spend Millions to Save Billions, An Ounce of CMCE Prevents A Pound of Corrupt Spending, and Clean Elections Save Taxpayers' Money.

As former Congressman and independent presidential candidate John Anderson said: "The American people instinctively know that when big money rules, ordinary voters are left out in the cold." I agree with this proud assessment that voters are in the know. All we need to do is light the fires for "can-do" Americans to take back their government.

Giving Discontent an Option

In our fading democracy, so many Americans are political Luddites—anti-politics instead of anti-technology, a symptom of decades of disillusionment with the two-party system and its dishonest and corrupt politicians. Politicians' concern about non-voters is superficial. Shunning elections is just fine with our power elites.

Popular cable TV commentator Bill O'Reilly tells his viewers that Americans have a responsibility to vote, even if it is for the lesser of two evils. The two major parties do a great job of delivering the message that a vote for a third party candidate is a "wasted" vote or, worse, may help someone get elected that you would never vote for. *Non-voting guilt works in favor of the status quo, as does voting for the lesser evil.* But non-voters may be expressing civic disrespect for the two-party duopoly, as well as for dishonest and corrupt politicians who criminalize politics.

Americans also deserve a simple fourth option—opting out of the two-party duopoly. In 1976, Nevada actually enacted a law that requires a box that could be checked "None of the candidates" on ballots, although those votes do not affect the outcome. Why? Because Democrats and Republicans had no desire to lose to no one, nor to document voter dissatisfaction. When then state Representative Greg Kaza in Michigan managed to get a bill passed in the House that would have allowed a None of the Above (NOTA) ballot line experiment just in his own district in the next election, it was killed in the state Senate. He observed: "You would have thought I was trying to take away their salaries, the vitriol [my proposal] attracted."

At the federal level, an attempt to require a "None of the Above" (NOTA) line on ballots for all elections attracted virtually no support in Congress when the bill was introduced in 1997. If the "None of the Above" option got the most votes, then another election would be required. Imagine if voters chose "None of the Above" and losing candidates could not run in the next election. New candidates, including third party candidates, could get on the ballot and win. Ralph Nader said: "A None of the Above line on the ballot—is a proper and long overdue expansion of voting choice at a time when citizens are staying away from the polls in droves because of their disgust, distrust, despair and disillusionment with tweedledum-tweedledee politics."

Representative Peter Hoekstra said: "This is a movement waiting to happen. But the American people will have to demand it." Demanding changes to improve American democracy has to come back into style. Movements focused on forcing change must make elections matter through reforms of the system. Election reforms should be seen as social change, just like the civil rights movement led to legal reforms.

Why would Americans want this option? The *Virginia-Pilot* interviewed two Virginia Beach residents in 1999. Part-time bus driver Thomas Hutchings, age 67, wanted a ballot with the NOTA option and a new election if "none" eclipses all the candidates and turns out to be the winner. "Either there ain't no difference between the candidates or no one else is running," he complained. Not voting was not good enough; he wanted a way to make candidates and political parties more responsive to citizens. Michael E. Rau, age 40, said "None of the above would help increase voter turnout while decreasing the influence of big money in politics."

In 2000, Californians had the opportunity to vote on Proposition 23 which would have created a non-binding NOTA on ballots as in Nevada. Other than opposition from the "establishment," the fact that it was non-binding fed the opposition. A telephone survey had found that 50 to 60 percent of California voters supported the idea. But it lost 64 percent to 36 percent, showing how difficult it is to break the status quo.

A national campaign already exists on Nota.org. Signaling that the appeal of the idea reaches across the political spectrum, *The Wall Street Journal* editorialized in 1996 for giving voters a real choice through the NOTA ballot option. Here are some of its salient points:

> More elected officials naturally oppose NOTA, but support for it is building among both conservatives and liberals. ...Citizens are increasingly showing their displeasure with the political process by not voting. Including NOTA on the ballot could give citizens a reason to go to the polls even if they aren't enthusiastic about the choices. It would offer a convenient way of protesting the status quo system.

Prior to the 2004 presidential election, attorney Elbert Lin wrote in the *Yale Daily News*: "Those people who are immune to civic guilt and the recurring get-out-the-vote drives will stay home" and "their utter dissatisfaction will be lost in a sea of other explanations for America's abysmal turnout—apathy, incapacity and indifference, to name a few." Lin argued forcefully for giving Americans the option of voting for None of the Above, because "their opinion...wouldn't be subsumed, diluted or misinterpreted." "With our essentially two-party system...we have narrowed the viable ballot choices and, in turn, weakened the expressive power of our votes," he said. His NOTA solution for presidential elections had a practical aspect, namely that no matter what the total NOTA vote was in a state, its electoral votes would go to the candidate with the most number of votes."

NOTA would be a powerful tool for political change. That's why two-party duopoly defenders fight it. Listen to Steve Lilienthal of the conservative Free Congress Foundation:

> Don't think the representatives of the people will be willing to give voters even a modest—but potentially very effective—tool such as NOTA. However, if enough reform-minded citizens in a state with the initiative process were able to put a binding NOTA proposal on the ballot, it would make for an interesting topic of debate and some interesting political coalitions could be forged.

Yes, it might make some elections messy and delay determination of winners, but NOTA would do wonders for making politicians serve the public interest and be more accountable and honest.

A Supremely Bad Decision

We need more political competition, opposition and dissent. But these are thwarted by two-party control of the illusory political system. As Lisa Jane Disch said in *The Tyranny of the Two-Party System*:

> The...two-party system as we know it shortchanges democracy because it 'wastes' the votes and silences the voices of dissenters. ...[It] has marginalized other forms of institutionalized opposition (such as community organizing and protest) and other forms of voting (such as fusion or stand-alone third party candidacies) by rendering them inefficient, incomprehensible, or patently illegitimate.

It also makes it difficult for status quo busters trying to change government and public policy. The two-party system status quo very much obstructs needed change.

Disch enlightened people by noting how "fusion" once was used effectively in this country and how it promoted third-parties. Fusion means multiple-party nomination. In other words, the same candidate can appear on more than one party line on ballots. Typically, a third-party backs a candidate from one of the two major parties. In doing so, it is able to document through the voting process that some voters are not totally supportive of the major party. It offers an option other than not voting for many people disgusted with the two-party system. Most importantly, it offers the opportunity to protest vote, yet does not throw the election to the candidate they least prefer. It also provides third-parties a route to greater visibility and ultimately the ability to run their own candidates.

Why be against the fusion option? The two major parties see nothing in it for them. In 1997 the Supreme Court justices ruled six to three to uphold state anti-fusion laws [*Timmons v. Twin Cities Area New Party*]. Because the two major parties have controlled state governments, they have mostly done so. Fusion has been long practiced in New York and is allowed in Connecticut, Mississippi, South Carolina, Idaho, Vermont, and South Dakota. The Supreme Court sanctioned a restricted voting system. Hardly what befits the "greatest democracy on Earth."

Worse than the court's decision was how the majority justified their action. In their view "the traditional two-party system" had offered so much "sound and effective government" that the cost to third-parties was justified. They said that the Constitution allowed states to use regulations that "in practice, favor the traditional two-party system." Fusion was deemed as a benefit that states could provide, but not a constitutional right. They praised the two-party system for bringing "stability" to elections and "integrity" to ballots. In truth, there was no basis *in the Constitution* for the court invoking two-party dominance. The dissenting justices noted an absurd aspect of the majority decision. Namely, that the state of Minnesota in defending its anti-fusion ban explicitly rejected the two-party preservation argument. Disch disparaged the strange decision:

> In the decisive paragraph where the Court attempts to forge the link between antifusion legislation and political stability, "two-party system" appears no less than six times and is partnered with explicitly celebratory adjectives such as "traditional," "healthy," "stable," and "strong." So excessive is this unsolicited testimonial to the two-party doctrine that it prompts Justice Stevens to wonder whether an "interest in preserving the two-party system" were not the "true basis" for the majority's holding. ...Unwittingly, the Court revealed the two-party system to be a social and political contrivance, no immutable foundation but a fragile construct that must be revered and protected if it is to be sustained. ...Antifusion statutes are themselves protections of two-party competition that force a preference for the party establishment.

In other words, fusion is anti-establishment and anti-status quo. Sounds like the Supreme Court made more of a political than legal decision. Few Americans know that the majority justices (with Republican or Democratic backgrounds) robbed citizens of the right to have stronger alternatives to the two-party duopoly.

The myth that a dominant two-party system is essential for American democracy is sheer nonsense. Generations of students have been brainwashed. In the textbook *Party Politics in America (third edition)*, this is how Frank J. Sorauf praised the two-party system:

> They encourage the political activity and participation that a democracy depends on. ...Because of the parties' simplification of political choices, the average citizen, often distracted by personal worries and limited in background, can participate more meaningfully in the affairs of politics. ...To put the matter briefly, the political parties have helped fashion a workable system of representation for the mass democracies of the twentieth century. ...[They] counter the social and economic advantages of small groups and powerful individuals. ...Behind the widespread preference for the two-party system lurks the experience of other [Western] democracies with multipartyism. ...By sheer contrast, and perhaps even by a little smugness, the value of two-partyism seems so great.

This is traditional two-party dogma. Despite his love of the two-party system, Sorauf was compelled to acknowledge: "We may well see the repeated emergence of third parties as expressions of deeper discontent with the parties and American society." Actually, the above statements were in the third edition of the book in 1976, but none of this thinking is in the seventh edition of 1992. What happened? Was it no longer fashionable to link the two-party system to democracy? Or had events over nearly two decades caused a less positive view of the two-party system? The later edition said: "Assertions that political parties are essential to or the keystone of American democracy may or may not be true, but simply as assertions they advance our understanding of politics and parties very little."

Know this: Contemporary third-parties usually see fusion as critical to their success. Indeed, where fusion has been allowed, third-parties have sometimes played a critical role, either in electing candidates supporting their key issues or causing the major parties to modify some of their positions. Here are some examples of third-party successes, often resulting from the benefits of having the fusion option:

- New York's Conservative Party in 1994 provided the margin of victory for Republican Governor George E. Pataki. Its support of term limits was instrumental in the 1996 defeat of proposed changes in New York City. President Ronald Reagan once remarked: "The Conservative Party has established itself as a preeminent force in New York politics and an important part of our political history."

- New York's Working Families Party, formed in 1998, produced the votes in 2001 necessary for the victory of Bill Lindsay running for the Suffolk County legislature. In 2003, the party, on its own, elected Letita James to the New York City Council; she was the first council member elected solely on a third-party line since the 1970s.

- Through fusion candidates, the Libertarian Party has done the best in New Hampshire in getting candidates elected to the state legislature.

Currently, the New Party, founded in 1992, says that "We believe that by building progressive fusion-based political parties on a state-by-state basis, we can invigorate electoral democracy in our country, demonstrate that it is possible to build minor parties that engage in serious electoral competition, and effectively force consideration of progressive public policy into electoral debates and the public arena."

Consider the views of the Working Families Party:

> Our democracy is in trouble. ...And most New Yorkers—like most Americans—are fed up with the narrow choices offered by the Democrats and Republicans. Polls show that 60% of voters would like to have a new political party of just the sort we're building—a party for working people and their children. ...What fusion allows us to do is build a third party incrementally, step by step.

You can see how important fusion is where it is allowed and practiced. If only the Supreme Court had valued political competition over the status quo two-party duopoly. Many polls have found that a majority of Americans want a third party. In commenting about public attitudes in the 1994 congressional elections, the *New York Times* said that the political mood "seemed driven not by particular issues, so much as a nagging sense that both parties are equally paralyzed by the influence of wealthy special interests."

In realty, two-party loyalty and membership has become less and less appealing. For the 2000 election cycle only 3 percent of Americans worked for a party or candidate, only 9 percent gave money to help a campaign, and only 10 percent put a sticker on their car or wore a button. What William Greider said in *Who Will Tell The People* about the Democratic Party holds equally for the Republican Party:

> The Democratic Party, as a political organization, is no longer quite real itself. The various strands of personal communication and loyalty that once made it representative and responsive to the people are gone. It exists as a historical artifact, an organizational fiction. ...It acts neither as a faithful mediator between citizens and the government nor as the forum for policy debate and resolution nor even as a structure around which political power can accumulate. It functions mainly as a mail drop for political money. ... Like candidates who run on the party label for convenience, voters would say their registration is a matter of historical necessity, not conviction.

When you add up all the registered voters who do not select either of the two major parties and all the eligible voters who have not registered, you have a majority of Americans. Yet the two-party duopoly has controlled which candidates the media focus on, defining the only practical choice. Note that the Supreme Court in 1998 held that an independent candidate for Congress did not have the right to be in a debate on a public television station [*Arkansas Educational Television Commission v. Forbes*]. The public did not have a right to hear the independent candidate on their public airways! Sounds like another political decision.

Without third-parties and real competition of exciting ideas, politics is not intellectually stimulating, nor interesting enough to attract mistrusting Americans.

Graduating from the Electoral College

Our democracy and Constitution are far from perfect. We should more frequently consider how democracy changes. James Madison saw the future:

> We are free today substantially, but the day will come when our Republic will be an impossibility. It will be an impossibility because wealth will be concentrated in the hands of a few. …when the wealth of the nation will be in the hands of a few, then we must rely upon the wisdom of the best elements in the country to readjust the laws of the nation to the changed conditions.

Today, with wealth concentrated in few hands and remarkably changed conditions, more courage is needed to "readjust" our laws.

The Electoral College is the ultimate status quo, a constitutionally mandated system in use for over 200 years. With it, there is a fundamental inequality for Americans. The Supreme Court has determined in other contexts that the Constitution's equal protection clause requires one person, one vote. Not so with the Electoral College. In the current system, the states' electoral votes on a per capita basis vary enormously, with a higher per capita allocation in small, low population states. Citizens in big states each have just a fraction of an electoral vote. There is a difference of a factor of four in the per person electoral vote intensity across the spectrum of states, mostly because of the standard two senators per state. Sure, original concerns about not letting big states control the federal government were appropriate. But now giving small states too much influence is just as important.

It took the Supreme Court until the early 1960s with its decisions on reapportionment to compel states to give voters equal representation, before which low population and usually Republican rural districts produced Republican control of state legislatures, and after which urban populations with more African-Americans produced more Democratic controlled legislatures. Why not extend the same one person, one vote doctrine to the Electoral College?

On this basis alone, there should be more interest in finding an alternative to the Electoral College, particularly since the presidential election of 2000. For the third time, the winner with the most electoral votes did not have the most popular votes nationwide. A USA Today/CNN/Gallup poll in December 2000 found that 59 percent of Americans supported elimination of the Electoral College.

People have caught on. In every presidential election, millions of votes do not matter, because the candidate who received the majority in a state gets all of the state's electoral votes. Winner takes all means many voters are ignored. In states with close elections, nearly half of voters on the losing side have their votes cancelled out, because electoral votes are not divided in proportion to the actual vote distribution. In presidential campaigns, a few "battleground" states having key electoral votes deemed up-for-grabs by candidates get campaign attention and visits, despite public funding for a national election. No wonder so few Americans vote. We have a nation of obedient, socially disconnected, time-poor, and cynical consumers, not enthusiastically engaged citizens.

Another fault with the Electoral College is that individual electors have voted for a candidate who didn't win the vote in the election; they are called "faithless electors." There have been nine cases in the past 60 years, just a tiny percent, however, of some 30,000 electors. The two parties create slates of electors who are not much of a risk, because they are major party contributors and supporters, elites. So defectors are far and few between. In 24 states, electors are legally free to vote their conscience and ignore the will of the voters, and in the other 26, they are required by state law to follow the popular vote. Legal experts say such state laws are unconstitutional and all electors are really free agents.

In 2000, before the final Supreme Court (political) decision to settle the presidential election, some people openly argued that several Republican electors should vote for Al Gore, the winner of the popular vote. If just three electors would have done so—just one percent of the Republican electors—Gore would have become president, and absolutely nothing could have been done about it. The Electoral College's fate would probably have been sealed because of screams about the injustice from Republicans and equally vociferous claims from Democrats that overturning the archaic Electoral College was proper.

In August 2004, the *New York Times* editorialized "Abolish the Electoral College," a reversal of its previous position. Why? Because the president could "be a candidate who lost the popular vote." "The majority does not rule and every vote is not equal—those are reasons enough for scrapping the system," said the *Times*. Also noted were: the bias in favor of small states, the undue campaign emphasis on swing states, and the potential for electors to switch sides.

In contrast, Ohio State University Professor Peter M. Shane had an article in the *Washington Post* about repairing the Electoral College rather than scrapping it. It showed status quo thinking and advocacy for tinkering rather than serious change. He said that the winner-take-all approach was good because it "bolsters the two-party system, which many think is the basis for our long history of relative political stability." Our political stability keeps us stuck on stupid, because our two-party system effectively narrows the range of debate, making sure that the stability is slanted in favor of those who rule. Stability should not be the slave of the two-party status quo. We can have national stability along with active political dissent that challenges the two-party duopoly.

Alas, protection of the two-party system is widely supported. In fact, the next day's lead editorial in the *Washington Post* was about the Electoral College. [A game played by newspapers is to solicit or select an op-ed article that reflects their point of view as a set-up for a subsequent editorial.] While saying that "it is time for serious discussion about reforming our presidential election system," the paper criticized direct election by popular vote because "Such a system could also encourage independent candidacies that would weaken the two-party system." What unfounded reverence for the two-party system. Anyone who fears third-parties opposes fixing our republic, which is especially disheartening when our free press feels this way.

The anachronistic Electoral College must be a prime target for status quo busting. Exactly what change is made is open to honest discussion. A constitutional change to replace the Electoral College with using direct popular voting is probably the best option, yet is awfully difficult. Rarely mentioned was the 1969 serious bipartisan effort to abolish the Electoral College. The House of Representatives overwhelmingly passed such a constitutional amendment calling for direct popular election. President Nixon and a substantial majority of the Senate favored it. But a Senate filibuster killed it. In 1977, President Carter proposed the same amendment, but it too died in Congress before it could be sent out for ratification by 2/3rds of the states. These defeats demonstrate the ability of the two-party duopoly to protect itself.

An easier way is for states to decide to proportion their electoral votes according to the popular vote. Also, requiring only a plurality of the popular vote in the Electoral College would promote growth in third-parties, while a majority requirement favors the current two-party duopoly. Another good idea is to eliminate the number of senators from the total of state electoral votes to better equalize the population basis for electoral votes based solely on the number of state members in the Houses of Representatives.

One-Two-Three-...Someone Wins

An election reform with strong support and a track record of use is Instant Runoff Voting (IRV); it applies whenever there are more than two candidates for an office and could be an important contribution to strengthening democracy. Here's how it works: Voters have ballots that allow them to rank candidates in order of choice—1, 2, 3, and so on. If any candidate receives a majority of first-choice votes, then that candidate is elected. If not, then the last place candidate is eliminated from the next, automatic and simulated round, in which all top-choice votes are counted again. If a top-choice candidate gets a majority, that candidate wins. If not, the last place top-choice vote-getter is eliminated, and another round of top-choice votes is simulated. Whenever a voter's initial top choice is eliminated, their next lower ranked choice moves up, and so on as rounds proceed. This explains why IRV has been upheld by courts. This sounds a lot more complicated then it really is with today's voting equipment and computer systems.

The intrinsic advantage of this method is that no candidate ever becomes a winner with less than a majority of voters' support. In other words, plurality winners are prevented. Also eliminated are separate runoff elections to determine a winner among the top two vote-getters. This is important for two reasons. Voter turnout can drop precipitously for runoff elections, allowing someone to win with relatively few votes as compared to turnout in the original election, and they cost significant more money for governments and candidates. With IRV, there is just one election that is guaranteed to produce a majority winner.

IRV has been chosen by many government and private entities, including: Australia to elect members of its House of Representatives, Ireland to elect its president, London to elect its mayor, San Francisco to elect its mayor and other positions, Burlington, Vermont to elect its mayor, Utah Republicans to select congressional nominees at its state convention, the American Political Science Association to elect its president, and the Academy of Motion Picture Arts and Sciences to determine nominations for Oscars. Some politicians have publicly supported IRV, including: 1980 independent presidential candidate John B. Anderson, Senator John McCain, former Vermont Governor Howard Dean, Ralph Nader, and Congressman Jesse Jackson Jr.

From a voter and democracy perspective, IRV gives voters more power and freedom, because they can express a range of choices. IRV will likely increase voter turnout, because citizens will feel that their vote is not wasted. There is no guarantee that third-party candidates have a better chance of winning. But in many respects third-party loyalists gain more respect by the major two-party candidates who become concerned about obtaining a high ranking that could help them if they fail to achieve a majority in the initial round.

Let Democracy Ring On Our Airwaves

At the federal level, the Alliance for Better Campaigns has been campaigning for an "Our Democracy, Our Airwaves" federal law. The goal is to require television broadcasters to provide increased candidate issue discussions in the two weeks before elections, and to provide financing for federal candidates to buy radio and TV ads. Radio and TV stations have increasingly focused on campaign coverage rather than substantive issues. Sixty organizations have supported the campaign, as well as former presidents Jimmy Carter and Gerald Ford, Walter Cronkite, and Senators John McCain and Russell Feingold. A 2002 poll found that 73 percent of the public supports free airtime to candidates to discuss issues. Time for issue discussions is needed. In 2000, just 20 percent of gubernatorial, senatorial and congressional debates held were aired by a network-affiliated local TV station. A good new law would let broadcast stations choose their own formats to air two hours per week of issue discussions.

A substantial sum of money would be raised every two years by charging radio and television broadcasters a small fee, less than 1 percent of their gross annual revenues, which are over $60 billion. A fee of just .615 percent would generate $750 million. Licensed broadcasters have paid nothing for their rights to use the public airways, and they earn profit margins of 30 to 50 percent. So it is reasonable to get a small fraction of their profits for serving the public interest. The money would provide vouchers that can be used to place advertisements on radio and TV. Candidates would use the vouchers to buy ads on broadcast stations of their choice; they would qualify by raising relatively small contributions. In a bill introduced in 2003, candidates would have to raise $25,000, not counting contributions above $250 and there would be limits on use of personal and family money. Qualifying parties could obtain $100 million. Third parties could qualify by having candidates in a certain number of House and Senate races. The idea is to give more candidates more airtime. Now, only two-party candidates in important elections can afford much media advertising. As with CMCE, Our Democracy, Our Airwaves must be seen by Americans as another tool to save their democracy. This option might be viewed as a mechanism to raise funds for CMCE or as a follow-up option should CMCE fail.

Primary Perplexity

Confusingly, there are three types of primary elections to select candidates for a general election:

Direct or closed party primaries: Only citizens who have registered a party affiliation are qualified to vote *in that party's primary*. Parties, especially third-parties, favor the direct party primary to assure getting their candidates on the general election ballot.

Open or crossover primaries: Regardless of party registration, citizens can choose to vote for a ballot of *any party*. Crossover primaries dilute the power of the two major parties; more moderate politicians can attract support from the other party's members and independents, and have a better chance of reaching the general election ballot.

Blanket primaries: Originally, every voter received the same ballot and did not have to choose one party across all offices. They could choose different party candidates across all ballot races. However, after California voters adopted a blanket primary system in 1996, the U.S. Supreme Court ruled against it in 2000. A Washington blanket primary system used for about 70 years was also stopped by court action in 2003. The key constitutional issue is whether a blanket primary nominates *party* candidates for the general election; if so, it is *unconstitutional*. Louisiana's non-partisan blanket primary system, with no candidates having a party affiliation, is constitutional, however, and became a model for initiatives in Washington and California. With less visibility, third-party candidates are disadvantaged in this non-partisan version. And is essentially a step backward for democracy.

To sum up: For third-parties, the open or cross-over primary offers an advantage, because disenchanted Republicans and Democrats can vote for a third-party candidate and a greater number of votes in the primary can help bring more public and media attention for the general election. Certainly, the non-partisan blanket primary is the worst possible option for third-party candidates and for restoring American democracy.

In 2004, Washington state voters considered an initiative that would create a new non-partisan blanket primary. A large array of groups opposed the initiative, including major newspapers, the League of Women Voters, the Democratic and Republican parties, the current and several past governors, and also the Libertarian and Green parties. Opponents said that "third parties, minor parties and even independents will be eliminated from the general election ballot." They noted that in the 2000 election the 180,000 voters who chose third party candidates in the general election would not have had that choice if the initiative had been law. And in the prior 12 years in 24 statewide races, 80 percent had more than two candidates in the general election. Here's what supported the two-party duopoly's *opposition* to the proposed non-partisan blanket primary: In one-third of elections for governor in the prior 25 years, the general election candidates would have been from the same party. In the ten years prior to 2004, two Republicans in 13 legislative races and two Democrats in 12 races would not have advanced to the general election. For those who wanted political choice the initiative was a bad idea.

The single proponent group spent $450,000 on creating and supporting the initiative called the "People's Choice Initiative," about ten times more money than spent by the opposition. The proponents touted the advantage of voting "for the person, not the party." Opponents said that it should be called the "People's Lack of Choice Initiative." What did Washington voters decide? *They accepted the non-partisan blanket primary*, with 60 percent voting for it. A court challenge was assured. In that 2004 election, Libertarian candidates in three elections garnered enough votes to decide the election, including the Washington governor's race in which the Democrat candidate won by just 129 votes after the third recount. The Libertarian candidate received 63,000 votes. Surely the Republican Party was not happy.

The *Seattle Post-Intelligencer* editorialized that voters wanted to "stick it" to the Republican and Democratic parties. Public antipathy toward the two-party duopoly and the pro-initiative messages of "people's choice" and "voting for the person, not the party" resonated with voters. However, relatively few voters in Washington vote for third-party candidates. Thus, preserving third-party access to general election ballots did not prevail and democracy was weakened.

In 2004, Californians faced a similar primary choice. A business-oriented group spent $2 million to get Proposition 62 on the ballot, which would create a non-partisan (anti-third party) blanket primary system. To complicate things, the state legislature put Proposition 60 on the ballot, which would create a traditional direct, closed party system that would allow third-party candidates to reach the general election. There were large groups of organizations behind Props 60 and 62. As in Washington, third parties were against Proposition 62, as were the state's two major parties. Also, as in Washington, those against Prop 62 and for Prop 60 were concerned about the impact on third-parties. The *Orange County Register* said: "Ironically, Prop. 62 would dramatically limit choices, because no third-party candidates would be on the final ballot unless they were among the top vote-getters. Third-parties are rarely competitive in elections, but they play a valuable role by bringing important issues before the electorate. Their voice would be effectively eliminated." The *Desert Sun* also pointed out that if Prop 62 had been in effect for the 2002 election, nearly 6 million votes for third-party candidates could not have been cast.

Those for Prop 62 and against Prop 60 focused on the promise of more moderate politicians (from the two-party duopoly) reaching the general election ballot. They asserted that they were opposing the status quo, because they argued it would promote more partisan moderates reaching the general election.

What did California voters decide? Californians *rejected* the non-partisan blanket primary option and passed Prop 60 by a 2 to 1 margin, preserving the ability of third-parties to be visible in California elections. Prop 62 lost, but by a much smaller 8 percent margin, probably because in the final weeks of the campaign Governor Arnold Schwarzenegger backed it, showing his anti-third party bias. Rich "big names" like Schwarzenegger see blanket primaries as safer ways to reach general election ballots than being chosen by voters affiliated with their party. In the end, democracy was strengthened.

Also, in 2003, New York City voters showed their penchant for healthy democracy when they rejected a non-partisan blanket initiative by a 70 to 30 vote. One argument against it was that it would favor self-financed, wealthy and celebrity candidates. Wealthy Mayor Michael Bloomberg had spearheaded the losing effort.

Involuntary Democracy

For voting, forget right and privilege. Some things must be legally required of citizens. Among 172 nations, the U.S. ranked 139th in the percentage of eligible citizens voting.

"Our democracy is becoming obese, the body politic grows fat and sluggish, through under-use and lack of vigorous exercise." So said United Kingdom pensions minister Malcolm Wicks in 2004, and it also applies to the U.S.

Research by Frederick Solt found that people living in countries with compulsory voting are roughly twice as likely to believe that their government is responsive to the public's needs and 2.8 times as likely to vote as compared to citizens in countries without compulsory voting.

So, there is good cause for supporting an additional and seemingly "radical" reform—compulsory voting for citizens. Despite its inattention here a Gallup survey in 1965 found that about 25 percent of people supported compulsory voting, and an ABC News survey in 2004 found that 21 percent said such a law would be good. Just imagine what public support might be if a well framed campaign for it was conducted. One result might be Republicans and Democrats running "Don't Make Me Vote" campaigns.

Though over 20 countries have compulsory voting, including many strong democracies, this option has not been pursued in the U.S. One reason is that the two-party duopoly does not really want large voter turnout that they cannot control; they want turnout from narrow groups predisposed to vote for them. But compulsory voting works. When Australia adopted it in 1924 turnouts increased from under 50 percent to a consistent 94 to 96 percent. Note that Australia uses a form of Instant Runoff Voting. Conversely, when the Netherlands eliminated compulsory voting in 1970 voting turnouts plunged from 90 percent to less than 50 percent. Enforcement is mostly minimal, but it is necessary. Some nations levy a small fine for not voting. In Australia it is about $35 but judges accept most excuses except "I forgot" and "I was busy." In a recent election when over 12 million Australians voted nationally, 500,000 non-voters received "please explain" letters. Regardless of fines it works, apparently because a social norm results. When voting reforms offer real options, nonvoting should be viewed as reprehensible, socially deviant behavior, unlike today's rational non-voting behavior of Americans.

The usual argument against compulsory voting is that it is inconsistent with personal freedom. This is ridiculous. We have compulsory education, jury duty, and taxes; these are more onerous than turning out to vote periodically. True, voting is a constitutionally protected right that suggests the option to not exercise the right. But voting is a "preservative right" that citizens must exercise to protect other constitutional rights. When the right to vote is not used, citizens surrender their sovereign control of their representative government. Many and probably most non-voters surrender their control because they no longer believe that voting within the two-party controlled political system matters. Yet this freedom to not vote weakens American democracy by strengthening forces that undermine it. The decline of American democracy is both a cause and consequence of low voter turnout.

Another argument against bringing most non-voters out is that there will be a lot of uneducated and uninformed people voting. In 1994 when the Republicans took over Congress and Newt Gingrich became Speaker a popular bumper sticker read, "Newt happens when only 37 percent of Americans vote." Research found, however, that among voters lacking a high school diploma just 30 percent voted for Republican House candidates, as compared to 62 percent with college degrees. What if the turnout would have been much greater? Wattenberg has shown that the Republicans would not have been victorious in 1994, prompting him to conclude that "Such findings regrettably make it less likely that anything will be done to increase turnout rates in America." It also shows why Republicans have relied on turning out more evangelical Christians rather than turning out all Americans.

For a better democracy we need better citizenship through compulsory voting. It can reduce the power of the two-party duopoly because many previously non-voting disillusioned citizens when facing a ballot will choose third-party candidates and exercise their political freedom. Citizen responsibility trumps the right to abstain. Anyway, with compulsory voting, citizens can still do what they want with their secret ballot—especially not voting for any or all candidates and ballot measures if the NOTA option is also used. Constitutionally, compulsory voting is actually just compulsory turnout, and the Supreme Court has ruled that voting is not an expression of free speech. Now, nonvoting can be seen as complacency, apathy, or dissent.

All things considered, compulsory voting is a no-brainer. It is a proven way to legitimize the meaning of "the consent of the governed." Australian Greg Barnes said his country is "a feisty and engaged democracy as a result of compulsory voting." Exactly what we need. J. F. Godet-Calogeras said "Voting is mandatory in Belgium because it is considered one's responsibility to society." Do Americans have less responsibility?

Justice Oliver Wendell Holmes Jr. said: "Taxes are what we pay for civilized society." Let's add: Voting is what we do for effective democracy. To those who find this idea of compulsory voting obnoxious, unnecessary or undemocratic, I say: consider how difficult it will be— even with the other election reforms—to overcome the cultural inertia about voting. Compulsory voting is definitely no substitute for greatly expanding political choice and competition to attract people to vote and it should NOT be pursued without other significant reforms. The best way to look at this reform is as a complement to all or some of the other election reforms presented here. Besides, it really works.

Futurize Your Thinking

When Kevin Zeese decided to run for the U.S. Senate in 2006 as an independent in Maryland he made the case for challenging the two-party duopoly:

> I want Americans to look back in 50 to 100 years from now—when we have a vivid multi-party democracy and say—"can you imagine in the last Century how there were only two major parties and dozens of colas? Boy, were we an immature democracy!

Even without necessary electoral system reforms he was committed to doing what was right. "The only way to create the politics we want is by challenging the corrupt system in place," he said. Amen. But exactly how much challenging and changing do we need?

It boggles the mind to imagine the impact on the nation of implementing *all* of the reforms discussed above. But that is exactly what is needed to re-legitimize American democracy. Without constitutional changes, nor total reliance on the federal government, the entire electoral system would be turned around to favor a more honest and politically diverse representative government. Individual reforms have some organized support, but virtually no group advocates a large set of mutually reinforcing and largely complimentary electoral reforms.

Here again are the reforms:

1. Expand the use of Clean Money, Clean Election programs.
2. Provide a None of the Above option on ballots.
3. Permit fusion candidates to promote third-party candidates.
4. Reform the Electoral College or its use by states.
5. Provide Instant Runoff Voting.
6. Pass the "Our Democracy, Our Airwaves" federal law.
7. For primary elections, support an open or cross-over primary that favors third-parties.
8. Make voting compulsory after other reforms

Now, there is fruitless competition among separate reform movements as if just one reform would be enough to reinvent American democracy. We should not be asking people to choose between, for example, IRV or NOTA or CMCE—all with their own advocacy groups—as if obtaining just one reform will do the trick for restoring American democracy. Fixing the republic is too big a job to think that only one or two reforms will turn democracy's arrow up. Today, many well-intentioned reform efforts are marginalized from the start because so many people know in their hearts that just one change will not do the job. This book is apparently the first to present and advocate that many reforms should be fought for and adopted through a unified effort—an ideal priority for a new third party. If one acknowledges the stubborn resistance and POWER of the corrupt political-business system, especially the two-party duopoly, to protect the status quo, surely a full set of democracy-strengthening electoral reforms is necessary.

Taken together, the eight reforms represent enormous change. This is not about pushing for one gigantic change all at once, however. It is about seeing the connections between many different efforts and their individual importance to a collective program of all of them to achieve the desired restoration of American democracy. This approach has the advantage of struggle over time on many fronts with no possibility of one single defeat killing the entire effort. The eventual whole would be greater than the sum of the individual reforms. See them being implemented piecemeal, in doable bite sized chunks spread geographically and temporally—BUT always within a larger framed national goal of implementing all of them to achieve their collective impact. This democracy-fixing "movement" must not be about individual technical reforms; it must be about fixing the republic through democratic means. It must be visibly passionate. Uniting separate activist dissenters and reform groups must be achieved if Americans are to be united behind a new competitive alternative to the two-party duopoly. Millions of Americans must perceive that if they were all passed, our democracy would be radically different and dramatically better. They must see that individually and collectively the reforms are worthy of careful consideration and dedicated effort to implement them.

Democracy-rescue is serious business. We must think in terms of presenting to the public and to the power elites a vision of large and dramatic change to restore American democracy and sovereignty to we the people. Let the right-wing conservatives, theocrats, corporate lobbyists, Republican and Democratic autocrats, and hateful fake patriots on talk radio and cable TV see a tsunami of democracy-reform coming at them. The function of democracy must be to produce active dissenters. Consider the conclusions of Cass R. Sunstein in *Why Societies Need Dissent*:

> It is usual to think that those who conform are serving the general interest and that dissenters are antisocial, even selfish. …But in an important respect, the usual thought has things backwards. Much of the time, it is the individual's interest to follow the crowd, but in the social interest for the individual to say and do what he thinks best. Well-functioning societies take steps to discourage conformity and to promote dissent. They do this partly to protect the rights of dissenters, but mostly to protect interests of their own.

Political tension in America is palpable even without the full blossoming of the discontent felt by so many Americans who have not yet said and done publicly what they think is best for our nation. What say you? Is the United States a well-functioning society promoting dissent? If not, then the interests of its citizens are not being protected. As Sunstein also said: "When injustice, oppression, and mass violence are able to continue, it is almost always because good people are holding their tongues." Loosen your tongue, spit out your outrage and infect others.

Chapter 8

Ballots Over Bullets: From Misrepresentation to Popular Sovereignty

> As I would not be a *slave*, so I would not be a *master*. This expresses my idea of democracy. Whatever differs from this, to the extent there is a difference, is no democracy.
>
> —Abraham Lincoln

> Every government degenerates when trusted to the rulers of the people alone.
>
> —Thomas Jefferson

Coups overturn governments with relatively few people, but a nonviolent revolution to restore a democracy requires many citizens. There is rightfully an enormous amount of discontent, disillusionment and disgust with government, big business, the mainstream media, and the relentless barking commercialism that invades our lives. When representative democracy fails we must seek direct democracy if we reject violent overthrow of the government. When corrupt "public servants" and their special interest partners have become our masters we the people must assert ourselves. Many election reforms will only be reached through citizen-driven ballot measures.

Better than Kicking Politicians is Sidestepping Them

Citizens deserve a means for sidestepping politicians and the institutions they control when they no longer serve the public interest. Local and state ballot initiatives and referenda provide a political safety valve. They are another check in our constitutional system of checks and balances based on power sharing among the legislative, executive, and judiciary branches. The ballot measure is a key tool to rise above the inherent constraints of the illusory political system.

It all comes down to whether you truly believe in the sovereignty of the people. If you do, then you must accept the principle that our republic with its representative democracy must honor the ultimate right of the people to express their sovereignty. The courts have many times considered the constitutionality of direct democracy and repeatedly established that the combination of sovereign citizen lawmaking and representative government fits a republican form of government. Leading Americans from diverse political perspectives have time and again expressed their support for the initiative and referendum process.[2] Here are some important endorsements:

> Woodrow Wilson: "We are cleaning house and in order to clean house the one thing we need is a good broom. Initiative and referendum are good brooms."

> Grover Norquist: "Organized special interest groups prefer that power be concentrated in state and national capitals, because it is much easier for them to influence when it is concentrated in the hands of a small group in one place. The initiative process is one of the very few effective tools citizens have for decentralizing power."

> Dick Armey: "It is very difficult to get good new ideas to be considered by Legislative bodies. New ideas have to be taken to the people. That's why we need the initiative process."

> Robert M. La Follette: "For years the American people have been engaged in a terrific struggle with the allied forces of organized wealth and political corruption... The people must have in reserve new weapons for every emergency, if they are to regain and preserve control of their government... Through the initiative, referendum and recall the people in any emergency can absolutely control."

The current failure of our representative government because of endemic corruption, manipulated incumbency, and misrepresentation more than ever—perhaps since the founding of our nation—justifies more use of ballot measures to assert popular sovereignty over our government.

A special dimension to this issue is the decline in Americans' support for both major political parties. Actually, outright antipathy toward the

---

[2]For clarification: anything on a ballot other than a candidate for office is a ballot measure; initiative refers to a petition process that enables citizens to propose new legislation on the ballot in a general election; some initiatives are for constitutional amendments; in some states initiatives must first pass through the legislature; referendum is a petition to call up existing laws for a vote

two parties has been growing. In the 1950s and early 1960s 70 to 75 percent of Americans identified with one of the two parties which has decreased in recent years to 60 percent. People see political parties as the institution most affected by corruption. Only 56 Americans believe parties are necessary to democracy, according to the Comparative Study of Electoral Systems. Worse, only 38 percent believe that political parties care what people think. Distrusting Americans are less likely to participate in party politics, 10 percent versus 26 percent for trusting people. This is what Russell J. Dalton and Steven Weldon of the University of California, Irvine concluded in a 2005 paper:

> In short, contemporary publics appear to view political parties as democracy's necessary evil, needed for running elections and organizing government, but they have doubts about how political parties represent their interests in this process.

In our corrupt pseudo-democracy, ballot initiatives are smart weapons for citizens to target problems and reclaim their power, to sidestep unresponsive and corrupt legislatures. Noam Chomsky in *Z Magazine* captured the essence of the problem:

> As usual, the [2004] electoral campaigns were run by the PR industry, which in its regular vocation sells toothpaste, life-style drugs, automobiles, and other commodities. Its guiding principle is deceit. ...As in the fake markets constructed by the PR industry, so also in the fake democracy they run, the public is hardly more than an irrelevant onlooker, apart from the appeal of carefully constructed images that have only the vaguest resemblance to reality.

How can Americans become relevant? Ballot initiatives help courageous citizens do battle with corrupt forces. It is Americans' major opportunity for civic power through direct democracy. It comes down to ballots or bullets to save our democracy. Ballot measures are held sacrosanct by most Americans and they have increased in recent years. They were largely responsible for term limits for elected officials in many local and state governments. Many Americans believe what Benjamin Franklin said in 1787:

> In free governments, the rulers are the servants and the people their superiors and sovereigns. For the former, therefore, to return among the latter is not to degrade but to promote them.

How many politicians today, when they are voted out of office or reach their term limit, feel they are being promoted from servant to sovereign? When elected officials now leave office they either seek another elected position, or work for the corporate or special interests that once supported them to strengthen the corrupt political-corporate system. In this nation's early years Americans understood that they did not elect *their* representatives to sell off *their* sovereignty. Time is long overdue for Americans to remember and internalize this understanding. In our republic, when we the people lose our sovereignty we lose our democracy. The correct view is that sovereignty resides in the people, not in government. When democracy is authentic government is subservient to the people and elected officials have a duty to determine and respect the current will of the people not just past expressions of the public will.

Research has found that voter turnout is higher in states with citizens' ballot measures. A study by NYPIRG found that between 1976 and 1996 the average turnout of eligible voters in initiative and referendum states was 52 percent and in other states averaged 46.5 percent.

When you cannot trust your public servants because they act like masters, what can you do? A 1999 survey of Washington residents found that 84 percent favored state initiatives. A 1997 survey of Californians found that 74 percent favored state ballot propositions, and another survey found that 51 percent cited initiatives as the main reason for voting in 1996, compared to 36 percent citing the presidential contest. A 1998 national poll found 64 percent supported state initiatives.

In the spring of 2001 a national poll conducted by the non-profit Portrait of America asked some revealing questions about ballot measures; the findings were sobering:

- 65.5 percent believed that, all other things being equal, voters were more likely than the legislature to produce laws in the public interest.

- 59.6 percent believed that if an organization supported a measure that would improve the way government works, voters would be more receptive than the legislature.

- 66.9 percent believed that when legislators propose regulations on petitioning they are trying to preserve their power, not protect the public.

These results show how disillusioned Americans are about trusting government to make things better. Rational, open-minded Americans watching what government has and has not done over recent decades cannot possibly have much confidence in it. Will they stay irrelevant and powerless? If not, then the answer lies in citizens' ballot measures.

Experimenting In Our State Laboratories

Initiatives and referenda have a long history in our states, over 100 years. Only 27 states now have some type of opportunity for citizens bypassing the legislature. Much more can and should be done to expand these opportunities. The Initiative and Referendum Institute website provides detailed information on states.

The recent upsurge in using ballot measures started in 1978 because of "two old geezers" who placed Proposition 13—to roll back and cap property taxes—on the California ballot. It passed with a 65 percent majority, despite opposition by all state political leaders. Howard Jarvis at 75 years old and Paul Gann at 66 years old had no formal power base, but they gave Californians what the legislature refused—tax relief. They tapped into real public dissatisfaction, an important lesson for others.

In 2005, Californians faced eight ballot initiatives and, with a 40 percent voter turnout, rejected all of them, including four strongly fought for by the governor. A subsequent poll of special election voters by the Public Policy Institute of California found some interesting views about ballot measures and California government:

- 53 percent were satisfied with the ballot initiative process
- 48 percent thought the public policy decisions made by initiatives were probably better than policies made by the governor and state legislature, versus 30 percent that thought they were probably worse
- 55 percent believed the wording of initiatives was too complicated and confusing
- 83 percent thought too much money was spent on initiative campaigns
- 85 percent favored more public disclosure of funding sources for

signature gathering and campaigns

* 77 percent favored both sides of initiatives participating in television debates

* only 17 percent believed that they could trust elected officials to do what's right always or most of the time

* 78 percent felt that state government is run by a few big interests rather than for the benefit of all of the people

Direct democracy was victorious in Colorado. The Taxpayer Bill of Rights (TABOR) constitutional amendment passed in 1992 with 54 percent voter support. It required a popular vote for all tax increases and linked the annual increase in local and state spending and debt to changes in population and inflation. Surplus tax revenues had to be refunded and billions of dollars have already been returned to taxpayers. Despite data showing many positive impacts of TABOR, politicians and special interests kept trying to regain more traditional power to expand government spending. A 2005 ballot measure was designed to let the state raise taxes with rising revenues and to withhold refunds for five years, some $3.7 billion. Most of the political establishment (including Governor Bill Owens an original TABOR supporter), most newspapers, the business community, and others backed the measure. Supporters spent $7.5 million on their campaign. State and national libertarian and fiscal conservative groups campaigned against it, arguing that the state did not really need the money. Douglas Bruce wrote the TABOR plan in 1992 and said: "They want to 'fix' TABOR the way a vet would 'fix' your pet: render it impotent." Would Colorado residents trust state government to spend more taxpayer money wisely? Yes, but barely. It passed by 52 to 48 percent; a second ballot measure to allow state borrowing of $2.1 billion for various uses failed with 51 percent rejecting it. TABOR movements in other states have attracted support, as well as a federal version, but the 2005 vote would surely be used to fight the efforts.

Oregon has used ballot measures more than any other state, including one that replaced polling places with voting by mail. Oregonians know why. Lloyd Marbet said, "business interests control the legislature, lock, stock, and barrel." Kevin Mannix said: "If you have a heartfelt issue that can engender a lot of public support, it can't be hacked to death by special interests the way it can in the legislature."

Montgomery County, Maryland is also known for having many ballot initiatives. In October 2004, the *Washington Post* offered this observation on the three ballot measures that year: "[They] are opposed by most elected officials in the county because the measures would, they say, place undue restrictions on their ability to govern. Other activists and community groups find the proposals attractive for exactly that reason." The county executive and most council members joined a coalition of business, labor and other groups to form the Vote No Coalition to campaign against all three ballot questions. What exactly was so disliked by those in power and their supporters?

One proposition would prevent the County Council from overriding a property tax cap that limited increases to roughly the rate of inflation. Another would impose a limit of three four-year terms on council members and the county executive. The last would replace at-large council seats with district representatives. A former county executive and six-term council member said this about the third proposal: "I think this is a way to improve democracy and get people closer to their representatives and the representatives closer to the people they represent."

All three initiatives failed. Never underestimate the ability of slick politicians to scam people and get them to vote against their own interests.

The ballot initiative strategy for saving our democracy has become increasingly difficult. A large number of signatures on a petition must be obtained to meet legal requirements for placing a proposal on an election ballot. Governors and state legislatures often try to make it more difficult for citizens to get measures on ballots by requiring more signatures and less time for obtaining them. Also, courts can and have nullified ballot initiatives that voters passed. In 2000, the *Wall Street Journal* noted how courts in Arizona and Arkansas removed citizens' proposals from ballots. It editorialized that: "The ideas of representative government and the right of petition should be viewed as complementary, not antithetical. ...Notwithstanding brickbats from elected officials of both parties, the initiative process is overwhelmingly popular. Voters want a trump card over entrenched incumbents, who often feel free to ignore voters."

As Professor Arthur Lupia noted: "The typical ballot measure asks voters to choose one of two alternatives—the piece of legislation described on the ballot or the status quo policy." However, new laws can create problems. For example, more state spending may be needed, but without any new revenue generation created. Or revenue generation may be cut, without consideration to what government services will be harmed. Not thinking about such problems can doom a proposal, because the opposition will focus on them.

Money from corporate and special interests is often used to defeat worthy status quo busting measures. A California initiative to provide government sponsored medical insurance was defeated by massive industry spending. Wal-Mart has used ballot measures to overcome citizen opposition to big box stores, sometimes succeeding. Sometimes business goes directly to voters. The gaming industry has used initiatives to get gambling approved, for example.

Turning On the Faucet of Dissatisfaction

Individuals with the right message can move masses, because a force for good can push a status quo off its unstable equilibrium when a "tipping point" is reached. New American Revolutionaries must find others dissatisfied with the status quo. With a well-framed message direct democracy can be made to work. Pursuing the ballot measure option means taking risks. In the *York Daily Record*, in 2004, what Gerry Turner advised people who were thinking about running for public office is equally applicable to status quo busters:

> Every aspect of personal and political indignation that current office holders and opponents can arouse from your public and private life will be used as ammunition in the fight to maintain their political control. ... All that is required is that you be opposed to the status quo as dictated by the political power brokers. ...Hold tightly your self-esteem and core convictions. Follow your heart and work toward change. ...Our open political system has been hijacked by those who would destroy the process rather than build an inclusive methodology for the common good.

Reaching success may mean depending on volunteers to get the legally required number of signatures in a relatively short time before an election. However, the opposition often can greatly outspend citizen efforts. A necessary tactic is then to find people and groups willing to bankroll a worthy proposal. For example, the group Arizonans for Clean Elections Committee that successfully achieved CMCE reported that only $547 of a total of $891,718 came in amounts of $25 or less. The initiative for CMCE in Massachusetts cost $1,066,770, but almost 75 percent came in amounts of $10,000 or more. Interestingly, in both cases, the opposition apparently did not take the citizen initiatives seriously, because they spent only $53,002 in Arizona and $60,957 in Massachusetts. Of course, after the initiatives passed, efforts were mounted to overthrow CMCE, and succeeded in Massachusetts.

Columnist David S. Broder fears and condemns the broad use of ballot measures. In *Democracy Derailed* he acknowledged that "public impatience with the 'system' has grown" and that "Overwhelmingly, polls and interviews demonstrate that most Americans believe their elected officials look out first for themselves, then for their contributors, and put serving the public well down on their list of priorities." Broder dislikes the large amounts of money that now go into creating and winning ballot measures. Yet this is nothing compared to the spending on lobbying officials and political contributions to them. Broder's error is thinking that fixing government is possible by the electorate choosing better representatives. But this requires truly better candidates to vote for, not likely with the two-party duopoly.

A Bold Rocky Road Initiative

Here is an example of issue framing that recognized the big picture injustice but was pragmatically focused on a specific solution. In 2004, Rick Ridder, a Democrat, took on the job of getting a ballot initiative in Colorado that would replace the usual "winner take all" method of determining which presidential candidate gets the state's electoral votes. Ridder's effort was named Make Your Vote Count, an excellent framing of the basic issue.

His group succeeded in getting about twice the required number of petition signatures for a ballot measure that would apportion the state's electoral votes according to the candidate's share of the popular vote. Moreover, if approved, it would apply to the 2004 presidential election. The measure drew national attention, because if it succeeded it might spur a national move by states to change the way the Electoral College was used, bringing it closer to a direct popular vote, but without the need for a constitutional amendment.

Here are public statements by Ridder who knew how to take advantage of the media interest in the ballot measure:

- "This is an affirmation of the basic principle of one person, one vote. It makes every vote count, and it gives greater weight to the individual."

- "It makes your vote count. It gives people a sense of empowerment."

Ridder's messages gave Colorado voters a rational, self-serving basis for voting for the ballot measure. Their individual vote would mean more in close elections. The measure was supported by many organizations, including the state's Libertarian and Green parties. The push for change was anger at injustice and unfairness, and the pull was making every vote count.

Not surprisingly, the initiative was opposed by Colorado Governor Bill Owens and other top state Republicans, who organized themselves as Coloradans Against a Really Stupid Idea. They argued that if the measure had held in 2000 Al Gore would have been the victor. Both the Democrat and Republican national parties were not happy with the prospect that they might lose the option to focus presidential campaigning in a few battleground states. What a potential disaster: *All votes in all states would matter equally!*

USA Today editorialized in favor of the measure: "All-or-nothing systems disenfranchise millions of voters… The Colorado initiative shines a light on the path toward more democratic elections, in which every vote really does count." The *San Antonio Express-News* editorialized that: "Voters deserve a more direct voice in choosing the president with a system that doesn't disenfranchise those who disagree with the majority in their state."

A few weeks before the election, a federal lawsuit was filed by a Colorado businessman. It challenged the application of the amendment to the 2004 election. A week before the election a judge quickly dismissed the suit. The amendment stayed on the ballot, but lost in the election by 2 to 1. Too many big political names went against it and national attention to the measure caused many Colorado residents to feel uneasy. The attacks on the initiative as a radical act, however, were undercut by the fact that two states had already made a change. Maine in 1969 and Nebraska in 1992 chose to allot two electoral votes to the statewide winner and the rest to the winner in each congressional district.

Lesson: Even with a great message, initiatives serving the public interest are often defeated by well-financed opposition protecting the status quo. In many cases creating a ballot initiative invites a fight against rivals with deeper pockets.

Initiatives must also be based on evidence that the electorate is predisposed to favor the change because of unrequited anger. To act prematurely and lose is to kill the issue more effectively than any other failure. Framing of the issue and the proposed change should anticipate what opposing forces are likely to use in their campaign.

All things considered, we need to make it easier for citizens to place proposals on ballots as long as government barely represents public interests.

Short-Circuiting Congress

Below the radar is a longstanding movement to give all Americans the opportunity to obtain a better democracy at the national level. There have been over 100 attempts to amend the U.S. Constitution to provide national initiatives and referenda. That we still do not have that opportunity only reveals how the entrenched power elites do not want popular sovereignty to check the ineffectiveness and inefficiency of the federal government. Here is a good framing statement from the National Referendum Movement:

> We the people have an immutable right to settle our grievances against government via petition, an authority that is declared in both federal and state constitutions. In fact, this is the people's most important power because it is through redress that all other rights are protected. Put another way, it is the citizens' ability to redress grievances in a convenient, timely and effective manner that prevents representative government from becoming misrepresentative of the people's will.

Only five major democracies have never had a national referendum: India, Israel, Japan, the Netherlands, and the United States. The democracy with the greatest use of national initiatives is Switzerland, a remarkably stable society. Other countries giving their citizens ballot sovereignty include: Canada, England, Ireland, Italy, France, Denmark and South Africa.

What stands in the way of giving Americans back their sovereignty? Certainly it is what the people want. A 1997 poll found that 67 percent of Californians favored *national* initiatives. The 2001 Portrait of America poll found that 56.7 percent believed that there should be a similar process where citizens can place laws on the ballot nationwide.

The biggest recognized obstacle is amending our Constitution and the basic conflict of interest for the Congress. It is fascinating that when the Confederate States wrote their constitution they made one very interesting change from the U.S. Constitution. They revoked the authority of Congress to draft proposed amendments. Instead, a proposed amendment would go to ratification when 25 percent of the states passed resolutions supporting the same proposal, a method apparently supported by the Founders but subsequently subverted by Congress. This states approach can still be pursued and would be even more feasible if more states introduced initiative and referendum opportunities by changing their constitutions. Another idea is that after a proposal passed through the states and was then placed on all ballots in the next federal election passage of the new federal law or amendment would require a two-thirds popular vote to ensure that the rights of minorities were being respected.

The downhill slide of America's representative democracy creates exactly the right atmosphere for more vigorous pursuit of the opportunity for citizens to bypass Congress and use their constitutionally protected sovereignty to retake their government.

Unconventional Conventions

Sooner or later people want to know how democracy-minded citizens can join together, face to face, to make change. How can direct democracy take form? Other than ballot measures, another way is through constitutional conventions that usually involve ballot measures. Here are three recent cases of attempts to use citizen conventions.

Rhode Island has earned a reputation for political scandals and bad government. Rhode Island's constitution mandates that a call for a constitutional convention be made at least once every ten years, a very good idea. However, this was ignored so the last convention was in 1986. Robert Arruda, head of Operation Clean Government, worked for years to pass the 2004 ballot measure calling for a constitutional convention. He argued that "A constitutional convention challenges the status quo." The convention would bypass "the vested interests looking to keep the status quo," he said. The convention would prepare amendments for the public to vote on—an important check on runaway conventions, and citizens would run to be one of the 75 delegates to the convention—an important procedure to avoid cronyism through political appointments.

Republican Governor Don Carcieri strongly supported the convention ballot measure:

> When I took office, I promised to shake up Rhode Island's political system. The State House is filled with special interest groups, lobbyists, and political operatives that care only about furthering their own agenda. Constitutional Conventions bring us one step closer to government by the people and for the people. ...Rhode Island must convene a Constitutional Convention if we hope to provide the people of the Ocean State with the system of government they expect and deserve.

One issue the governor wanted the convention to consider was giving the governorship a budget line item veto; another was imposing term limits on legislators. His support was consistent with the results of studies by Syracuse University that Arruda cited:

- "Rhode Island is one of the worst managed state governments in the country—perennially so."

- "Rhode Island is among the least likely states to want to change" the way it operates

There were a large number of supporters for holding the convention, including several members of the state legislature. Former state Representative Rod Driver said: "A constitutional convention actually provides an opportunity to rein in some of the abuses we have suffered from the legislature and from the executive and judicial branches of state government."

Unexpectedly, a number of public interest groups opposed the ballot measure for the convention, including Common Cause, the American Civil Liberties Union and Planned Parenthood. They expressed a lack of confidence in a convention and felt threatened by it. They also argued that the $2 million cost was too expensive and unaffordable. These "liberal" groups seemed to lack trust in citizens, trust normally expected from the political left. That the Republican governor had been so public in his support made the opposition all the more curious.

So what did Rhode Island voters do? The ballot measure lost 52 to 48 percent. Arruda said it was "a total surprise," because two weeks earlier a poll found voters 2 to 1 *in favor* of holding the convention. He blamed the opponents to the convention for "effectively putting doubts in the minds of voters, enough for a loss by a slim margin. Rhode Islanders lost an opportunity they won't have again until 2014 to directly effect their government. Now, we have no choice but to go through the legislative process—and we see how ineffective that is. It will be a long time before we can see systematic change that needs to take place to bring about accountable government and that's sad."

As to the opposition, "That was an organized effort with money put into it, and we don't know where it came from. People need to realize that special interests came together and each group involved had paid lobbyists. People who earn their living going to the Statehouse to lobby want to see the work done there, rather than at a convention," Arruda explained. Apparently opposition groups did not want to upset their relationships with the legislature that opposed the convention, because it would likely cut its authority. For example, one of the stated goals for the convention was giving citizens the right to have ballot initiatives, which the legislature opposed. So, liberal groups chose certain but limited status quo influence on the legislature over gambling that their support of the convention might reduce that influence. Lesson: Never underestimate the power of the status quo, especially when money is spent on conning citizens to preserve it.

As in Rhode Island, a constitutional convention proposed in New Jersey to reform its property tax system faced considerable opposition. Property taxes have been a huge public policy issue because New Jersey has had the highest property tax rates in the nation, 50 percent higher than the national average, creating enormous burdens on many middle and low-income households. Burdened garden state taxpayers wanted relief. Governors and state legislatures, however, did not take action over many years, creating a need for a citizens' constitutional convention. A Governor's task force led to a bill passed in the Assembly that would have given voters the opportunity to consider a ballot measure to form the convention, whose recommendations would then be placed on a subsequent general election ballot. Citizens would vote for nearly all the convention delegates (80 with 10 appointed by various elected officials). All these steps represented true direct democracy to handle a politically loaded issue of finding other ways to raise state revenues through taxes. A poll early in 2005 found that 78 percent of people supported the convention.

There was a broad coalition of groups actively supporting the convention, including: the New Jersey State League of Municipalities, the League of Women Voters, AARP, and the Sierra Club. *The Trenton Times* editorialized frequently in support of the convention; its view was that "the standard lawmaking process" had failed because "they are too beholden to powerful lobbies and that benefit the status quo," making the convention "the only real hope for [tax] relief."

But special interests concerned about being hit with tax increases and government spending cuts, including business associations and teachers groups, were opposed to what a special task force member called "democracy in action." In 2004, writing in the *Asbury Park Press*, Carl Golden described what the constitutional convention faced:

> [It] is in jeopardy, torpedoed by a combination of powerful private-interest groups guarding their economic turf and protecting the status quo from which they've benefited handsomely all these years. ...The [New Jersey Education Association] likes the status quo—why shouldn't it? Change represents things unknown. Things unknown are to be fought.

What happened? The Senate headed by the acting governor refused to pass the Assembly bill to put the convention proposal on the 2005 ballot. All the support for the convention remained, however, and groups vowed to keep the convention option alive, especially if the legislature did not accomplish tax reform on its own.

Here is another recent experience. In Memphis, Tennessee a battle raged over the desire by many city residents to establish a charter review commission to meet and recommend revisions to the city's charter, including possible term limits and changes in the powers of the mayor and city council members. Concerned Citizens of Memphis in 2004 obtained about three times the required number of certified signatures (10,485) within 30 days. The group's leader attributed the success to pent-up anger among residents about the status quo in city government. Guess what? City lawyers fought what citizens wanted and were able to get a court to delay creation of the commission. The *Commercial Appeal* editorialized in October 2005 in support of moving forward, noting that no changes would occur "unless approved by citizens in a public referendum. In other words, democracy in its purest form." The referendum was likely to occur in 2007 when all city officials would be up for reelection and be pressured to take positions on charter changes. The editorial concluded: "Democracy might just prevail here, after all."

In sum, all three cases document how status quo forces effectively blocked citizens' conventions to address issues of vital concern to the public. They should cause one to think about what John Adams, our second president, observed:

> There was never a democracy yet that did not commit suicide.

More recently, Sean Wilentz author of *The Rise of American Democracy: Jefferson to Lincoln* said:

> Democracy can come undone. It's not something that's necessarily going to last forever once it's been established.

So, the essential challenge for Americans is fighting complacency and resignation about their democracy. We need ways to regularly reexamine what we have, what's wrong, and what needs to be fixed. Otherwise, democracy will inevitably sow the seeds of its own destruction because of the many who take advantage of its freedoms and opportunities for corruption.

From a democracy perspective, there are many more benefits than costs of well conceived constitutional conventions, especially when they are followed by elections to adopt or reject proposed changes to constitutions or charters. Conventions are an alternative to more narrowly conceived ballot measures that are voted on. If there is to be a national "movement" to rescue American democracy, the concept of citizen conventions merits attention. To fear conventions is to fear the wisdom of Americans and to reject Jefferson's belief in citizens' active participation in government. If you believe in authentic citizen participation and the sovereignty of citizens, then you should support conventions. Opponents are those who fear losing their power, money or influence. Nor should people assume that the absurd corporate-studded conventions of the Democratic and Republican parties represent what can be done with citizen conventions. More states should require periodic constitutional conventions as a democratic check on their executive and legislative branches.

Chapter 9

Respecting Our Roots:
From History to Inspiration

The fact that we've been a great democracy doesn't mean we will
automatically keep being one if we keep waving the flag.

—Norman Mailer

We the people, to *reform* a more perfect Republic, must
regain our sovereign power and use it. Time to reclaim our
government and make it what it was supposed to be—*ours*.

As Hendrik Hertzberg said in *The New Yorker*:

> If we kept in mind the ways in which our constitutional arrangements
> distort our democracy and hobble our politics, we might gain a deeper, more
> useful understanding of the sources of our various national discontents. If
> we didn't assume that the system was perfect, we wouldn't assume that
> everything we don't like is the fault of bad people. ...our system is a lot less
> democratic than it should be.

Fixing the system is the goal. There are too many opportunities for
bad people to act badly. Countless politicians take special interest money
to stay in office, and then serve those interests more than the public. A host
of legislators and governors have been criminally prosecuted in recent
years, usually related to taking illegal money or gifts from corporate
interests, often from government contractors. And shame did not prevent
Massachusetts Governor Mitt Romney from refusing to veto a law that
tossed out the Clean Elections law passed by citizens. Morality has not
stopped legislators and presidents from shackling us to international
trade agreements that erode our sovereignty and export our national
wealth. Yet immorality, dishonesty and corruption in American politics
continues, despite public scandals and prosecutions. A bad system makes
an ideal home for bad people. Business as usual is corruption as usual.

This much is clear: Our Constitution was not meant to maintain
a status quo system that no longer provides effective representative
government to the sovereign, self-governing people. That is too high a
price to pay for government stability.

As to the hallowed rule of law, anyone who still has faith in laws made by (corrupt) legislators and interpreted by (partisan) judges is as blind as the statue of justice is. Above the law are those promoting the American dream for the masses but benefiting from the restricted political system. In our deMOCKracy, the rule of law hardly applies to the rulers, the power elites, the masters. No greater proof of this can be imagined than the federal government's sloth in stopping the invasion of illegal immigrants through our porous borders, a massive disrespect for the rule of law. To add insult to injury, those illegal immigrants as well as legal non-citizens are counted in the national census. This increases congressional representation in some states. As a result of the 2000 census, that counted 18.6 million non-citizens, California gained six House seats it would not have otherwise received, for example. Representative Candice Miller has introduced a bill to amend the Constitution so that non-citizens would be excluded from the census. "Immigration takes away representation from states composed almost entirely of U.S. citizens so that new districts can be created in states with large numbers of non-citizens," observed Steven Camarota of the Center for Immigration Studies.

Federal inaction on illegal immigration can only be explained by powerful business interests that want immigrant "slave labor." Indeed, by allowing millions of illegals to enjoy the privileges of citizenship, our rulers have used cheap labor to make the U.S. economy look better than it really is. Profits have trumped national security. Meanwhile, Americans subsidize the costs of poorly paid illegals who take advantage of government benefits and services paid for by taxpayers, not employers of illegals. The Minutemen working to detect and publicize illegal immigration across our borders are activist dissenters, stepping in to fill the gap left by our corrupt and inept federal government.

Ignoring the will of the majority on this issue shows the tyranny of misrepresentation in our fading democracy. Yes, historically, we have been a nation of immigrants—but not massive numbers of illegal immigrants. Lifeboat America is sinking. Local governments and states are footing the bill for costly social and educational services to illegal immigrants just like an unfunded mandate from the federal government. The rule of law has been made a mockery. Wages have been depressed across the nation. Business interests benefiting from cheap labor have called the shots rather than the voice of the people, overwhelmingly angry about the poor response of the federal government to take border security seriously.

Will the Real Enemies Please Stand Up

American democracy is not threatened by those opposing democracy, by dissenters and status quo busters, or by foreign forces. It is threatened by fake patriots and citizens who blindfold themselves with the flag they wrap themselves in or the Bible they immerse themselves in. The real threats are corporate power, wealth inequality and politicians who feed on these. They perpetuate America's delusional democracy.

An ironic and inevitable truth is that all the conditions that justify major change are also the biggest obstacles to change. Yet they must be overcome.

Some things do not need proof—they are self-evident truths. Americans can be proud that they are overwhelmingly smart (regardless of their formal education), generous (regardless of their income), and morally grounded (regardless of their religiosity). Many of them feel that they are bearing some pain, cost, or penalty because of government or corporate corruption. The question for this new century is this: Are these Americans willing to unite and fight for disruptive but necessary systemic change in the public and private sectors?

Rejection of America's distractive consumer culture must be part of the solution. Americans are kept so busy working, driving, borrowing, and consuming—trying to stay out of financial ruin, trying to afford health care, and trying to cope with daily fatigue and stress—that they do not focus on the breakdown in the democratic structure of their country. Yes, they see bad politicians, bad government, and bad public policies, but that is not the same thing as grasping something wrong with their democracy, with the foundation of representative government. Surveys may find many Americans seeing the country headed in the wrong direction. But most think simplistically, namely that changing the political party in the White House or running Congress, or getting better people in the party they favor elected, will steer the ship of state in the right direction. We need to imagine something else and ask: Do we need a different kind of change? Should new thinking be steering the nation into the future? Should we the people take charge and turn the nation around?

In past times Americans faced what we face today. Hope for the future is found in America's history. Our nation has gone through serious, periodic reforms. The lesson is that money in politics remains the major impediment to true reform. Senator Mark Hanna, chair of the Republican National Committee, said, "There are two things that are important in politics. The first is money and I can't remember what the second one is." That was said in 1895. The first reform cycle occurred in the late 1800s and early 1900s in the form of the Populist and Progressive parties. The Populist Party was a farmer-worker challenge to corporate power. The Progressive Party was a middle-class and intellectual effort to clean up government corruption. They both were successful. Now, no political party is focused on fighting corporatism and corruption. Our nation is ready for another cycle of citizen outrage-driven reform. The statements of Populists and Progressives from about a century ago apply today. Eltweed Pomeroy wrote these sentiments in 1900:

> The theory is that [the people] choose the wisest and most trustworthy and that these officers, when chosen, retain and exercise these qualities. …it soon became evident that the interest of the ruler after election did not coincide with justice to all the people. …Representative government has been tested on these shores for over a century. …Representative government is a failure.

Populist Washington Governor J. R. Rogers said:

> The people are helpless against the bribery which is resorted to by the great corporations and interests which fear the people and deal with their corrupt officials.

Progressive Wisconsin Governor Robert M. LaFollette said:

> The forces of special privileges are deeply entrenched. Their resources are inexhaustible. Their efforts never are lax. Their political methods are insidious.

The original progressives believed in an idealistic, anti-corruption, nonpartisan approach to efficient and productive government. Today, liberals and others often use the word progressive indiscriminately.

Despite facing enormous resistance, both the Populist and Progressive movements proved that entrenched well-financed status quo defenders can be defeated. But victories turn into complacency and defeated power elites regroup and develop new strategies. What has happened in the last century? *O-n-e h-u-n-d-r-e-d years* of failed efforts to keep American democracy faithful to our Founders hopes. Corporate power and government corruption became smarter, less visible, more entwined, and more institutionalized. Buying government became more expensive, not more difficult. Lesson: Faces change, but the powerful stay powerful and the powerless stay powerless.

For the most part, persons born into an economic class stay in that class. Socioeconomic mobility in the U.S. had declined sharply and is now lower than in most other advanced industrialized democracies. In 1944, conservative economist Friedrich A. Hayek in *The Road to Serfdom* warned of industry-government power leading to "totalitarianism." In his 1948 book *Economic Policy for a Free Society*, University of Chicago conservative economist Henry C. Simmons lamented:

> America might now be better off if the corporate form had never been invented or never made available to private enterprise.

True fiscal conservatives concerned about liberty and democracy should be against the axis of corrupt government and corporate power. It is time for another strong political effort aimed at restoring government's integrity by reducing corporate power everywhere, including the media. Can we afford to waste another *o-n-e h-u-n-d-r-e-d years*?

One of the best statements on American society came from Senator John Edwards when he ran for the Democratic presidential nomination in 2004; it was his "two Americas" declaration:

> One America that does the work, another America that reaps the reward. One America that pays the taxes, another America that gets the tax breaks. ...One America—middle-class America—whose needs Washington has long forgotten, another America—narrow-interest America—whose very wish is Washington's commands. One America that is struggling to get by, another America that can buy anything it wants, even Congress and a president.

Things might have turned out differently if Edwards would have stuck with this class-struggle message and John Kerry would have bought into it, and both would have denounced their previous funding from those running the restricted political system. Words without steadfast commitment and action are hollow. Edwards was more of a party loyalist than a New American Revolutionary.

Complicit Conformity

As the power elites have become stronger, we have lost the spirit of the Founding Fathers, status quo busters to their cores. What has gone wrong? The federal system they created has provided political stability and individual freedoms. But at what price? Dysfunctional government has been stabilized.

An all-powerful set of private interests that trump public interests is more powerful today than it was a century ago, as shown by greater economic inequality and more outrageous government actions, including preemptive war. One problem is that the court of public opinion has been corrupted along with government. Public opinion is measured more than ever and more than ever it is manipulated by propaganda. Those in power use opinion survey information not to better serve the public interest, but rather to devise tricky messages that take advantage of a public paying little attention to issues and getting little help from the mainstream media in understanding them better. Combine better information about the public with special interest money and you get weapons of mass deception.

Largely unknown is how the legal entity called a corporation has produced a "business aristocracy" and removed the power of the people. It all started with a Supreme Court decision in 1886 [*Santa Clara County v. Southern Pacific Railroad*] that allowed corporations to be considered "persons." This started a long series of court decisions that gave corporations constitutional rights and protections, which a rational person would think were meant only for individual citizens. Does this seem like more of a political than legal interpretation of our Constitution? With it, corporatism became a permanent plutocracy, with the president as plutocrat-in-chief.

Writing about economic injustice in the *Baltimore Chronicle* in 2005, Jason Miller got it right:

> Sadly, the notion of "of the people, by the people, and for the people" is in its final throes. A corrupt, plutocratic government "of the rich, and for the rich" sucks the marrow, leaving the rest of America to hungrily gnaw the bones. Bearing a striking resemblance to the feudal lords of the Middle Ages, America's plutocrats plunder and hoard the wealth of the land while their serfs fight over the remaining scraps.

It may seem abstract, but when corporations obtained *human rights* something historic happened. Corporations obtained more power. In return, corporations give little respect to their country, their investors, their workers, and their customers. The result has been cancerous corporatism. Corporate citizenship is an oxymoron. Corporate abuse is fostered by corporate corruption that curtails government control of corporate behavior. Power has shifted from "we the people" to "we the corporations." Americans struggle more as corporations use offshore tax havens, receive corporate welfare, and export our prosperity. We have not listened to Jefferson, Lincoln and Roosevelt, so our democracy has morphed into a corporatist state.

What the corporate world does has also changed dramatically. As the U.S. shifted from a manufacturing to a service economy, the corporate world became dominated by financial, health care, land development and home building, law, accounting, information technology, software, telecommunications, entertainment, media and publishing, consulting and government contractor companies. The corporate pressures on government changed from protecting classic manufacturing (such as textiles and steel) to serving the interests of the broad services sector, especially companies obtaining business directly from government. Globalization has harmed manufacturing by expanding imports, but aided the services sector by opening up foreign markets and providing cheap foreign labor. The privatization of government has been critical to multitudes of contractors, servicing every type of government department. They employ former government officials (think The Carlyle Group), provide huge amounts of campaign money (think Enron), and send their officials into government to exploit opportunities (think Dick Cheney). This has created an enormous amount of corporate corruption that hits the news periodically with scandals of illegal bribes and crooked contract procurement.

One insidious development is using contractor personnel to represent government agencies at meetings with the public—privatization of democracy. Elected and bureaucratic public officials don't want to face angry citizens to defend their policies, programs and plans. *Washington Post* columnist Marc Fisher examined this phenomenon of "diffusing dissent" in 2005 and noted: "Don't look now, but American democracy is being privatized. ...[Government is] using contractors to separate the public from decision makers." When government officials do not personally listen to and answer citizens concerned about their decisions you know your "representatives" don't give a damn about you. Just another sign that things today are really worse than 100 years ago.

Besides big business and corporatism, there are a set of collective special interests, including professional sectors, such as lawyers, physicians, and teachers, and various narrow interests, such as gun owners (NRA) and older Americans (AARP). Some seek profits, others seek power, and some seek protection from government regulation and civil lawsuits. All have subverted and corrupted our republican, representative form of government, with no end in sight. In 2005, through NRA lobbying Congress passed a law to shield gun makers from lawsuits by victims of shootings; 56 Democratic Representatives voted for it and only four Republicans voted against it. In the Senate the Democratic Minority Leader and other Democrats also voted for it. Do you think most Americans favored this legislation? No way.

Money buys generous access to elected officials. Only token access is offered to the general public or interest groups that do not provide money. It takes effort for ordinary people to get a meeting with a staffer to a governor, mayor, county executive, or U.S. Senator or Representative, or perhaps a perfunctory short meeting with the official or a quick handshake and a few words at some public event. These interactions are profoundly unequal to what lobbyists and corporate officials obtain at plush receptions, private dinners, golfing events, corporate jet travel with politicians, corporate boxes in sports stadiums, and fund raising events, for example.

A Revolting Situation Requires a Revolution

American democracy is not dead—yet. The question is: With our democracy deficit and our corporatist state with its distractive consumerism, can Americans think in terms of "revolution?"

In early 2005, many residents of Loudoun County, Virginia called for the "Catoctin Revolution." Residents in the western part of the county wanted a new county, because business interests in favor of more suburban sprawl development had taken control of their county government. The dissidents wanted to protect the rural character of the western region against the onslaught of suburban sprawl. A leader of the revolt, county commissioner Karl Phillips said: "We have a right to have our own government. ...the current board is disenfranchising all of us." *Washington Post* columnist Marc Fisher said "it's hard to imagine legislators in Richmond embracing a rebellion against development when so many lawmakers seem to believe developers are their primary constituents." True enough. Sprawl industry money had long controlled the state legislature. Would the voice of Loudoun citizens be honored? Not likely with so much legal corruption.

The nation's sprawl pushers won a huge victory with the Supreme Court's 5-4 June 2005 decision in *Kelo v. City of New London*. Local governments won the right to use eminent domain to seize private property for private commercial use if it can be deemed economic development. Any commercial activity, including building more sprawl subdivisions, shopping malls, and Wal-Marts, that could provide more tax revenues can now displace any existing homeowner or business owning land that the commercial developer wants, unless state laws prevented it Four conservative justices wrote an extremely strong dissent and said:

> The beneficiaries are likely to be those citizens with disproportionate influence and power in the political process, including large corporations and development firms.

Interestingly, Republican justices went against corporatism and the plutocracy, because of their stronger commitment to private property rights. Yet the Democratic ones (with the help of one conservative justice) supported it in the name of urban revitalization. Justice Thomas pointed out this sad irony in his own dissent:

> Something has gone seriously awry with the Court's interpretation of the Constitution. Though citizens are safe from the government in their homes, the homes themselves are not.

Taxation without representation provoked the First American Revolution, now taxation with misrepresentation is the right call for action—for a Second American Revolution. But today, no one is shouting or marching in the streets with signs saying, "Taxation with MISREPRESENTATION is tyranny." Consider the wisdom of Walt Whitman, still relevant today:

> We have frequently printed the word Democracy. Yet I cannot too often repeat that it is a word the real gist of which still sleeps. ...It is a great word, whose history, I suppose remains unwritten, because that history has

yet to be enacted.

Our politicians act as if the story of American democracy is over. It is not. This is not the time to rest or celebrate and believe we have a democracy product worthy of export. It is the time to face the truth. Today's unaddressed the-emperor-has-no-clothes-crisis is that private interests have been able to literally steal our government—by buying elected representatives at every level of government. Nothing done to date has changed this, not term limits, not restrictions on campaign contributions. As David Broder said before the 2004 election: "Elections are the great accountability device in our system of representative government—and accountability has never loomed larger than it does now." But if money determines election outcomes and third-party candidates are kept off ballots, out of debates and out of media coverage, then accountability fails. Representative government fails. Broder also bemoaned the reality that "except for a few whistleblowers, a handful of independent, opinionated legislators and some few enterprising reporters, there is no accountability mechanism operating." You might think that this deserved a headline on page one—something akin to "the Red Coats are coming!" Where is Paul Revere when you need him—again?

When someone changes sides—from corruption to conscience—it has historic importance. After the horrific aftermath of hurricane Katrina in 2005 one of the most senior and important lobbyists in Washington, D.C., Frederick L. Webber, president of the Alliance of Automobile Manufacturers, went public with a remarkably honest message about the "crazy" and "diseased" system of congressional fundraising. He said, "Political fundraising in this town has gotten out of control." The hurricane's devastation and the thousands of Americans needing aid prompted him to reflect: "All of a sudden I asked, 'What are the priorities here?' It was an easy decision to make. I couldn't justify making those $500 to $2,500 [campaign] contributions. It just didn't' fit." But in the days after Katrina, most congressional fundraising events went on shamefully as usual and corporate vultures dived for disaster dollars.

Special interests have perfected the art of lying or deluding themselves. Michael Kinsley captured the cynical but true nature of things:

> American democracy is a conspiracy of special interests against the general interest, but every special interest thinks that it is the general

interest.

Or more correctly, special interests work hard to convince or deceive politicians, the media, and the public that their objectives serve the public interest. More lies.

It comes to this: When does a genuine democracy become a fake democracy? When the "consent of the governed" no longer applies. Consent becomes meaningless when: too few citizens vote, there is too little difference between candidates that have a chance of winning, corporate money shapes the policies and actions of government, corporations have human rights, and gerrymandering promotes reelection of incumbents. In fake democracies, citizens are hostages to raw state power despite some personal freedoms. In the U.S., distractive consumerism replaces brute force. America's economic slaves have freedom; but their values, opinions, and behavior have been shaped by economic oligarchs and political plutocrats who have benefited from a weak education system, unappealing elections, cowardly news media, activist judges, and myopic globalization.

John Kenneth Galbraith said that "the deepest instinct of the affluent, whether in America, Germany, or Argentina, is to believe that what's good for them is what's good for the country." As long as that perspective among the ruling class holds sway thoughts of making a new revolution will stay imprisoned in peoples' heads. When the consent of the governed becomes a joke the historic, sacred, and patriotic duty of Americans is to think revolution.

Bipartisanship Betrays Democracy

What is bipartisanship? Through magical molecular chemistry one party not only neutralizes the toxicity of the other, but also produces some new beneficial substance—Demopublicans. Two poisons are mixed to produce a healthy concoction. Sit back angry Americans and wait for another dose of bipartisanship. But if you keep your eyes on the wicked brew you will see that it is like a mixture of oil and water that in time separate into their natural states.

Step back and think about the historical presumption that American democracy is served by bipartisanship and the constant mantra that more bipartisanship—especially in Congress—is a remedy for representative government's failures. Rather than examining the many fault lines in our crumbling democracy there are calls for more bipartisanship, mostly from the least extreme adherents of both major parties and (worse yet) many Americans disenchanted with both parties. But this seemingly reasonable approach or compromise, usually articulated by the moderates in both parties, is yet another example of the politics of distraction. No need for fundamental reforms, just mix Ds and Rs—like mixing some blue and red inks—to smear another coat of deception on our Constitution. Bipartisanship gives us the worst of two worlds. It is an opportunity to reward two sets of special interests. Remaining out in the cold are third-parties and politically smart independents and dissenters.

Bipartisanship creates the illusion of choice, but at a deeper level of reality the two major parties are not all that different. In 2004, Nader called the two presidential candidates "corporate politicians with the choice being between heart disease and cancer" and that we have "one corporate party with two heads." Those two heads lie to each other and citizens; in secret conversations they work together to keep out third-party competition and split the riches. The system offers the choice of which party gets which corporate dollars. *What differs is the set of private, special interests that the Democrats and Republicans are indebted to and then favor when in office.* Both major parties sacrifice the public interest through equal opportunity corruption.

But you think: Surely on many important issues there are critical differences between the parties and especially between Democratic and Republican presidential candidates. Listen to Nader:

> The parties are polarized on certain social issues. But on the fundamental issues affecting the future of democracy, they're on the same page. They sell elections to the highest bidder. They are unwilling to challenge John Corporation. To me that's on the same page of hypocrisy, instead of democracy.

The Republicans are more open about being corporate whores—as they practice *compassionate corporatism.* At most, the two major parties offer near-term incremental change to tweak things, rather than more radical, systemic and status quo busting change. The bipartisan support for the preemptive Iraq war will go down in history as a dagger through the heart of democracy. That neither party has given the public what is wants—universal health care—is another blow to democracy.

There is little room in the Democratic and Republican parties for "moderates." And that is good, because the moderates are used to make both parties look more reasonable than they really are—to provide cover for their true agendas, to make dissent-minded Americans take comfort in bipartisanship. Forget the "big tent" crap the partisan spinners serve to pundits. Let each party be seen for its true subservience to its financial backers. Moderates aside, two-party extremism and loyalty among politicians has increased over time. Consider that in the House of Representatives the average member backed the party position 65 percent of the time in the 1970s, which increased steadily and reached 87 percent in 2001-2002, and is probably higher now. Party loyalty earns campaign money, something that Tom "The Hammer" DeLay took to new levels.

Bipartisanship must never obscure the need to crush the two-party duopoly. In the creative "A Declaration of Independence from the Republicans and Democrats," H. Sternlieb made the case for Americans freeing themselves from the shackles of the two-party system, as they once did from British tyranny:

> The recent history of those parties is a history of repeated injuries and usurpations, all having a direct object, to establish control of our national government by large monied interests. …they have placed the wealth of the few above the welfare of the many. …they no longer serve the interests of the vast majority of the citizenry and they should be cast aside and replaced by parties that will protect our livelihoods, our health, our environment and our freedom.

This version of the Declaration of Independence should be required reading in all schools.

Arianna Huffington spoke of "breaking the stranglehold of two party politics in order to challenge the broken status quo." The two-party duopoly gives the public highly visible combat that entertains and offers false hopes for Americans, and in a more subtle and sinister way maintains the status quo illusory political system.

Justin Raimondo of Antiwar.com made these important observations upon attending a 2004 Nader for President rally in San Francisco:

> Nader explained that his campaign is important "pictorially" because the two major parties, left to themselves, will merely consolidate the status quo, there will be no one to pull the political dialogue in a new direction. …Nader's views are attractive to the Left but are rooted, at least in part, on

the libertarian and populist Right.

Few Americans appreciate that third parties have brought about real social change. A third party called the Republicans helped end slavery. The Greenback-Labor Party helped give women the right to vote. The Socialist Party helped create the Social Security system. The Progressive Party helped bring about direct election of U.S. Senators and spearheaded the use of ballot initiatives, referenda and recalls. So much of the time when the term "nonpartisan" is used, it is a lie, because the correct term should be bipartisan—or better yet "buypartisan." *The dirty little secret is that bipartisanship is just a mutual protection pact against third parties and greater political freedom.*

Too many public interest and political pressure groups have become resigned to making incremental changes in the system to keep a relatively small number of supporters (and funders) happy. This has certainly been the case for environmental groups (the Sierra Club) and trial lawyers for the Democrats, and evangelicals and gun owners (through the National Rifle Association) for the Republicans. They do not seek larger status quo busting changes. Holding onto their preferential treatment and incrementalism are less risky. Often highly partisan, they are content with developing a choir they can preach to and maintaining organizational stability, rather than taking more risk to convert more people to their way of thinking. The big exception is usually small, independent groups focused on revealing information that would otherwise be withheld from the public; examples include the Project on Government Oversight, Citizens for Responsibility and Ethics in Washington, and the Electronic Privacy Information Center.

In sum: Skepticism is warranted when, in an effort to launch a revolution through a new third-party, bipartisanship is touted by the two-party duopoly and the corporate world as the better solution to maintain our political stability and strong democracy. Think B.S.—bipartisan spin!

Illusionary Choice

In the early 1980s, Waylon Jennings said this of the two major parties: "There ain't a dime's worth of difference between them." It has gotten worse. In 1994, Kevin Phillips said this in *Arrogant Capital*:

> Aspects of Republican-Democratic rivalry can seem as staged and phony as American professional wrestling. ...Since [1992], several different surveys have shown a clear national majority continuing to call for a new political party to contest the Democrats and Republicans in elections from president down to those for Congress and state legislatures.

In fact, survey data over several years showed the greatest support for a new party from those calling themselves independents, followed by Republicans and then Democrats. The rigged two party system is a major distractive feature of the illusory political system.

This is how Jim Hightower saw the 2000 presidential election choice in *If the Gods Had Meant Us to Vote They Would Have Given Us Candidates*, which can apply to just about every two-party race:

> This is choice? Which one of them is going to stand up for your family against the whims of the global speculators, the polluters, the downsizers, the tax loopholers, the corporate welfare barons, the HMOs, the media conglomerates, the finance industry finaglers, and all the rest of the establishment, which is flanked by an elite corps of $500-an-hour Gucci-clad lobbyists and armed with enough campaign cash to build an impenetrable wall around Washington?

Sure, with the two-party duopoly, over time the political pendulum swings from Democrats to Republicans, but such change masks status quo power. The larger issue is: What force is moving the pendulum? The electorate is visible, but the pendulum's movement is just the illusion of change that distracts us from urgently needed structural changes. As to the corporatist state, it prospers under both Democrats and Republicans. *Forbes* has pointed out that economic inequality as seen through the gap between the pay of some CEOs and their workers has grown for decades and widened greatly during the Clinton era. Of the 2005 roster of the *Forbes* 400 richest people, 374 were billionaires. Cloud Morris wrote in to comment: "Every Administration since 1981 has pursued roughly the same economic policies—increasing wealth in the hands of a few." As economic inequality has increased, economic security for most Americans has decreased. The rich become super-rich and the middle class becomes poorer. What a system.

Few Americans want to believe that there is political repression in the world's self-proclaimed greatest democracy—as the United States *brands* itself. Not in America! But there is. We have our own style of repression, despite considerable *individual* freedom. We have rulers too—power elites in government and business, with their two-party duopoly to conceal the repression of wide political discourse. We have a working class too—non-elite Americans struggling to survive in an economy that seems to only care about their capacity to spend, not save, to work, not be politically engaged, to think globally and lose locally.

Repulsive Repeat Offenders

Gerrymandering—political distortion of congressional district boundaries has been elevated from an infrequent misdemeanor to a frequent felony—the two-party duopoly now rapes our democracy. Meaningful political choice is violated. But the victims mostly remain silent, for so many non-voters are raped in absentia.

Evidence of third-party candidates being locked in political prison is the remarkable fact that about 95 percent of congressional districts have been carved up so that they are dominated by either the Republican or Democratic parties. Over 98 percent of congressional incumbents get reelected. The party in power in a state is able to redefine congressional districts to maximize the party's capture and retention of seats. *Rather than voters choosing politicians, politicians are choosing their voters.* Incumbency is now like royalty that our Founders revolted against.

Patrick Basham of the conservative Cato Institute observed:

> Incumbency is now so entrenched that many voters lack any real say in who represents them. Incumbents share a semi-perpetual easement on their seats that more nearly resembles hereditary entitlement than the competitive politics we associate with a democracy.

Exactly the point—this is strong evidence of a declining democracy. Steve Weissman of the Campaign Finance Institute commented: "Political competition, the lifeblood of democracy, is under siege."

Tom DeLay, democracy-rapist and the epitome of plutocrat politics (and member of the Council for National Policy), corrupted the congressional redistricting process in Texas to defeat four out of five targeted Democrats. His criminal indictments in September 2005 for breaking the Texas prohibition against corporate campaign money prompted Craig McDonald, head of Texans for Public Justice, to comment: "the justice system must punish those who criminally conspire to undermine democracy." In December 2005, it was revealed that the

U.S. Justice Department had kept secret from the courts and the public a 73-page memo by seven career lawyers and analysts that said the redistricting that DeLay and his cohorts had constructed violated federal law because it reduced minority voting strength. Political appointees had covered up the report. So much for justice in the Justice Department.

Ralph Nader observed that the current system "takes away the voices and choices that would listen and respond to your concerns, your desires for a better future for your children. Also remember, the replacement of democracy with autocracy in our country comes not with heavy boots and smashed doors. It is coming, to use the words of the poet Robert Frost, 'on little cat feet.'" So many voices have been ignored by Americans who have paid scant attention to congressional redistricting—the mapping of democracy. Listen to Peter Gruenstein, an attorney in Alaska:

> The loss of equal voting rights caused by gerrymandering taken to new depths of precision through computer programs and immunized by jelly-kneed courts has disenfranchised the vast majority of Americans just as effectively as King George did, and more insidiously. ...Gerrymandering fundamentally undermines the democratic process itself, and there is essentially no rational basis for opposing reform.

In 2004, there were 35 House members who faced no opponent. Though a small percent of all House members, it is still shocking. Columnist David S. Broder wrote "What Democracy Needs: Real Races." He pointed to the Senate and House elections where there were very few competitive races and concluded: "That is where our system of representative government really failed." What a commentary on our government by someone who has been examining it up close for many decades. And still Americans do not rise up in angry rebellion.

In January 2005, Governor Arnold Schwarzenegger emphasized that not one of the 153 California congressional and state legislative seats in the 2004 election changed parties. He asked, "What kind of democracy is that?" [Of course, his four ballot measures were rejected by voters in November 2005.] This prompted the *Washington Post* to editorialize about "the depressing state of electoral democracy." Later, in August 2005, the California Supreme Court cleared a ballot measure to reform the state's redistricting process. The *Post* supported replacing "the state's corrupt system...with a cleaner one in which a panel of retired judges" would periodically redraw state and federal legislative districts. While attacking the current "undemocratic and unacceptable" system, the *Post* also said that the current system "weakens two-party democracy." In other words, the *Post* defined American democracy as "two-party democracy." What status quo thinking.

An interesting analysis by Eli Rosenbaum of Yale University showed that in states using autonomous, bipartisan commissions there was no more competitive races or reductions in incumbency. Rosenbaum explained that "equal representation on the panel for both parties tends to favor the status quo...and of course nobody on either side really wants a competitive district." Moreover, unlike legislators doing redistricting, independent commissions are not accountable to voters, so they "can hardly be seen as democracy in the voters' hands," said Rosenbaum. Still, he was overly pessimistic; better-designed commissions may be the only answer, including actions to reverse current gerrymandered districts. Iowa's commission has proven successful, making four of its five congressional districts competitive. Ballot measures for redistricting reform in California and Ohio failed in 2005, principally because the dominant state party and its allies feared change—Democrats in California and Republicans in Ohio. The California measure proposed a three retired judge panel selected by the legislature and was opposed by many public interest groups and unions with Democratic ties. In Ohio a bipartisan panel would have replaced a redistricting commission dominated by Republicans, so they and business interests campaigned against the measure. The real winner in each state was the status quo.

Federal legislation to compel state commissions without any party bias is necessary and has been introduced. One bill came from Democratic Representative John Tanner who said that this redistricting issue "goes to the very essence of our democracy." He argued that rigged redistricting has fostered victories by Democratic and Republican extremists with no interest in appealing to the political center and without "a broad sense of the public welfare."

Our nation's Founders designed the House of Representatives with the shortest terms to best represent shifts in public opinion. But with rigged districts, why bother going through the motions of electing Representatives every two years when it has become nearly meaningless? Besides commissions, solutions for curing this malaise and reinvigorating this aspect of democracy include the Clean Money/Clean Elections way of financing campaigns and the other election reforms discussed previously. Honest politicians would also help. Our anemic democracy desperately needs a transfusion for a healthy body politic.

One of the few honest House members should introduce a bill for renaming the institution to reflect reality. We have a House of Misrepresentatives, increasingly not the peoples' house, but the lobbyists' mansion, composed of lawbreakers, not lawmakers. At the very least, the media should refer to the "House of Misrepresentatives."

Majority Math: Despair Divided by Hope Equals Victory

Filmmaker Michael Moore said: "The reason you, the majority, no longer vote in America is because you, the majority, realize there is no real choice on the ballot." So, who cares? Who wants a lot of voters? Politicians only care about what they can get from those who do vote. Perversely, fewer diverse voters (in terms of interests, concerns and geographical location) just make the job of winning an election easier for liars.

Importantly, winners rarely win by large margins and often with less than a majority. What is disturbing is how *non-landslide* winners nevertheless are arrogantly unresponsive to all citizens. Bill Clinton received only 43 percent of the vote in 1992, and 49 percent in 1996. George W. Bush received 47.8 percent in 2000 and just 51 percent in 2004. From 1948 to 2003, 80 governors were elected with less than 50 percent of the vote, including 10 with less than 40 percent. Third-party candidate Jesse Ventura won with 37 percent in 1998. Arnold Schwarzenegger won with 48.6 percent, which was better than Gray Davis who was recalled and had won a year earlier with 47 percent. Votes for third-party candidates often prevent the "winner" obtaining a majority of those voting—and even less of all *eligible* voters.

Historically, this has happened with minor third-parties splitting a relatively small number of votes. The two-party duopoly can accept such illusory (non-mandate, plurality) victories that keep third-parties marginalized. Now imagine a strong, viable third-party intent on winning! In thinking about such an alternative to the two-party duopoly keep in mind that so many Republicans and Democrats have won without majorities. So splitting the total among three competitive parties and winning with a plurality should be viewed positively. If Americans want greater political freedom, then they must get over seeing plurality winners as "weak" or expecting them to cater more to the losing parties. Tripartisanship should be no more prized than bipartisanship. We need parties with distinct and clear goals and agendas, competing against each other and giving voters sharp choices. What plurality winners should be mindful of is being responsive not to the other political parties but to the broad spectrum of American citizens.

Back to the issue of all eligible voters versus the fraction voting. A big winner might get 55 percent of the vote, but if only 60 percent of eligible voters vote, then the winner actually received just 33 percent of the total electorate—not a majority. Two-thirds of all eligible voters had not voted for the winner—so you might say that the "winner" actually lost by 2 to 1, because there certainly is no logical reason to presume that 55 percent of the non-voters would have voted for the "winner." The total breakdown for the eligible voter population is 33 percent for the winner, 27 percent for the loser, and 40 percent not voting. Notice that the "loser" only needs to attract a small fraction of the non-voters to become the winner, a much smaller fraction than that obtained from the voters. Importantly, "none of the above" or "who wins doesn't matter" non-voters are the biggest fraction or plurality, surely not a ringing endorsement of contemporary American electoral democracy.

In truth, the ruling elites "have no problem with disaffected citizens dropping out—it keeps them from making waves. ...In many ways, it is easier to play to, control, and manipulate a smaller audience," as Arianna Huffington observed in *How to Overthrow the Government*. And as William Greider noted in *Who Will Tell the People*:

> [Elected officials] may occasionally lament the decline in voting, but incumbents are not threatened by this. The fewer who are paying attention and actually voting, the easier it will be for the status quo to endure.

With a high fraction of non-voters, winning an election, even with a majority, is far from winning a mandate or directive from the "the people." In his essay "Fake Democracy," Dave Stratman made this good point:

> The illusion of popular approval bestowed by fake democracy can convince people that politicians who in fact represent only the interests and outlook of a small elite really do represent the voice of ordinary people.

The effect of this is devastating. It can make people feel that they are all alone in opposing the policies of a "democratically-elected" politician, and that change is impossible.

The democratic process gains legitimacy when the voter turnout is high even though the victor is a plurality winner. That's better than a low voter turnout with a small-majority winner.

Look at the positive side. Change is possible. Do the math. President Bush received 51 percent of the nearly 60 percent of eligible voters who voted in the 2004 presidential election; but less than 31 percent of eligible voters. It would have been perfectly correct for news media to shout that *"Bush received the support of less than one-third of all eligible voters."* Those who focus on election frauds might accomplish more by emphasizing the undemocratic basis of victory. But to win by a minority is not a fraud, just not as powerful as a landslide. Claims by Bush that he had a "mandate" were quite absurd. Bush's a now famous post 2004 election statement "I have gained some political capital and I intend to spend it," reflected a delusional mindset. The media should have been saying, "No, you have very little political capital." Remarkably, Senator Kerry only needed less than 10 percent of the non-voters fraction nationally to beat Bush.

Also note that in many non-presidential elections, far less than 50 percent of eligible voters actually vote. For example, for the 2002 congressional elections, just 33 percent of eligible Americans voted, and the big Republican win was achieved with just 17 percent of eligible voters, another phony undemocratic mandate. Such numerical realities have received scant attention by the mainstream media.

The media watch group Fairness and Accuracy in Reporting put out a press release immediately after the 2004 election titled "Defining Bush's Mandate." Its point was that Bush's claim of a mandate with just a 51 percent majority "caught hold in the mainstream media—a sign perhaps that White House spin was triumphing over the actual numbers recorded on Election Day." Indeed, every major new media outlet subscribed to the mandate spin. This mandate madness illustrated successful framing, propaganda and media-sellout. No reporters did the math, totally ignoring the 40 percent of eligible voters who chose not to participate in America's "democracy."

Worth attention is that non-voters may be more than lazy or alienated;

they may be more resistant to the lies of the duopoly's politicians. Simmering outrage keeps many Americans away from voting. To add insult to despair, after an election like Bush's in 2004, the dissent-minded non-voters got hit with 24/7 media coverage about a "mandate" from the voters. Such experience likely makes them even more estranged from society, more hopeless. The mainstream media is no help at all. They just make a bad situation worse for democracy by ignoring the uncounted, ignored part of the citizenry voting with their absence. Isolated and divided despair ends up serving the power elites. Collective, unleashed outrage is the enemy of plutocracy and fortunately we have so much pent up outrage to do the job. What will bring it out? That's *the* question. Answers follow.

Think back to the 2004 presidential election. Within minutes of winning it the Bush Propaganda Machine actually sent forth three lies. Beside the claim of a mandate, was the incessant talk that Bush had received more votes than any other presidential candidate EVER. This was actually true, but irrelevant. With a growing population, it's no surprise the winner, whoever he was, would get votes than anyone in past elections. The relevant statistic is not the number of votes but the percentage of the electorate the winner received, a statistic deliberately underplayed. These word games showed a sinical disrespect for the public's intelligence and for democracy itself. But lies revealed must become nourishment for dissent and outrage.

There was also constant talk that the voter turnout was historic. In fact, three elections in the 1960s had the same or higher percent voter turnout. Worse, a 60 percent voter turnout was nothing to be so proud of compared to a far more ambitious goal, say 90 percent, as found in other democracies. In reality, the two-party duopoly has never sincerely wanted to increase voter turnout across the board. Nearly all partisan-related voter registration and turnout efforts target specific groups that they believe will support their party or candidate. In 2004, those efforts for the two major parties worked, but largely cancelled each other out. The 18 to 29 year old youth vote was greatly increased and favored Senator Kerry, while the increase among religious and evangelical voters favored President Bush.

Fools Fool Our Citizens

Changing our system is purposefully made difficult. In *Democracy for the Few* Michael Parenti pointed out the difficulty of obtaining fundamental change in our corporatist state:

> Change, if not impossible within state-supported capitalism is always limited by the overall imperatives of that system and is usually of a cosmetic or marginal nature. …Quite simply, those who have the interest in fundamental change have not the power, while those who have the power have not the interest. …meaningful changes are not embarked upon because they would literally threaten the survival of privileged interests; like most other social groups the elites show little inclination to commit class suicide.

Marginalization is the opiate of committed but tentative reformers. Well-meaning persons and groups that aim low at incremental changes only get what the power elites can accommodate. New American Revolutionaries must aim higher and face the wrath of those with real control over the system.

George Bernard Shaw said "power does not corrupt men; fools, however, if they get into a position of power, corrupt power." If you buy this, then power in America has been so corrupted that it rarely serves public interests. Corrupted not just by fools (as in lacking judgment or prudence)—but by many greedy, arrogant and evil people. While many people have been chagrined by the clear loss of civil liberties and privacy through the 2001 USA Patriot Act, the other insult to democracy was how the law was passed by Congress. A sound bill had been thrashed out by Republicans and Democrats on the House Judiciary Committee, though at the request of the White House there were no public hearings. But within hours of the vote on the bill the Bush administration had substituted new language and the new bill was printed up for distribution to House members. Yet the several hundred page bill could not be read and was not read by congressmen before it was passed by a huge majority, including most Democratic members. What a breakdown in democracy, even in the aftermath of 9/11. What shameful behavior of the peoples' representatives. Who could trust such "fools?"

So many younger Americans say that labels such as Democrat, Republican, liberal, progressive, conservative and the like mean nothing. Yet millions of disgusted, disillusioned and disenfranchised Americans have not coalesced around one political movement or party. Oddly, breaking the two-party duopoly was not helped by the success of Jesse Ventura, Ross Perot, and Pat Buchanan. Ventura had personality but was unqualified and voted into office out of sheer frustration in Minnesota. Perot had enough money to get considerable attention that eventually showed how unqualified he was. And Buchanan profited from his media celebrity status and brash language to appeal to some frustrated voters but not those giving some thought to his rhetoric. Ventura became governor and Perot got nearly 20 percent of the national vote because both had access to televised debates. All three had a certain charm and spoke plainly, but in the end gave true political reform a bad name. There was also the third-party racist George Wallace (who received nearly 10 million votes for 13 percent of the popular vote for president in 1968) and the perennial, bizarre presidential candidate Lyndon LaRouche, who has received about $6 million in federal campaign funding.

With little access to third party candidates and their messages, the electorate, at least the part that votes, aligns itself with one or the other of the two major parties. The Libertarians, the Greens, and independents really do have important political perspectives. Yet we stay with the tyranny of simplicity. Voters decide whether Democrats or Republicans offer some personal benefit, or which one causes the least cognitive dissonance. Some hope that one party's largesse to special interests may "trickle-down" and offer personal benefits. Ignored is whether either party consistently serves the broad public interest. American society is polarized by special and self-interests and distractive cultural issues (such as gun control, abortion, and gay marriage), rather than being united by shared civic demand for public servants serving public interests. Keeping America on edge with fear and anger over social issues has always paid off for the power elites.

Both major parties are populated by lying politicians, who "*talk* for the people, and *work* for the corporate elites," as Michael Parenti observed. Electing liars chips away at democracy. As Ralph Keyes said in *The Post-Truth Era*: "One sign of a healthy democracy is its citizens' capacity for outrage when they are deceived." Outrage requires letting in the truth about our deMOCKracy. Americans without outrage perpetuate placebo patriotism. The worst aspect of our plutocracy is how outrage has been suppressed and sublimated into consumerism. Combine simmering outrage with a glimmer of possible political change to unshackle outrage, and when it surfaces shared personal dissent becomes collective political power. People can discover that this feels better than silently suffering personal anger and despair, not voting, or voting for a third-party candidate only because it feels good for a few minutes.

Blasphemous Objective Reality

In theory, good citizens vote. In practice, better citizens work to bust negative status quo conditions or support those trying to do so for the sake of restoring American democracy.

To help understand the voting behavior of Americans, we can examine whether they believe that their personal success in life depends in some way on government. In fact, the percentage of Americans who believe that personal success depends on forces outside their control fell from 41 percent in 1988 to 32 percent in 2004. Think about this; it is remarkable. Only about a third of Americans, therefore, have much reason to think that who wins elections really affects their lives. They are dead wrong. They are buying into the American dream rhetoric—the myth that opportunity is there for everyone to take advantage of, that success is just up to you, which is exactly what our ruling power elites want you to believe rather than demanding government that really works for we the people.

Residents in other advanced, industrialized nations with higher voter turnouts and civic engagement feel differently: 59 percent of Germans in 1991 believed that forces outside their control determine their success and this rose to 68 percent in 2004. In other nations government is important in peoples' minds. For them government is a necessary good. For many Americans, government is a waste of taxpayer money. And to a large degree it is, but only because of bad government serving the corporatist state. Americans really do want effective social programs, they want the government to provide assistance to the poor, they want universal health care, and they want economic security.

American politicians, when campaigning and when in office, make headlines by supporting various kinds of benefits, such as a few hundred or even a few thousand dollars of tax cuts to middle-class Americans. But most people know that such inducements for loyalty to a political party matter little, especially when health care and other costs are rising, real income is stagnant at best, and consumer debt is skyrocketing. With strong emotions about wasteful and corrupt government spending, the old distinction between Democrats-want-more-government versus Republicans-want-less-government no longer holds. The two parties emphasize different special interests to lavish government spending on and hand-outs to. They know how to pander and whom to pander to, and the fewer voters the easier is their job.

A largely shared perspective on the 2004 presidential race was that a vote for President George W. Bush was a vote for the status quo. As is true of most elections for incumbent presidents; they are referenda on their administrations. Bruce Kunkel of Hillsboro, Kansas explained his vote for Bush in 2004 "I went with the status quo." He explained the similar vote of his neighbors and the majority of all Americans as "they don't like change." After the election when Bush elevated several close advisors to cabinet positions, the *New York Times* editorialized: "Optimists can regard the new team as a more efficient packaging of the status quo."

Yet in 2004, Kerry failed to convince enough Americans that he could take the country in a new and better direction. His supporters mostly were "pushed" by what they viewed as a disastrous administration—the-anyone-but-Bush state of mind. But a candidate must "pull" people with likely benefits. Kerry did not present a clear vision of a better America. Bush, the status quo preserver, could only have been beaten by a perceived status quo buster. This line of argument was supported by data, as Dick Polman reported in the *Philadelphia Inquirer*:

> What made Kerry competitive in this race was that he won the voters (25 percent of the electorate) who wanted change; he beat Bush among those voters by 95 percent to 4 percent. But there was also strong sentiment, elsewhere in the electorate, for the status quo—for the traditional dictum that it is unwise to change presidents in wartime.

Not that anyone would suggest that Bush went to war with Iraq to win reelection or that The Carlyle Group sought the financial bonanza from the war. Sure.

Winning politicians like to refer to their parties as "majority parties." But rarely do winning parties get into office through anything close to a majority of the electorate. To the contrary, what we normally see is a fairly equal split among voters. Consider this hypothesis. The fact that the nation's voters are so evenly divided between Republican/conservative versus Democrat/liberal candidates is evidence that objective truth does not prevail. If true facts prevailed, then one of these groups would have a lot more supporters than just half the population. Standing on the sidelines are the many people having escaped both groups' paradigms—unbelievers of both sets of lies, the moderates and independents, third-party supporters, and the totally alienated who do not participate—the "none of the above" eligible voters. They are the most likely to see the lies of Democrats and Republicans. Stuck with their better grasp of reality and their own belief systems they remain outside the two-party power game.

Consider this question: In 2004, in the context of a war on terrorism and a war in Iraq as well spiraling government spending, borrowing, and debt, how could nearly equal parts of society want either more of the same (Bush) or a change (Kerry)? Such splits can be interpreted as resulting from the absence of a perceived truthful, objective reality seen by open-minded citizens. More likely, fairly even splits reflect the war of campaign lies and efforts aimed at offsetting the opposition's incremental achievements to obtain votes above and beyond reliable core constituencies. The fight for the middle, for the center, and for the undecideds is a battle fought with lies, propaganda and deception.

Yes, it is reasonable to believe in a true, objective and causal reality, notably about the consequences of decisions, policies and programs of an incumbent. There certainly were a large number of certifiable effects of the Bush administration, many of them negative and contrary to the personal interests of voters, such as dire economic conditions. The question is: Why did half of the voters not see and accept the information that they had access to. The exposure to considerable information is proven by dramatic changes in public opinion as revealed in surveys. Bush-supporters minimized their cognitive dissonance by blocking or ignoring key negative facts, while Kerry-voters did not. And they assigned more importance to other information, particularly social issues positively connected to Bush. On many issues, however, voters could not perceive enough difference between the candidates, which was objectively true. As columnist Robert J. Samuelson said: "The post-election elation of Bush voters and the wretchedness of Kerry supporters cannot be explained by objective differences on policies. ...Politics, news and entertainment merge, because all seek to satisfy psychological needs." So Bush won with less than 31 percent of eligible voters in 2004 not because of the absence of all truth about the negative impacts of his presidency, though certainly more information could have been produced by the media, such as reporting about the Bush bulge.

To invoke moral judgments and choices as determinants of political outcomes without recognizing the role of objective facts is folly. In making moral judgments and choices about real-world things we process information and make conclusions based on that processing— on evaluating or ignoring the truthfulness of information—that is used to reach moral decisions. Bush-supporters reached different moral judgments than those of Kerry-voters and those differences resulted from different status quo bias beliefs and reality models that greatly impacted how generally available information was used. It is either using this line of reasoning or believing that one group's morality is superior to the other's. And this quickly brings you into the realm of the radical evangelicals who see God only on their side and Satan's influence on their political enemies. Or it causes you to place too much importance and blame on the media's control of information. In advocating for a new and better political system we need to believe that something more than religious and moral beliefs are determinative; we need to hope that providing truthful and well framed information can lead thoughtful people to reach rational conclusions consistent with their religious and moral beliefs. When Bush says, "the United States does not torture," we must hope that abundant information about the torture of people by U.S. agents is heard, processed, remembered and used by ALL Americans to causally conclude he had lied.

The split in the population also resulted from the illusion of choice, because issues masqueraded as principles. Yes, the choice of president would determine how the government pursued the Iraq war, dealt with social security, defended the nation against terrorism, spread the tax burden, and addressed health care. Neither Bush nor Kerry talked about the need to repair our representative government. Neither one would stand up to corporate corruption of government. Neither would crack down on corporate welfare, just spread it around differently. Neither would treat the public with honesty. So why vote for change. The liar you know is safer than the liar you don't know. We desperately need radically different principles in the public arena so that the political spectrum widens.

There was not enough difference in 2004. As Barry Crimmins said: "The two party system just means that the corporations cut two checks instead of one." And Robert F. Kennedy, Jr. said: "The biggest threat to American democracy is corporate power. …[The Democrats] just quash discussion about the corrosive impact of excessive corporate power on American democracy."

A far different scenario would hold if a third-party candidate, who has demonstrated commitment to the public interest could become president. Believers in the two-party duopoly argue that with no allies in Congress such a president would have little ability to change the system. Third-party advocates counter that given the power and prestige of the presidency, including putting in new heads and managers of Executive Branch agencies, a third-party president could make a big difference. What we do know is that in 2004 the Democrats could not blame Ralph Nader or insufficient money for their loss; they had raised about the same amount of money as the Republicans. Paradoxically, Nader was able to maintain that the Democrats ran on the wrong issues and that if they had adopted many of his positions, they could have won. But that's the view of a status quo buster.

Chapter 10

Retaking Democracy:
From Dysfunction to Rebirth

In a democracy dissent is an act of faith. Like medicine, the test of its value is not in its taste, but in its effects.

—J. W. Fulbright

It is easier to say that loyalty is not than what it is. It is not conformity. It is not passive acquiescence to the status quo. ...It is the realization that America was born of revolt, flourished on dissent, became great through experimentation.

—Henry Steele Commager

We have it in our power to begin American democracy over again.

Many thoughtful people have a very negative view of the state of the union. Conservatives on the right, progressives on the left, and independents in the middle are disgusted with the political system controlled by the two-party duopoly. Reaching the Promised Land enshrined in the American Dream requires serious consideration of a new and unique third party.

Overcoming Bad Choices

What an intellectual treat to read the words of people from the political left and right as they explained their votes in the 2004 presidential election. True conservatives and progressives lost in 2004, because neither had an authentic choice and they were vastly outnumbered.

First, consider the political left, especially many people casting themselves as "progressives." Based on Gore's defeat in the 2000 election and Ralph Nader's relative success, the Democrats did a hatchet job on Nader in 2004 so that he would not appear on ballots in some major states (California, Ohio, Pennsylvania, and Oregon) and draw votes away from Senator John Kerry. They were even able to hijack the Green Party and keep its nomination from going to Nader. Nader had received more than three times the votes in Green Party primaries than the ultimate candidate, David Cobb. Now, the evil that Democrats did lives after them.

In October 2004, Greg Bates on Counterpunch.org offered an open, unscientific survey to people committed to voting for Nader in the 2004 presidential election. What they said sheds light on the thinking of many Americans disillusioned with the two-party system. Here are extracts from some of those comments:

> History shows plainly that neither the Democratic Party nor the GOP gives a damn about democracy. Both groups exist to preserve the status quo and ensure corporate hegemony at the expense of workers and the environment. All of this is so well-documented that it simply underscores the complicity of mainstream media in maintaining the veil of ignorance that rests firmly over the eyes of most of my fellow citizens.
>
> This year, more than at any previous time, I have been conscious of the amount of money and effort spent by the state and its various apparatuses (including the mainstream media) to create the illusion of democracy and choice in the political process. And yet, never before has the lack of both been so glaringly apparent.
>
> The last 4 years have proven to me that the Democratic Party is dead and serves no useful purpose other than to preserve the illusion that the United States is a democratic country.
>
> The Ds sat on their asses for almost four years and now they expect the voters to jump up and notice them because they say they have a plan. I don't want to join the delusional crowd that feels that as soon as Kerry is in the oval office, things will immediately change for the better.

Democracy only works when we vote for what we truly believe in. "Strategic voting" and the lesser-of-two-evils politics have no place in a successful democratic society.

Immediately after the defeat of Senator John Kerry, Donna J. Volatile published on Counterpunch.org, a kind of manifesto for the Kerry downfallen and a call to status quo busters. Here are her key ideas:

> Your guy lost, plain and simple but was he really your guy to begin with? ...I wonder if it ever occurred to any of you just how un-democratic the Democrats truly were throughout the course of this election? The Democrats didn't promote democracy, they impeded it and in the end, they decimated the third party alternative and spent millions of dollars doing it. ...So, here's the reality, slowly sinking in, as another day dawns over the evil Bush Empire: we cannot change the system from within. ...There was no choice in this election! Repeat after me: There was no choice in this election, only the illusion of choice, more than that, the bill of goods you

were sold was the illusion of democracy. ...Out with the old worn out two party system. ...We need to get busy organizing the third party alternative: the party of, for and by the people! ...Every society needs a little revolution now and then. The Revolution starts now!

Anis Memon also published an article on Counterpunch.org that castigated progressives who voted for Kerry:

> The Democratic Party savagely undermined democracy by obstructing ballot access for progressive third party candidates. ...Now it's up to the progressives to realize that if they want a progressive candidate to win, they have to vote for one. ...The Democratic Party, which has survived for years by co-opting progressive movements, has ceased making any effort even to pretend to change the system of which it is an increasingly useless part.

From the political right, great thinking and writing was given on the Internet site of *The American Conservative* in a series of essays representing justifications for different votes by conservatives in the 2004 presidential election.

In "The Right to Remain Silent," Kara Hopkins made these dazzling points about the value of not voting in the two-duopoly system:

> They will be accused of sloth, though indifference is more apt—and remains the appropriate response to irrelevance. ...Elections maintain the illusion of opposing parties, exchanging ideas rather than political animals competing for power. Selling voting as the ultimate expression of citizenship serves two purposes. It legitimizes the process that keeps them in control and makes the public docile by enforcing the notion that we rule ourselves. But what value is participation if those who cast ballots go unrepresented? Is there virtue in the act if it allows no choice? ...By declining to be coerced, we may yet salvage a scrap of liberty. We won't be letting democracy down, for it has already disappointed us.

In "Libertarian Resistance," Allan W. Bock made the case for conservatives voting for the Libertarian candidate rather than George W. Bush:

> The question is what kind of vote will best send a message to the system about the importance of your core political values. ...By its nature the electoral system does not offer ideal choices, simply those that have managed to claw their way to party nominations and ballot status. ...George W. Bush richly deserves to be punished at the polls. ...The Libertarian Party, whatever its many shortcomings, has been around since 1972, running candidates at every level. ...It is much better organized at a national level than any of the minor conservative parties (which may not be saying much) and it has presented a coherent philosophical alternative

to the major parties for decades. ...A vote for a Libertarian is the best way for a small-government, constitutionalist conservative to let various establishments know there is still a constituency for the Constitution.

In "The Real Deal," Taki made the case as a conservative for voting for the Constitution Party candidate Michael Anthony Peroutka over George Bush:

> Yes, I know, it sounds like a wasted vote, but is it? ...The point of voting for Peroutka is to help create an alternative. ...Without big ideas, elections become about personalities—popularity contests, nothing more. Both major candidates are filching each others' rhetoric and pandering. All that matters is sell, not the content.

In "Kerry's the One," Scott McConnell took on the challenge of justifying a conservative vote for Kerry rather than Bush:

> If Kerry wins...the most important battles will take place within the Republican Party and the conservative movement. A Bush defeat will ignite a huge soul-searching within the rank-and-file of Republicandom: a quest to find out how and where the Bush presidency went wrong. And it is then that more traditional conservatives will have an audience to argue for a conservatism informed by the lessons of history, based on prudence and a sense of continuity with the American past—and to make that case without a powerful White House pulling in the opposite direction. ...George W. Bush has come to embody a politics that is antithetical to almost any kind of thoughtful conservatism.

Finally, in "Coming Home," Patrick J. Buchanan made the case for true conservatives swallowing hard and voting for Bush despite substantial disagreement with many of Bush's positions and actions:

> Assuredly, a president who plunged us into an unnecessary and ruinous war must be held accountable. And if Bush loses, Iraq will have been his undoing. But a vote for Kerry is more than just a vote to punish Bush. It is a vote to punish America. ...The Constitution Party is the party closest to this magazine in philosophy and policy prescriptions, and while one must respect votes for Michael Peroutka by those who live in Red or Blue states, we cannot counsel such votes in battleground states.

No idealism here, just pragmatic rationalization amounting to choosing the lesser evil.

Hit the Gas for the Future

Now, the only way you see the promise of American democracy is in the rear view mirror. Coke is now more of the real thing than is American democracy. We no longer have the fairy-tale American democracy long advertised to us and marketed to other countries. Nostalgia and complacency have replaced rage—except on roads. Americans work hard for their money, but not for their democracy. They must see a return on their investment of time and energy in fixing the republic. That requires seeing that current circumstances ideally support what this volume concludes and prescribes—that a major shakeup in our political system is possible.

Our stable electoral, representative government—along with the entrenched legacy belief that we live in the greatest democracy on the planet—blinds most Americans to the truth and in others prevents discontent from becoming outrage. It is instructive that George W. Bush has rarely put himself in front of unscreened and unapproved American citizens to directly hear their views and experience their passionate dissent, nor does our system compel him to face his political opposition in person and in public. The British parliamentary system that regularly puts its prime minister out in public confronting and debating his political opponents makes our president's isolation all the more repulsive and more empowered to use propaganda and lies to keep Americans in tow.

To love our nation, but believe it has been squandering its democratic principles is to be branded as unpatriotic or subversive. The right to make money is deemed more important than the right to dissent and have third-party candidates offering true political discourse.

It is important for people to see the possibility of making substantial systemic improvement in our political system without, however, wholesale constitutional change. People have lost hope for change through a third-party candidate. They also discount dramatic change that can happen outside of electing new office holders, as through ballot initiatives and protests and other forms of social action. They must recall our early revolutionary days when there were British loyalists and American patriots. Today's loyalists owe allegiance to the political-economic power elites running the country. And today's patriots fight the corrupt corporatist and autocratic status quo.

Think Positive: The Invincible is Destructible

The media ensure that the public's attention is steered away from truly fundamental problems with government and democracy and toward social and cultural issues. And toward scandals, but scandals are no substitute for solutions. All this helps the two major parties to differentiate themselves, obscuring their sameness and subservience to status quo political-corporatism. When consumers get suckered into this game and feel good about choosing one side or the other, they have empowered the two-party duopoly, political-corporatism status quo and erosion of democracy. When others align with a third-party or do not vote, they too empower and sustain the status quo. A United Americans Party that seeks to destroy the restricted political system and defeat Democrats and Republicans is the way out of this.

In commenting about the 2004 presidential election from the progressive perspective, Jeffrey St. Clair said this on Counterpunch.org:

> Freedom can come from such losses. Freedom from illusions, for starters. There's a crisp clarity to the political landscape now that will cloud up as the days and months go by. The time to bolt is now, while the guards are changing. There are many fellow travelers, leftists and libertarians, wandering out here in the wilderness searching for a new party of resistance to corporatism and imperial wars that will be led by those who will not flinch under fire.

Futurists tend to be wrong in the short-term but correct in the long-term. In 1982, John Naisbitt said this in *Megatrends*: "The demise of representative democracy also signals the end of the traditional party system." In 1993, Alvin Toffler said this in *Powershift:* "Our existing political decisionmaking structures are now recognized to be obsolete." That same year *A Call for Revolution* by Martin L. Gross decried historically extreme conditions that he could not imagine getting even worse. His view that those conditions would produce an imminent citizens' revolution was dead wrong. Here are some excerpts to give the flavor of Gross's analysis:

> The stirrings of revolution are afoot in the land. ...[The] American government [is] now a model of bipartisan excess, even stupidity. ... Representative government in the United States no longer works. ... Citizens of every tribe and stripe have become the victims of America's manipulators. ...Without fear of reasonable contradiction, we can state

that the U.S. government, circa 1994, has evolved over three decades into the worst in the history of the Republic. ...[The] apocalypse of the U.S. government comes nearer every day as the critical mass of taxes, debt, and expenditures becomes impossible to sustain. ...Politicians have always been somewhat deceptive, but the corruption of words is reaching new heights. ...More and more, the lying seems pathological—the mouthings of untruths almost by reflex, a dangerous new precedent. ...*Either the American people will defeat the oppressive excesses of Washington, or Washington will defeat us, ending the story of the most successful nation in history.* ...What is needed is a *Citizens Revolution*, one organized by an educated populace with an agenda for real change. ...To remake America we must understand that it will not happen without citizen intervention. ...those who know that tinkering with the broken engine of Washington is not going to do the trick—are gaining exponentially in number every day. ...Who are these people? They are Democrats. They are Republicans. They are Perot people. ...There will be a peaceful revolution. Of that I am sure. And as it moves forward each day, we can feel confident that it will be the American citizen, as it was in 1776, who will save our blessed land.

Clearly, overturning status quo forces to fix the republic is much more difficult than Gross, an experienced social critic, imagined. Despite a correct diagnosis, his simplistic prescriptions for making Americans more educated and politically engaged proved inadequate. His focus on addressing problems in *government* did not fathom the depth and scope of cracks in American *democracy.*

Another important analysis was made by two senior political reporters, Dan Balz and Ronald Brownstein, in their 1996 book *Storming the Gates.* They examined American history and how third-parties had played important roles in improving the nation. They considered "the third way," meaning an independent third-party candidate becoming president and said "mounting frustration with Washington is accelerating political instability. If disenchantment continues to mount, the nineteenth century precedents suggest greater turbulence could lie ahead." Public disenchantment certainly has mounted since 1996. Here are more of their insights:

> Historically, the emergence of new parties has been one of the clearest signs of dissatisfaction with government and the political system. ...As in the nineteenth century, discontent with the two major parties is again increasing agitation for a new choice.

As to the pathway for this to happen, they expressed some optimism about one scenario:

> As more established voices join the chorus urging alternatives to
> the two parties, the idea is bound to seem less radical and risky. And as
> the prospect of new alternatives becomes less forbidding to voters, more
> established political leaders may see an advantage in aligning themselves
> with it—further increasing the idea's credibility.

It is not obvious, however, at this time which "established voices" having public recognition and stature could take a third-party to success. But Balz and Brownstein were optimistic that diverse "groups can be united in their dissatisfaction with the nation's direction and the two major parties." And that "the longer majorities of Americans continue to distrust Washington and view politicians as controlled by special interests, the greater the opportunity will grow for a credible independent presidential candidate to make the case that both parties serve themselves and not the nation. ...The question is whether any political entrepreneur can organize that discontent by offering an appealing alternative to the existing choices... ...The procedural barriers to providing such a new political choice are formidable. But there is no question that the market for it exists."

So, *demand* for democracy-rescue is not the issue, *supply* of political leadership is the problem.

Interestingly, Balz and Brownstein invoked public opinion survey results over the years that showed public support for a new third party: 20 percent in the 1960s, 40 percent in the 1980s, and 60 percent in 1995. Recall the 70 to 80 percent support found in 2005 mentioned in the Preface. Could anyone ask for a more significant trend?

In 2005, David S. Broder wrote a column titled "A Pox on Both Parties." It and ended with: "When both parties have lost public confidence, where do voters turn?" Do they turn away or do they engage?

Now fast-forward to 2016. Circumstances are bringing an end to 164 years of two-party rule because the next president is from a new party, according to a head-scratching 2005 article by James Fallows, "Countdown to a Meltdown" in *The Atlantic Monthly*. In looking back at what created this historic change through a memo to the certain next president Fallows noted: "having created our new party, you are already assured of its nomination, whereas the candidates from the two legacy parties are still carving themselves up in their primaries. ...The story of the parties, then, is that the American people mistrust the Republicans' economic record, and don't trust the Democrats enough to let them try to do better. That is why—and it is the only reason why—they are giving us a chance." As to the "unspoken deal with China," Fallows said, "each time Congress raised benefits, reduced taxes, or encouraged more borrowing by consumers, it shifted part of the U.S. manufacturing base to China. …In retrospect, the ugly end is so obvious and inevitable. Why didn't people see it at the time?" He was referring to the "hard landing" of the economy in 2009, when the dollar "bought only 2.5 Chinese yuan—not eight, as it did a year earlier." Economic meltdown hit hard. "The two-party system had been in trouble for decades. It was rigid, polarizing, and unrepresentative. The parties were pawns of special interests," Fallows recounted.

Step back and reflect on all of these views from 1982, 1993, 1996, 2005 and 2016. Failed American government leads to more public discontent that leads to more disgust with the two-party system and its ability to address genuine public interests that leads to a successful citizens' revolution that leads to a third-party candidate winning the presidency. It could happen. It must happen.

Most people have been overly optimistic about timing. What this demonstrates is not that the two-party duopoly, dual political system, and corporatist plutocracy has turned around enough to merit broad public support. To the contrary, the Bush II reign of incompetence and dishonesty has only exacerbated and underscored the failure of America's traditional political system. No, this is what must be acknowledged: *Though public discontent, disgust and dissent have reached new highs, what is still lacking is a critical mass of public outrage—or tipping point—to produce the organized active dissent capable of beating the corruption status quo.*

What now? We must believe that the tipping point is on the horizon of hope, that the future is soon arriving. That the beginning of the 21st century is the right time for challenging America's two-party duopoly and political-corporatism status quo, because democracy's decline has reached new depths with the Bush II administration. Never have so many Americans become so disillusioned with politics as usual. The case presented in this volume for a Second American Revolution is not pie-in-the-sky optimism. Achieving major societal change too easily seems improbable if not impossible. So consider this wisdom of noted historian Howard Zinn:

> There is a tendency to think that what we see in the present moment will continue. We forget how often we have been astonished by the sudden crumbling of institutions, by extraordinary changes in people's thoughts, by unexpected eruptions of rebellion against tyrannies, by the quick collapse of systems of power that seemed invincible.

In other words, even the strongest status quos can be busted. Okay, the glass was hardly filled in the 2004 presidential election, but Ralph Nader received 504,000 votes in 34 states, Libertarian Party candidate Michael Badnarik received 360,000 votes in 49 states, Constitutionalist Party candidate Allen Petrouka received 131,000 votes in 36 states, and Green Party candidate David Cobb received 106,000 votes in 46 states. Considering that third-parties do not get on many ballots and do not get any significant access to voters during campaigns, it is heartening that over one million Americans went against the popular grain, did not succumb to the giant propaganda machine, and voted their beliefs and conscience. Do the math. Remember those roughly *80 million eligible voters who did not vote*—ultimately they are the truly persuadable voters, the most likely to viscerally feel our democracy deficit and support true structural change. Their internalized dissent must morph into loud outrage.

Fusing Left, Right and Middle

Wisdom *is* out there. After voting for independents for 20 years New Jersey resident Frank Demartino observed in December 2005: "Why can't these [independent political] parties get together and support the basic principle of the need for a third political party. Spearheading this campaign could be Ross Perot, Ralph Nader or Jesse Ventura. They should forget their agendas in order to put up a united front. ...the time has come and gone for the two-party system. Let's bring on the third." For the good of the country former independent candidates (and free-thinking public figures) ought to patriotically band together to support a new and larger effort to overturn the political status quo. They would tell Democrats and Republicans "a pox on both your houses" and by example show Americans the need to unite and fight our democracy's assassins.

Recall the split among eligible voters for the 2004 presidential election, with some 40 percent not voting. Now, imagine convincing half of them and 15 percent of those voting for the two major parties to vote for a United Americans candidate. You end up with a plurality for the new party. A straight-talking, non-lying United Americans candidate, with a message focused on repairing our democracy and ridding it of all forms of corporate subsidies, corruption, and abuse, could pull this off. The candidate would not be seeking the "middle" or the "center" for political purposes but all Americans who recognize the failure of the two-party duopoly and the need to get back to basics—the quality of American democracy. Unite and fight.

Think about the voices from the progressive left and the conservative right who, to a large extent, share a common rejection of the two-party duopoly, because the Republican Party has let conservatives down and the Democratic Party has let progressives down. In so many ways, these people are the most thoughtful and politically engaged Americans, and the most energized to bust the two-party status quo. True, at first you see their opposite views on many contemporary *issues*. Yet, at another, deeper level of reality, they have a common belief in the finest American *principles and aspirations*. Cultural issues of the day divide and polarize Americans, but core principles that define the noblest American ideals can unite people. A good example is that many people on the political right and left share a commitment to removing the corporate corruption of our government.

When it comes to principles, however, unprincipled politicians would rather blabber and lie about cultural issues, often dressing them as "values." Cultural issues matter, but principles of democracy matter more. In September 2005, after hurricane Katrina, Newt Gingrich acknowledged that "We're not in a values fight now but over whether the system is working. The issue is delivery. And that's true at every level— city, state and federal. …it is a mistake to get trapped into defending the systems and processes which clearly failed." *Washington Post* columnist David Ignatius echoed this view about the need to change politics as usual: "The yearning in the country for something different has been palpable this year."

Issues must be framed and debated in ways that link them to democracy. To talk issues is to focus on facts and squeeze status quo bias beliefs, but to talk democracy principles is to stress American ideals sought but not yet reached. If one candidate talks issues and the other talks principles, they likely talk past each other. Cultural issues must not distract Americans from focusing on American democracy's decline. Protecting democracy should trump issues used by politicians to divide Americans.

The point of fusing conservative and progressive goals is not to achieve a compromise-middle, but to align interests in restoring American democracy. This requires a focus on three central needs: revitalizing our democracy, promoting citizen participation, and stopping corporate aristocracy and corruption. A historic opportunity awaits the disenfranchised and disillusioned from the right and the left—and the distracted in the middle—to work together for a better America. A new party could select and prioritize among the following ideas; those recommended for top-10 consideration are bolded.

To revitalize democracy:

- **replace the Electoral College with the popular vote or at least proportional state systems**

- **eliminate the number of senators from state electoral college votes**

- **promote None of the Above options on ballots**

- seek news media reforms to better serve the public interest, including reinstating the Fairness Doctrine and the News Distortion Rule

- remove barriers to fusion candidates

- adopt Instant Runoff Voting

- pass a federal requirement for independent state redistricting commissions free from any political party bias to reverse rigged districts and prevent new ones

- pass the Our Democracy, Our Airwaves Act

- remove obstacles to third-party candidates, such as blanket primaries

- lower qualifying criteria for televised presidential debates to allow leading third-party candidates to participate

- put the League of Women Voters or the Citizens' Debate Commission in charge of presidential debates
- criminalize use of false and misleading information in political campaign activities
- require that a Supreme Court majority have a two-vote margin to eliminate narrow 5-4 decisions
- remove judicial immunity
- enforce the constitutional requirement that only Congress can declare war, and ensure that it explicitly does so when necessary (it is unconstitutional for Congress to transfer its war power to the presidency, as happened with Bush II and the Iraq war)
- modify the 14th constitutional amendment so that only legal citizens are counted to in the national census to establish the number of congressional districts in states
- to expand public support for non-corporate media provide public funding for the Public Broadcasting System through a voluntary $10 check off on federal income tax returns
- pass a federal Taxpayer Bill of Rights law that constrains increases in spending and debt
- fight globalization and withdraw from international trade agreements that remove the sovereignty of Americans and their local, state and federal governments, and that impoverish the world
- eliminate fast-track status for trade negotiations that limits the role of Congress
- require all political parties to hold state primaries for presidential candidates on the same day
- to expand political discourse and competition allow foreign born persons with at least 20 years of citizenship to be president
- change the presidential succession to replace the Secretary of State with the Senate majority leader so that an elected, not a political appointee can become president
- make the secretive Federal Reserve Board accountable to Congress

and the public through more public reports and more open congressional oversight

- for persons born on U.S. soil, but with parents here illegally, make them legal residents but not U.S. citizens

To promote citizen participation:

- **make Election Day a national holiday**
- **create a federal ballot initiative or national referendum process with ballot measures for congressional and presidential elections**
- **expand state ballot initiative options by providing necessary enabling laws and reducing procedural requirements**
- **implement same day registration everywhere**
- after making critically needed election reforms make voting compulsory
- support regular required state constitutional conventions
- restore voting rights to felons who have fulfilled their penalties

To stop corporate supremacy and corruption:

- **use state and federal Clean Money/Clean Elections campaign financing**
- **end federal corporate welfare and subsidies through the tax code and regulations**
- **prohibit no-bid federal contracts**
- block the invasion of illegal immigrants that gives business cheap labor through markedly greater physical barriers and policing of borders as well as reversing our globalization policies
- remove constitutional protections and human rights for corporations
- prohibit fund-raising for presidential libraries during a presidency and require full disclosure of contributions afterwards
- prohibit former federal officials from lobbying their former agencies

and working on contracts or grants from them for five years

- prohibit use of eminent domain to transfer private land to different private commercial interests for the sake of economic development and increased tax revenues

- pursue petroleum independence through, for example, conservation, alternative fuels, higher motor vehicle fuel efficiency, removal of government subsidies for vehicle use

- remove government incentives for exporting jobs

- prohibit use of government funds for work outsourced to foreign countries

- prohibit use of non-disclosure requirements in civil settlements that protect corporate interests but keep valuable information from the public

- through legislation of executive order require federal executive branch agencies to explicitly serve the public interest as their chief priority rather than any business sector; for example, the Food and Drug Administration would not support the pharmaceutical industry and the Department of Agriculture would not aid the beef industry

- aggressively pursue corporate crimes and criminalize Internet spamming, phone telemarketing, and junk mailing

- adhere to the polluter pays principle through aggressive enforcement of environmental laws and regulations with criminal prosecutions not just civil fines

- for corporate fraud levy fines that really hurt bottom-line profits, and make them non-tax deductible as a business expense

- make it a federal crime (felony) with mandatory long prison sentences for companies that knowingly hire illegal residents

- remove federal funding to jurisdictions with sanctuary policies that protect illegal immigrants

- impose an offset sales tax on companies, like Wal-Mart, that externalize costs to government by paying low wages and giving poor benefits, with an exemption for truly low income people

- require businesses that collect data on individuals to obtain permission from them before they can sell such data

- fight elitism by requiring official presidential inaugural balls (where the president or vice-president attend) make at least half the tickets low-priced and available to the general public

- require that government-oriented non-profit groups, such as the National Governors Association, that receive federal funds make their public meetings open to the general public at low cost

In contemplating these many reforms it pays to focus on the potential for state governments—"the laboratories of democracy"—to initiate action under the pressure of citizens, rather than depend on the federal government in Washington, D.C.

Let's Surprise the World

Sweeping reform of the political-economic system is the goal. The key question is: Will enough Americans welcome a new unifying political party to save *their* democracy? By providing a forum for lively and broad political debate that connects citizens to politics, such a party would provide the venue for implementing the Second American Revolution. It must expose and break the underground restricted political system—the power mafia that some enter because they are born into it (like George W. Bush) or work their way up the ladder of corruption (like Dick Cheney and Tom DeLay).

Imagine *millions* of third-party supporters, non-voters, and lesser-evil voters (Republicans and Democrats) uniting around the need to regain the basic principles and virtues that our Founders believed possible for our nation: democracy, fairness and the rule of law. Think of a unified third-party as more than a rejection of both the Republicans and Democrats, but as a national party "of, for and by the people." A party that would be based on Clean Money/Clean Elections principles, taking no money from any special interests and only small amounts from individuals. In the end, differences on social and cultural issues are less important than unifying Americans in regaining an honest and effective democracy. Our Founders did this and so can we.

Such a party would truly represent the best, most principled "moral values" to unite Americans. Recognizing that divided we stand, together we fall, uniting Americans would be the priority. This new party could be called the "United Americans Party." Much like the original Progressives, it would be a reformist movement to mobilize the latent power of people now trapped in the illusory political system and exploited by the restricted political system. It would fight the plutocrats, oligarchs, and theocrats that undermine American democracy. It would attract Americans who honor the magical words of Tom Paine:

> We have it in our power to begin the world over again.
> He also said something else that merits reflection:
> A long habit of not thinking a thing wrong gives it a superficial appearance of right.

Blocking the reality that American democracy has become delusional is the problem. We have it in our power to reboot our democracy. Also, the words of Mark Twain should guide a new reformist effort:

> [The people] have *at all times* an undeniable and indefeasible right to *alter their form of government* in such a manner as they may think expedient. ... Loyalty to the country, always; loyalty to the government when it deserves it.

Today's politicians intentionally conflate patriotism with loyalty to country and government to protect themselves when what is needed is patriotism based on loyal dissent.

The new party must have charismatic leaders committed to battling the two-party duopoly, condemning it for pushing us toward a fake democracy, economic ruin, and reduced national sovereignty and security. They must tell Americans that no democracy is worthy of imposing its military and economic power on other nations, supposedly to spread democracy, if it ignores its own serious imperfections. They must help Americans understand that by admitting our own shortcomings and having the courage to correct them, we will regain international respect and peace. A bumper sticker message for the new party might be: **Give Government Back to the People**. This would also be a pledge to Americans.

We need leaders willing to risk their personal future for the good of the nation. They must be many things: Willing and able to take the country back to Jeffersonian ideals. Able to think like our Founders, because saving a democracy is as important as creating it. Dedicated to placing people above politics. Determined to earn the consent of the governed by representing the public interest. Courageous to do what's right—not just raise money—but raise hopes—inspiring millions of Americans to have conversations with their family members, relatives, friends, co-workers and neighbors about fixing our shared democracy. Honest enough to tell Americans that what the country needs is not governing *from* the left or right or center but solely governing *for* the people, that dissent in the name of democracy is patriotism, that providing pleasure today through tax cuts and deficit borrowing means pain for tomorrow's children. Politically savvy enough to lay out a vision, strategies, tactics, and specific projects. Daring enough to tell Americans that it's morally right and necessary to tax the rich and super-rich again—to get *really* progressive, at least until there's no more deficit. To bring back the idea of a balanced budget constitutional amendment and maybe put together a **Contract With Democracy**.

Who is out there to take us to the Promised Land? Think of a grand genetic blender combining the pointy-headed simplistic honesty of Ross Perot, the political and speaking skills of Bill Clinton, the gutsy revolutionariness of Newt Gingrich, the quiet, take-charge charisma of Rudy Giuliani, the political honesty of Jon Stewart, the intellectual courage of Ralph Nader, and the media integrity and savvy of Lou Dobbs. You have to imagine someone willing to risk everything (after winning) to rescue American democracy. Think of some character right out of an Ayn Rand novel willing to go up against the many power elites to win the presidency.

In December 2005 columnist David Brooks wrote about the "New Age of Skepticism." He referenced the results of an NBC/Wall Street Journal poll that found only 24 percent of Americans believed Republicans represented their priorities and just 26 percent felt that way for Democrats. That leaves 50 percent disappointed with BOTH PARTIES. Plus, two-thirds of Americans felt the country was headed in the wrong direction. Brooks observed:

> In this atmosphere of general weariness, the political pendulum is no longer swinging on a left-to-right axis. ...Problems on the right do not lead to a resurgence on the left, or vice-versa. ...In this atmosphere of exhaustion, the political pendulum swings from engagement to cynicism. When polarized voters lose faith in their own side, they don't switch to the other. They just withdraw. ...In theory, skepticism leads to prudence, not a

bad trait. But when it is tinged with cynicism, as it is now, skepticism turns into passivity.

What Brooks calls "passivity" is better seen as deep political but passive discontent. Passive Americans are revolution-ready citizens. The national mood spells optimism about a United Americans Party appealing to a majority by acknowledging and addressing our democracy deficit.

Moral Imagination is Necessary

New political leaders need moral imagination—more than money and same-old political tactics—to successfully fight the deception, corruption and hypocrisy used by those who wrap themselves righteously in the American flag. New leaders must call for a Second American Revolution, not fought with weapons but with straight talk, facts, and passionate discussion. They must confront domestic tyranny. People will ask: What do we need to revolt against? An enemy a lot tougher than the colonial British is the answer. Fellow Americans oppress us, not foreign powers. If passionate Americans could fight the tyranny of the British for independence, then today's Americans can fight the tyranny of crony capitalism and corrupt government to repair their democracy. Talking openly about fake patriots taking us to a fake democracy will help Americans see the truth. And help them reject cruel credit card democracy that enslaves them.

Our current distrusted government no longer deserves the loyalty or consent of the governed. In *Superpatriotism*, Michael Parenti made this important point:

> Democracy is not about trust; it is about *distrust*. It is about accountability, exposure, open debate, direct challenge. …We have to get our fellow Americans to trust their leaders less and trust themselves a lot more, trust their own questions and suspicions, and their own desire to know what is going on.

The proposed new party must leverage citizens' mistrust in corporate-corrupted government. Then it can win, if not at first, then in a few election cycles. A United Americans Party must educate the millions of Americans who have open minds and who sense that America is on the wrong track. The majority is not Democrats and liberals or Republicans and conservatives, but the disenfranchised, disillusioned, and distracted. Forget those with closed minds who block out facts and the truth because of chronic cognitive dissonance. They have been too brain washed by the likes of Rush Limbaugh, Sean Hannity, Karl Rove (a.k.a. George W. Bush), and Fox News. Let the faith-driven and morally righteous stay glued to the myth that we still have the greatest democracy. Let the rest respect the truth and unite and fight.

Call me crazy, but I see enough common interests among moderates, conservatives and liberals, as well as hundreds of public interest groups and their supporters, to form a competitive alternative to the two-party duopoly. Importantly, a majority of Americans consider themselves independents or moderates, not liberals or conservatives, nor Republicans or Democrats. And a majority believes we should do away with the two-party system. The two-party duopoly persists because of public apathy and alienation more than commitment. What we need is widespread rejection of our pseudo-democracy, plutocracy, oligarchy, and corporatist state, and then the determination to change it.

Consider the discontent of Texas Republican (but libertarian) Congressman Ron Paul, complaining about the neoconservatives controlling the Republican Party:

> They believe lying is necessary for the state to survive. They believe certain facts should be known only by the political elite, and withheld from the general public. …They are very willing to use force to impose American ideals. …They view civil liberties with suspicion, as unnecessary restrictions on the federal government.

Such sentiments are shared by many liberals, moderates, and progressives.

In our deMOCKracy, "competition" in the marketplace is the Holy Grail. Yet, under the thumb of corporate power, the two-party duopoly works against competition where it is most needed, in the political, electoral arena.

Moral imagination is essential. We must imagine historic change for the better, the kind of change that looks remarkable and revolutionary when looking backwards into history and extraordinarily difficult when looking forward into the future. Remember the past as it really was and visualize the future as you want it to be. Hope is needed. The kind of hope expressed by Gar Alperovitz in *America Beyond Capitalism*:

> Major eruptions and political realignments are the rule, not the exception in U.S. history. …There are numerous indications of underlying

political instability in the U.S. system. ...A major electoral shift or political realignment is easily conceivable...

The greatest uncertainty is whether major needed change will only result from some type of national crisis—after the corruption hits the fan. Or whether it can result from a number of mutually reinforcing status quo busting victories that gather momentum to increase Americans' outrage and energize them to demand and work for structural change.

On reality and hope, listen to the poetry of Leonard Cohen:

> Sail on, sail on
> O mighty Ship of State!
> To the Shores of Need
> Past the Reefs of Greed
> Through the Squalls of Hate
> Sail on, sail on, sail on...
> I'm sentimental, if you know what I mean:
> I love the country but I can't stand the scene.
> And I'm neither left or right
> I'm just staying home tonight,
> getting lost in that hopeless little screen.
> But I'm stubborn as those garbage bags
> that Time cannot decay,
> I'm junk but I'm still holding up
> this little wild boquet:
> Democracy is coming to the U.S.A.
> [From his song *Democracy*.]

Set the Table for the Party

What should concerned Americans do before a new revolution-minded third party is created and the many reforms presented above are enacted? In broad terms there is a two-part strategy for stepping in to stop America's democracy decline and reverse course. In the near-term passive dissenters must set the stage for new political leadership to take advantage of historic conditions of widespread public discontent; this is the reaching-tipping-point stage. In the longer-term a newly empowered and motivated dissenting citizenry recognizes their common goals and bands together to support the new third party; this is the organizational stage aimed at electing a president from the new third party, such as a United Americans Party.

Here are some near-term tactics. First, if you believe the messages of this book, then stop participating in the two-party duopoly's game! Stop voting for Democrats and Republicans in primary and main elections. In presidential elections, fight the urge if you are in a swing state to vote for the lesser evil. In the long run you will only be disappointed. Do not attend any event sponsored by these parties. Withdraw registration in these two parties. Stop watching two-party debates. Stop voting for the lesser evil. Reduce the power of these two corrupt groups and create space for a new political party.

Yes, you have a responsibility to vote. Yes, you can help fix our republic in a nonviolent way. Yes, you can help remove the legitimacy of the current two-party-controlled illusory political system. Yes, person by person we can bring the nation closer to a tipping point for major changes.

Do not underestimate the power of lowering support for the two major parties. Imagine how the power elites will contend with, say, only 25 percent of eligible voters voting for Democrats and Republicans. Such a reality would help dispel the myth that the United States is the greatest democracy. The only meaningful protest vote is a None of the Above message. De-legitimizing the current system means removing the claim of two-party politicians that they represent the majority and the will of the people and that they have the consent of the governed. It also means dispelling the myth that we the sovereign people still rule, even if indirectly.

The more votes for third-party candidates the better the message sent to the two-party duopoly, better even than staying home and not voting.

A second tactic is for many groups organized to fight for a specific election reform to form some type of umbrella group that frames the political goal in terms of a set of necessary election reforms to accomplish large scale political system reform, with reforms established in states and where possible at the federal level. This is a pre-third-party-formation effort, where new leaders can become successful.

A third tactic is for angry citizens to demand that *criminal* charges be brought against elected and appointed government officials whose abysmal performance causes substantial harm to the public. Recall the Katrina catastrophe in New Orleans where there was overwhelming consensus that all levels of government had failed to safeguard public health and safety. It would be reasonable in such cases to demand that criminal charges be brought against the mayor, governor, head of FEMA, and possibly President George W. Bush for negligent homicide, because their incompetence caused over one thousand deaths.

Similarly, the public should be screaming for criminal prosecution for "corporate homicide," which is far more widespread than most Americans comprehend. Thousands of workers in many industries are killed yearly because of criminal recklessness, negligence, and willful violations of health and safety regulations. Consumers also die because companies knowingly sell hazardous products or use unsafe manufacturing processes; think of cars that burn up on their own, tainted poisonous foods, and cigarettes, for example. Don't forget mistakes made in hospitals and callous actions by HMOs. No greater shame exists in our corporatist state than the failure of government to criminally prosecute corporate officials and their companies, especially for homicide. Periodic convictions for fraud—white-collar crime that harms investors and others financially—are just the tip of the corporate crime iceberg. Neither tough-on-crime conservatives and Republicans—or Democrats—have shown enthusiasm for aggressively prosecuting corporate homicide and risking corporate campaign funding. White-collar crime is as damaging to the nation as street crime and probably more so, because street crime has not damaged our democracy.

Saving Our Republic is Saving Ourselves

You rarely hear or read the word "republic" other than when the pledge of allegiance is recited.

Nevertheless, now is the time for all good Americans to come to the aid of *their* republic—and take it back from the power elites to repair their democracy and fill their nation with civility. Thinking strategically and acting boldly empowers status quo busters to harness the latent dissatisfaction among millions of Americans and channel it for change. Winston Churchill said it all: "The cure for what ails democracy is more democracy."

To do this, however, you must risk reprisal and being labeled a "subversive" or worse. In *Toward an American Evolution* Jerry Fresia captured an unsettling truth about our society:

> The claim that common people govern ourselves in the United States is a false claim. And the claim that common people can freely and fundamentally criticize our political and economic system *and work to build one that is more democratic without risking reprisal* is a lie. ...Ours is a government which rests on the assumption that 'the people,' especially when they become politically excited, interested, and alive, are thought of as subversive. ...The common person then who is not responsibly obedient but who is politically active, who is a *citizen*, is subversive. ...The responsible citizen obeys. The democratic citizen is subversive.

Yes, it has come to that: A politically engaged, truth-seeking, corruption-fighting citizen is branded subversive and risks reprisal. Such citizens exist, of course, but more are needed so that a United Americans Party can act like a magnifying glass to convert diffuse sunlight, concentrate and focus it on a spot that is vulnerable to change. Focus public dissatisfaction carefully and a sudden change can erupt as a tipping point is reached. The old corruption status quo can figuratively flare up from the heat of scrutiny and revelation.

More Americans must have a thirst for the real thing, a thirst that provoked the First American Revolution and then a century later the Populist and Progressive movements. Another century has passed and we again face the loss of true democracy. Follow your heart. Don't accept any more decline of our representative government—there's been enough to be alarmed and outraged. Don't accept any more corporate corruption and disregard for consumers, workers, and investors. Don't be demoralized by the constant barrage of lies from right-wing commentators, pundits, Christocrats, and politicians. Listen to your inner voice of dissent.

We urgently need New American Revolutionaries. Read again what Abraham Lincoln said in 1864:

> I see in the near future a crisis approaching that unnerves me and causes me to tremble for the safety of my country...corporations have been enthroned and an era of corruption in high places will follow, and the money power of the country will endeavor to prolong its reign by working upon the prejudices of the people until all wealth is aggregated in a few hands and the Republic is destroyed.

That crisis *has* arrived. Americans *should* be trembling. Corporations *have* been enthroned. We *are* in an era of corruption in high places. The money power of our country *does* effectively prolong its distortion of our representative democracy. Most wealth *is* in the hands of a few. We the people are saddled today with the responsibility to prevent *our* Republic from being destroyed. To restore American democracy many Americans must accept personal responsibility for accomplishing this. Unite and fight.

Lincoln echoed what Thomas Jefferson had written much earlier: "The spirit of the times may alter, will alter. Our rulers will become corrupt, our people careless..." Jefferson was all too correct in his dark forecast. Times have changed. Misrepresentative government and corporatism have conspired against citizens.

It's enough to make you cry. Especially when you see what is really going on—if you let in painful truth. As Thom Hartmann said in *We the People—A Call to Take Back America*:

> The real agenda, relentlessly moving forward with hardly a notice in corporate-owned media and hardly a peep from corporate-owned politicians, is the dismantling of democracy.

There are those still defending the wisdom of the Founding Fathers in rejecting direct democracy in favor of representative government, mostly on the basis that majority rule would wipe out constitutionally protected freedoms. Their fear of direct democracy, however, ignores our current condition, a misrepresentative democracy under the domination of corporatist power. We must make real what President George W. Bush uttered as spinspeak: We believe that the voice of the people ought to be determining policy, because we believe in democracy. Unite and fight.

Reaching the Finnish Line

To face the truth about America it helps to examine foreign thinking and experience. Decades of the Cold War had an unanticipated cost for America, the democratic winner. By getting in the habit of supporting many repressive governments in the fight against communism, the U.S. tarnished its image as the best democracy. And our government persists in this practice. Foreigners are well aware of our crime, violence, low voter turnout, immoral pop culture, lack of social safety nets for the poor and homeless, absence of universal health care, poor school performance, and huge prison population.

By believing domestic propaganda we ignore a repugnant fact. Much of the world sees the gap between the theory and practice of American democracy, despite our military and economic power. U.S. politicians like to talk about the thirst for democracy throughout the world and hold up the U.S. as a model. But very many people in other nations are not impressed with the U.S. They question the business, commercial and compulsive consumption dimension to American society—a shallow culture. They see a nation overly focused on dollars and possessions. They see the only superpower serving business interests, not noble causes. They see religious fanaticism shaping our government policy even as the U.S. fights it in other places. Yes, our politicians always remind us that foreigners want to come to the U.S. For many there is the attraction of a consumer economy and material affluence, though economic success is far harder to obtain once they get here. And for their children we have an education system that ranks 16th among the top 20 developed nations in the fraction of students completing high school and 14th for college graduation rates.

Consider that the European Union nations give their citizens complete universal health care at one-half the per capita cost of health care in the U.S. Europeans spend only one-quarter to one-third the hours Americans spend shopping in a year; and Europeans have less than half the rate of mental disorders of Americans. Europeans are more engaged with their governments. For them, government is a necessary good. They pay high taxes, but most know they get valuable things in return. [Of course, they are not utopian places and there is increasing problems with foreign immigrants, as the 2005 rioting in France revealed.]

In so many ways, Finland makes the USA look second rate. It is a great democracy but not a consumer economy like us. The Finnish consumer spending accounts for 52 percent of the economy, compared to 70 percent in the U.S. Citizens receive incredible social benefits; their infant mortality rate is half ours and their life expectancy greater. Whereas Finland is first in reading literacy, the U.S. is 15th. In terms of the fraction of people who are quite happy, Finland is 2nd with 72 percent and the U.S. is 30th with 53 percent. Finns receive good unemployment benefits indefinitely.

Here are some of the certified hallmarks of the Finnish society relative to all other countries: the least corrupt nation; the best free press; the greatest practice of sustainable living; the most competitive economy; very low economic inequality; the best education system and which is totally free through graduate and professional school, including law and medical schools. Total circulation of all newspapers is 3.6 million in a population of 5.2 million, third in the world after Norway and Japan.

Constitutionally, sovereign power belongs to the people who are represented through 200 members of parliament. The members are elected on a proportional basis. There are a number of political parties and, as in most other parliamentary systems, coalitions govern. Finland has nearly three times as many women in their parliament than we have in Congress. Without compulsory voting, Finland had a turnout of 76.8 percent for the latest presidential election and 65.2 percent for local parliament elections. Finns vote on a Sunday but almost 40 percent vote by mail.

Washington Post editor Robert G. Kaiser summed it up this way:

> Ours is a society driven by money, blessed by huge private philanthropy, cursed by endemic corruption and saddled with deep mistrust of government and other public institutions. Finns have none of those attributes. ...[Finland] has effectively removed many of the tangible sources of anxiety that beset our society. ...Finland has no private schools or universities, no snooty clubs, no gated communities or compounds where the rich can cut themselves off from everyday life. ...Finns have extraordinary confidence in their political class and public officials. Corruption is extremely rare.

Miapetra Kumpula, a 32-year-old member of parliament commented on the American dream: "Sure, anyone can get rich—but most won't." One fascinating aspect of Finnish government is that traffic fines are pro-rated according to the wealth of the law-breaker. So a 27-year-old heir to a fortune was fined the equivalent of $204,000 for driving 50 miles per hour in a 25 miles per hour zone in downtown Helsinki.

Finnish political leaders pursued a clear vision of the society they deemed valuable to its citizens. The public interest has been paramount and an intentionally well educated citizenry is politically engaged. Rather than U.S. politicians selling American democracy they should serve their country by humbly learning from better performing democracies, like

Finland.

What merits recognition is that Europeans still have civic faith. Disappointed with government, many Americans have replaced civic faith with religious faith. With the help of the sanctimonious and media-savvy right-wing movement, they want an American theocracy. Where others see economic, political or environmental crisis, they see God's will, quite to the liking of the power elites.

Truth be told, in an objective global democracy competition, don't bet on America winning or even coming in second or third. Citizens in the democracies of the European Union, India, Israel, Canada, Australia, Japan, and many others do not see American democracy as better than theirs. Note that eligible voters in other democracies turnout at much higher rates than in the USA: roughly 75 percent in Great Britain and Canada without compulsory voting and 90 percent or more in Italy and Australia with compulsory voting. Mere voting opportunities do not define genuine democracies—witness Cuba and Egypt. The U.S. is a great nation with great *people*, but we no longer have a great government and political system serving the people. Perhaps this explains why the respected General Social Survey found in 2004 just 40 percent of Americans believed that "America is a better country than most other countries." And only 25.6 percent were "very proud" of America's "fair and equal treatment of all groups in society."

We the people have allowed a corrupt political system to persist through our own irresponsibility and we should not dismiss how foreigners view our political system. Listen to Peter S. from the United Kingdom:

> Nearly everything about America is fake. From fake tits to fake democracy. And they want to inflict all this on the rest of us! ...The whole notion of America (at present and past) as something worthwhile is, in a word, obscene. ...But like all vast controlling nations, America is crumbling.

This view came from a third-world country with a struggling democracy:

> Many in the pro-democracy movement were inspired by the U.S., but lately we have been very disillusioned. You take your democracy for granted.

So said Smita Notosusanto, an electoral reform activist from

Indonesia.

According to a 2005 survey by the Program on International Policy Attitudes, while 78 percent of Americans believed that democracy is the best form of government, only 50 percent believed that it is the best for all countries. The United States must stop trying to save the world and start saving itself and spending its wealth at home. To paraphrase Edward R. Murrow: "We cannot defend democracy abroad by deserting it at home." When Secretary of State Condoleeza Rice condemned Egypt and Saudi Arabia in June 2005 for democratic failings what she said could be applied to the United States: "It is time to abandon the excuses that are made to avoid the hard work of democracy." If only our leaders accepted this challenge for themselves and us. If only Rice understood how other countries see our government's hypocrisy and lies. Rice's hands are dirty from her complicity in misleading the American public about the pretenses for the Iraq war, and for buying into the prisoner-torture-is-necessary-sometimes fiction. She was promoted when she, as other Bush sycophants, should have been fired. Talk of Rice running for president should inflame even more outrage and motivation for activist dissent.

As a soldier Brian Cain spent time in Iraq and Qatar and was proud of his service, including promoting democracy. But when he came home he found that his county government had approved the expansion of a landfill, overturning the recommendation of the Planning Commission, and putting his community and a marsh area "in harm's way." In October 2005, in the local newspaper *The Reporter*, he framed his views wisely:

> Over time we have learned that [democracy] is not perfect and needs to be sheparded closely. When I returned home from my last tour I was shocked to find that democracy was blatantly in jeopardy right here in Solano County. ...The Board of Supervisors did not represent the interest of people in Solano County. Their votes only benefited the corporate landfill owners and their outside investors. We all deserve better. How can we bring democracy to others if we don't practice it at home?

When America's foreign policy emphasizes spreading democracy abroad, it's important to see the truth about our homeland deMOCKracy. As Jonathan Alter observed in November 2005:

> The same president who seeks democracy, transparency and dissent in Iraq is irritated by it at home.

Should we be surprised about such hypocrisy from a president so isolated from the public? No, but neither should we be surprised that so many foreigners are not buying what our government is selling and what too many of our citizens are ignoring or resigned to. Canadians really know us and 70 percent of them in 2004 agreed with this statement: I value and respect the United States and its citizens — it's just that I disagree fundamentally with their government. When foreigners respect us but not our government, then *our* government does not represent us and that is *our* problem to fix.

Will the Real Patriots Please Get Mad as Hell

Say this loudly: All democracy is local...**All democracy is local... All democracy is local!**

American democracy peaked in the post-World War period. We are now descending into the hell of a fake democracy. As the great contemporary writer David Mamet said, "the question is how long we Americans, Democrat and Republican, will continue to engage in self-destructive behavior and call it democracy." Our democracy is committing suicide, just as John Adams feared. Will a critical mass of Americans try to forestall total collapse? Only if this holds: **For people to possess democracy, democracy must possess them**.

A republic is a fragile thing and Americans have not taken care of theirs. Not one of the branches of government, at every level of government, has effectively protected American democracy. American democracy is dying in a slow downward spiral. The only question is whether we the people will intervene to save it. God knows, the usual politicians will not. They have demonstrated ad nauseam their lack of trustworthiness and commitment to maintain American democracy in its highest state.

Our citizens work hard to take care of themselves, not noticing how American democracy has been unraveling. *Like a victim of an accomplished pickpocket, con artist, or identity-thief, most Americans are oblivious that their democracy has been stolen by corporate interests and corrupt politicians.* Status quo busters must wake them up, and provide well framed truth-telling messages that grab their attention and break through mental blocks.

In *Patriotism, Democracy, and Common Sense*, Alan Curtis grasped the full shape of today's challenge:

> Democratic power is not given. It has to be taken, aggressively defended, and retaken when it slips from our hands, for the moneyed powers relentlessly press to gain supremacy and assert their private will over the majority.

Retake democracy is more accurate—this is why we need a Second American Revolution.

Time for Americans to accept responsibility for letting down our Founders and subsequent great leaders And most importantly for letting down ourselves, people in other lands and, in great probability, future generations. We have allowed our republic to steadily decay and become more and more dysfunctional and delusional. Betrayed are the untold thousands of men and women who gave their lives, limbs and sanity to save our nation in time of war. Save it for what? For all the corporate vultures caring more about money than about the nation, the public good and future generations?

Great American leaders like Jefferson, Lincoln, and Teddy Roosevelt saw the vulnerability of American society to corruption. For too long, Americans have dulled their senses with an illusionary view of their government. In return, they received the illusory political system. Cognitive dissonance keeps many people from seeing the truth. As good consumers, patriotic Americans buy the two-party line that we live in the greatest nation on Earth. Meanwhile, politicians continue to sell them and our democracy out.

On the dark side of democracy is the confession of Frederick T. Martin in the 1934 book *The Robber Barons*:

> It matters not one iota which political party is in power, or what President holds the reins of office. We are not politicians or public thinkers; we are the rich, we own America; we got it God knows how; but we intend to keep it if we can…

The rich who own America can deal with either Democrats or Republicans. And things have gone downhill for a long time. We have a lot more rich people and powerful special interest organizations that have corroded our political infrastructure and rusted our representative government. Just as bridges and roads crumble without maintenance, so does a democracy. Going forward, we have three central needs: revitalizing our democracy, promoting citizen participation, and stopping corporate aristocracy and corruption.

As Jefferson feared, Americans have become careless about their democracy. Settling for less when it comes to political candidates is one thing, but settling for less democracy is nationcide. *Americans need a slap on their brain and a kick in their conscience to wake them from complacency, conformity, cynicism and resignation.* We also need impassioned leadership from people with a clear vision, objectives and road map for restoring our democracy—charismatic leaders who are self-evidently honest, who can wake up Americans to ugly realities that provoke outrage sufficient for them to become rebels with a cause.

When the world's only superpower, *pretending* to be the best democracy, pushes democracy on other nations, can its citizens face facts? Can its political leaders admit that the superpower has no clothes and is becoming a fake democracy? Will the working class keep buying the lies and (literally) all the crap that keep the power elites fat and happy?

What should morality, patriotism and conscience require of Americans? They must repair their democracy. Taxation with misrepresentation is just as bad as taxation without representation that angered our nation's Founders enough to revolt. Why work to finance a government that does not work for us? To fix our republic, we must put politicians in their proper place, servants to we the people, we the sovereign. Real patriotism requires this. We must tell elected officials they no longer have "the consent of the governed" because they have squandered it. Through new laws we must put corporations, business leaders, and lobbyists in their proper place, acting responsibly for the good of their workers, customers and country, not just for the rich and powerful.

More is needed. It is up to us, we the people, to put honesty back into fashion. A democracy without honesty is like a computer with a worm-infected operating system. It seems to work, but it really is serving the nefarious purposes of whoever has corrupted the system. And, as history has shown, it is likely to shutdown when you least expect it. We need leaders in the public and private sectors whom we can trust. *Oppression by dishonesty and corruption within a representative democracy is as repulsive as oppression by a king, tyrant, general, or foreign power.* Like a frog thrust into boiling water that jumps out, if a military coup had suddenly taken over the government, Americans would rise up to fight for their democracy. But in our declining democracy Americans seem like the frog in cold water that stays calm as the water is slowly heated, until it dies in the boiling water. Unruffled Americans are letting their government boil them—slowly. Americans must use their democracy muscles and jump out of the corruption cauldron by building democracy one piece at a time along the lines of the extensive checklist provided earlier.

An occupation force has gradually invaded the United States—the corrupting power elites—though the Constitution and all the trappings of representative government and personal freedoms remain. What is the important yet underused freedom? It is the freedom to peacefully fix the republic without violently overthrowing the government. Over decades of two-party rule Americans have been distracted by the illusory political system, delusional prosperity, self-absorption, job and financial security concerns, compulsive consumption, health care worries, infotainment, gambling, pornography, sports, and now the fear of terrorism. Like a law of physics, *distraction destroys democracy*. Widespread public distraction is not accidental.

Power elites use every means to keep Americans time-poor, distracted, and politically negligent—and make money in the process. Like watching a terrific magician, Americans are mesmerized by the tricks of the illusory political system, disinformation from mainstream news media, and 24-7 corporate marketing messages—either oblivious to their democracy's dismantling or dispirited and downtrodden by it. When did Americans vote for trading democracy for a rampant consumer economy? When did they choose being compulsive consumers over engaged citizens? When did fake news become more truthful than real news? When did a nation of laws become a nation of lies? When American democracy became delusional, that's when.

When democracy-loving Americans are passive patsies for false patriotism, they abet democracy's dismantling. Facing facts about our crumbling democracy is, in the end, more patriotic than deluding ourselves about it. When pressed by frightening circumstances Americans have shown their courage, confidence, and commitment to work hard, get their hands dirty, speak truth, and meet the challenge head-on. We must believe that the future is where the next "greatest generation" will step up and fix our republic. We must stop lesser evil compromises, reject the misinformation and lies bombarding us, and become engaged with politics without supporting the two-party duopoly. We must imagine being what we are becoming—a weaker nation with a fake democracy.

As said before, divisive social and cultural issues, kept inflamed by the two-party duopoly and fanatical special interests, keep Americans from focusing on what matters more, especially corrupt corporatism and plutocratic rule. Ponder the words of Martin Luther King Jr.: "Our lives begin to end the day we become silent about things that matter." Democracy matters most. Sensible Americans must put repairing their representative government first. Distractive issue-conflicts and victories perpetuate an unprincipled pseudo-democracy that no longer serves the public good. The moral imperative of the 21st century is restoring our democracy.

Along with our budget and trade deficits, we have a democracy deficit, resulting from decades of civic distraction and irresponsibility. The longer we wait, the more difficult repairing American democracy becomes. A wonderful American tradition is national renewal and reinvention and we need it now more than ever.

Most critically, Americans need to distinguish personal freedoms from trustworthy democracy. Freedoms obscure negative conditions. They allow Americans to feel that they live in the greatest *country*, despite not living in the greatest *democracy*. Threats to constitutionally protected freedoms must always be of concern, but even with freedoms intact democracy is still a larger issue. Besides, there is more to freedom than what our Constitution addresses. Americans have the freedom to drive anytime and anywhere, but few have the freedom to walk or use quality public transit instead of driving. Americans have the freedom to consume from the world's greatest array of products and services. But we lack the freedom to choose among diverse and equally visible political candidates and parties. With free speech, there is the foul freedom to lie and misinform, and too little freedom for individuals and the press to be brutally honest about things political without being branded un-American. We are free to vote for the illusory political system, that no longer means much, but not for the more controlling restricted one that the power elites own.

This is what must be learned. Legally protected personal freedoms are necessary but not sufficient for effective democracy. Discussion about the quality of our democracy must not be framed in terms of freedoms, but only in terms of whether government deserves public trust and serves public interests. Note what Roman orator Cicero said: "Freedom is participation in power." Do you participate in power?

We have unused citizen-power. More of us must use it or risk losing it. So much is at stake. Will American democracy be forever forfeited to corporate profiteers and corrupt misrepresentatives? Will our descent into fake democracy continue? Or, will our country be saved by a Second American Revolution that recaptures what the First American Revolution sought? Democracy is very hard, even when it seems easy. Fixing a delusional democracy with delusional prosperity is especially hard. It is up to us. It *is* them or us. The U.S. is US. We the people must decide what's best for us and the U.S.

Epilogue

Now is the time to heed the wisdom of Socrates: The unexamined life is not worth living. Likewise: The unexamined democracy is not worth trusting or paying and dying for.

Some say that people get the government they deserve. The question is—when? The answer is—as soon as the Americans who are ready for revolution take action.

The time must come when America's democracy arrow starts to turn up again. The rich will stop getting richer, the corrupters will be spurned, and the working class will wake up and retake their sovereign power. Americans can and must unite and fight, because they believe they have the power to begin American democracy over again—democracy as if people matter, not just dollars. Americans can and must use their collective power to resuscitate their democracy. Otherwise, future generations will look back and conclude that we were stuck on stupid.

Americans are not stupid, just too distracted, held in thrall by corrupt and unworthy leaders, and held captive by a cruel economy. From their considerable discontent outrage must explode and become the anger heard round the world.

We *can* retake our democracy.

You can retake *your* democracy. Make it so.

Bibliography

Getting Smarter for the Revolution

A Call for Revolution—How Washington is Strangling America—and How to Stop It, Martin L. Gross, 1993, Ballantine Books

All the President's Spin—George W. Bush, The Media, and The Truth, Ben Fritz, Bryan Keefer and Brendan Nyhan, 2004, Touchstone

America Beyond Capitalism—Reclaiming Our Wealth, Our Liberty, and Our Democracy, Gar Alperovitz, 2005, John Wiley & Sons

American Democracy in Peril, William E. Hudson, 1995, Chatham House

Arrogant Capital—Washington, Wall Street, and the Frustration of American Politics, Kevin Phillips, 1994, Little, Brown and Company

Breaking the News—How the Media Undermine American Democracy, James Fallows, 1997, Vintage Books

Crashing the Party—Taking on the Corporate Government in an Age of Surrender, Ralph Nader, 2002, Thomas Dunne Books

Dangerous Democracy?, Larry Sabato et al, editors, 2001, Rowman and Littlefield

Democracy At Risk—Rescuing Main Street From Wall Street—A Populist Vision for the Twenty-First Century, Jeff Gates, 2000, Perseus Publishing

Democracy for the Few, Michael Parenti, 1977, St. Martin's Press

Dirty Little Secrets—The Persistence of Corruption in American Politics, Larry J. Sabato and Glenn R. Simpson, 1996, Times Books

Don't Think of an Elephant! Know Your Values and Frame the Debate, George Lakoff, 2004, Chelsea Green Publishing

How to Overthrow the Government, Arianna Huffington, 2000, ReganBooks

If the Gods Had Meant Us to Vote They Would Have Given Us Candidates, Jim Hightower, 2000, HarperCollins

Is That a Politician In Your Pocket?, Micah L. Sifry and Nancy Watzman, 2004, John Wiley & Sons

Manufacturing Consent—The Political Economy of the Mass Media, Edward S. Herman and Noam Chomsky, 2002, Pantheon Books

Patriotism, Democracy, and Common Sense—Restoring America's Promise at Home and Abroad, Alan Curtis, editor, 2004, Rowman and Littlefield

Pigs At The Trough—How Corporate Greed and Political Corruption Are Undermining America, Arianna Huffington, 2003, Crown Publishers

The Politics of Lying, David Wise, 1973, Random House

Rich Media, Poor Democracy—Communication Politics in Dubious Time, Robert W. McChesney, 1999, University of Illinois Press

The Activist's Handbook, Randy Shaw, 1996, University of California Press

The Cheating Culture—Why More Americans Are Doing Wrong to Get Ahead,

David Callahan, 2004, A Harvest Book/Harcourt, Inc.

The Exception to the Rulers—Exposing Oily Politicians, War Profiteers, and the Media that Love Them, Amy Goodman, 2004, Hyperion

Gag Rule—On the Suppression of Dissent and the Stifling of Democracy, Lewis H. Lapham, 2004, The Penguin Press

The Good Fight—Declare Your Independence & Close the Democracy Gap, Ralph Nader, 2004, Regan Books

The Impossible Will Take A Little While—A Citizen's Guide to Hope in a Time of Fear, Paul Rogat Loeb, editor, 2004, Basic Books

Off Center—The Republican Revolution and the Erosion of American Democracy, Jacob S. Hacker and Paul Pierson, 2005, Yale University Press

The Post-Truth Era—Dishonesty and Deception in Contemporary Life, Ralph Keyes, 2004, St. Martin's Press

The Radical Center—The Future of American Politics, Ted Halstead and Michael Lind, 2001, Doubleday

Storming the Gates—Protest Politics and the Republican Revival, Dan Balz and Ronald Brownstein, 1996, Little, Brown and Company

Superpatriotism, Michael Parenti, 2004, City Lights Books

The Real State of the Union—From the Best Minds in America, Bold Solutions to the Problems Politicians Dare Not Address, Ted Halstead, 2004, Basic Books

The Tipping Point: How Little Things Can Make A Big Difference, Malcolm Gladwell, 2000, Little, Brown and Company

The Tyranny of the Two-Party System, Lisa Jane Disch, 2002, Columbia University Press

We the People—A Call to Take Back America, Thom Hartmann, 2004, CareWay Media.

What Comes Next—The End of Big Government and the New Paradigm Ahead, James P. Pinkerton, 1995, Hyperion

What's the Matter With Kansas?—How Conservatives Won the Heart of America, Thomas Frank, 20004, Henry Holt & Company,

Who Will Tell the People—The Betrayal of American Democracy, William Greider, 1992, Simon & Schuster

Why Societies Need Dissent, Cass R. Sunstein, 2003, Harvard University Press

Index

About the Author

Joel S. Hirschhorn's views about American democracy have been shaped by a multidimensional career that included long stints in the academic world as a professor (the University of Wisconsin, Madison), in the federal government as a congressional staffer (at the Office of Technology Assessment), in business as a consultant (to many large companies, grassroots groups, and government agencies), and in state government as an advisor to governors and their staffs (at the National Governors Association).

Throughout his life he has championed what others usually saw as lost causes, radical ideas, new ways of thinking, and the right or moral thing to do. Writing has always been his passion, his way of supporting and spreading new information and ideas. He has published hundreds of papers and articles, lately on many progressive Internet sites. Most of these are available through his web site www.sprawlkills.com. The name refers to his previous book *Sprawl Kills—How Blandburbs Steal Your Time, Health and Money*, a stinging attack on suburban sprawl as housing, land use, lifestyle, corrupt government and politics, and culture, as well as a strong case for Americans choosing smart growth or new urbanism alternatives to sprawl.

He welcomes opportunities to discuss with readers of this book their ideas for moving forward with the election and other reforms discussed, the Second American Revolution, a new third party such as the proposed United Americans Party, and ways to unite the many dissent-driven groups into a stronger collective force for change. He can be reached through his web site.